European Volleyball Championship Results

Since 1948

Tomasz Małolepszy

THE SCARECROW PRESS, INC.
Lanham • Toronto • Plymouth, UK
2013

Published by Scarecrow Press, Inc.
A wholly owned subsidiary of The Rowman & Littlefield Publishing Group, Inc.
4501 Forbes Boulevard, Suite 200, Lanham, Maryland 20706
www.rowman.com

10 Thornbury Road, Plymouth PL6 7PP, United Kingdom

British Library Cataloguing in Publication Information Available

Library of Congress Cataloging-in-Publication Data
Małolepszy, Tomasz, 1979–
    European volleyball championship results : since 1948 / Tomasz Małolepszy.
        p. cm.
    Includes bibliographical references and index.
    ISBN 978-0-8108-8785-5 (cloth : alk. paper) — ISBN 978-0-8108-8786-2 (ebook)
    1. Volleyball—Tournaments—Europe—History.   2. Volleyball—Records—
Europe—History.   I. Title.
    GV1015.45.E87M35 2013
    796.325094—dc23
                                                            2012038681

Contents

Abbreviations

App.:   appearances
G: games
W/L: won/lost games
GM: number of gold medals
SM: number of silver medals
BM: number of bronze medals
TM: a total number of medals
Pts.:   number of points (before 2011 edition 2 points for won game, 1 for lost game, in 2011 edition 3 points for 3-0 or 3-1 win, 2 points for 3-2 win, 1 point for 2-3 loss and 0 points for 1-3 or 0-3 loss)
SW/SL: sets won/sets lost

Abbreviations of some countries used in this book:

USSR: Union of Soviet Socialist Republics, simply Soviet Union
FRG: Federal Republic of Germany, simply West Germany
GDR: German Democratic Republic, simply East Germany

Preface

In sports, 2012 was the year of the Summer Olympic Games in London. For most Olympic athletes, Olympic medals are the culmination of their careers, a special prize awarded for many years of laborious training. The winners are surrounded by their well-deserved glory, and their names almost immediately find their way into the sporting annals. Those who manage to win medals in several Olympic competitions become particularly famous. The list of such multimedalists is the starting point of any discussion about the greatest athletes of all time. But comparison of medal achievements of athletes from different sports is often a mistake because it does not take fully into account the kind of discipline in which the given player competed. It is rather obvious that it is much more difficult to become a multimedalist in team sports than it would be for most of the individual sports (extreme examples are swimming and gymnastics). This was one reason why I have always been a fan of team sports. Over the years I realized that the history of team sports, for various reasons, is also more difficult to examine. But in some ways, this is not surprising. In principle, team sports require individual team members to utilize their sometimes very different skills and ambitions for the good of the whole team at the cost of their own anonymity. After many years, fans usually do not remember the names of individual players (with the exception of a few stars), but only which country they represented.

At first, in the late 1980s, I became interested in the history of basketball. There was no Internet easily available then in my homeland of Poland, so even basic facts were extremely hard to find. This was the beginning of my interest in the history of team sports. I then continued with research into volleyball, ice hockey, and other team sports. After many years of research and collecting data, this book is the final result of these activities, the first of a series of books documenting the history of the main team sports. My goal is to create a kind of compendium of several books in which the reader will find the detailed results of any of the games played in the most popular team sports in the most important events such as the Olympic Games, World Championships, and European Championships, with the full rosters of the winning teams and the most interesting records related to these events. You may wonder why I begin with the presentation of the complete results from the European Championships in these team sports and not the results of the Olympic tournaments. There are at least two reasons. First, continental championships, such as the European Championships, are today, together with the World Championships, a direct roads to the Olympic Games in most of these disciplines. Second, most of the Olympic laurels in team sports were gained by athletes from Europe and the United States. The history of the Old Continent's championships is very rich, and I believe it is worthwhile to trace how over the years the European hierarchy in team sports changed, often finding its reflection in the final standings of Olympic Games. It is also important to know that, to my best knowledge, such a book collectively documenting the results of the European Championships in main team sports has never been published.

This book is about volleyball. Interestingly, the Fédération Internationale de Volleyball [FIVB], the international governing body for volleyball, has 220 affiliated national federations, the most among international sport federations (for comparison its football counterpart, the Fédération Internationale de Football Association [FIFA] has 209), which clearly shows the popularity of volleyball. This book is the first ever published that allows the reader to find in one place details such as the date and place of each edition of the European Championship in volleyball, a complete set of results with dates and places of each game, and the full rosters of the teams that won medals. The only data I was not able to find is the result of one set in one game from the 1948 European Championship in men's volleyball. Sometimes I found different details in various sources, but I then tried to determine the true ones.

This book surely would not have been completed successfully without the support and help of many friendly people. Special thanks to all the workers from international and national federations of various team sports and national libraries all over Europe who were willing to answer my many questions. I am grateful to my publisher, Scarecrow Press, Inc., for a chance to publish my results of several years of work. But most important for me was that I could, as always, count on the support and understanding from my family, especially my beloved wife, Paulina, and our lovely daughter, Karolinka, who was often my faithful companion in the library. I would also like to thank my mother, Bożena, for supporting my sport hobby from my childhood, even in times when it was not easy.

Volleyball: Introduction

The first European Championship in men's volleyball was played with six teams in 1948, just a year after the creation of the Fédération Internationale de Volleyball (FIVB; International Federation of Volleyball). As the European Volleyball Confederation (Confédération Européenne de Volleyball [CEV]) was officially established in 1973, the first eight editions of the European Championships were played under the auspices of the FIVB. They were played without any qualification system, which meant that every national team could compete in them just by registering. Because the popularity of volleyball grew steadily, the 1971 championship was contested by a record number of 22 teams. This was the main reason that when the CEV took over the organization of the championships, the number of teams in the final tournament was reduced through the introduction of qualifications, starting with the 1975 championship. Today, there are 55 members (national federations) of the CEV, but only 16 of them can play for the gold medal in the European Championship.

Over the years, the rules of volleyball have evolved. The most important modifications were made to increase the attractiveness of the sport, mainly through changes in the way points are counted. The main changes are:

1988   Introduction of the rally point system (a point is given after each play, in contrast to the earlier system when only the serving team could score a point in a given play) for the fifth set (so-called tie-break); the final score per set is limited to a maximum of 17 points.

1992   For the fifth set, the maximum limit of 17 points is removed, and in order to win a tie-break the team must have at least 15 points and a minimum two-point advantage.

1998   Introduction of a 25-point rally point system for the first four sets, while preserving the minimum two-point advantage rule at the end of each set.

1

These changes have significantly shortened the duration of games, and volleyball has become a much more dynamic sport and, hence, more popular around the world.

In the history of the European Championship in men's volleyball, two teams have been the most dominant: the Soviet Union and Italy. The former team was the best in Europe 12 times, including nine times in a row from 1967 to 1987. The names of players such as Aleksandr Savin, Vyacheslav Zaytsev, Vladimir Kondra, Viljar Loor, Yuriy Panchenko, and Vladimir Chernyshyov are known to volleyball enthusiasts all over the world. Interestingly, after the dissolution of the Soviet Union, Russia, the inheritor of the records of the Soviet Union according to the FIVB, failed to win the European Championship even once! As of 2011, the Italian team has won the gold in the European Championship six times. In the 1990s, when their coach was the famous Julio Velasco, they were indisputably the best team in the world, but ironically never managed to win Olympic gold. In Europe, they had only one notable rival at that time–the national team of the Netherlands–and their encounters were a demonstration of volleyball at the highest possible level.

Until the political changes in Europe in the early 1990s, the best women's volleyball team in the Old Continent was arguably the Soviet Union. In each of its 17 European Championship competitions, the women's Soviet team captured at least a silver medal and was the best 13 times. What's more, it won the championship six times without losing even one set in the whole tournament! However, even such a wonderful team was not unbeatable. This was especially apparent in the 1980s when the GDR (twice) and Bulgaria (once) turned out to be better teams in particular European Championships. After the collapse of the Soviet Union, the Russian women continued the tradition of Soviet volleyball, winning four times in their first five championships in which they appeared as an independent country. Their coach was the famous Nikolay Karpol, who won a total of nine European Championships medals in his career, including a record seven gold medals (first in 1979, the last in 2001). Today the level of the best European teams (Italy, Turkey, Germany, Russia, Poland, and Serbia) is more balanced, and each of them has the potential to win a championship. It is also worthwhile to note that since 1995, the champions of Europe in the years preceding the Olympic Games do not receive a direct Olympic qualification. To play at the Olympics, they must win pre-Olympic tournaments, and they have not always managed to do so (such as the Polish women's volleyball team in 2004).

The tables that follow summarize the important data for all 27 editions of the men's and women's volleyball European Championships.

European Championships in men's volleyball (all-time table)

Country	App.	G	W	L	SW	SL	GM	SM	BM	TM
Italy	26	184	**116**	68	398	289	6	3	2	11
USSR	16	121	**108**	13	342	86	12	0	2	14
Bulgaria	25	179	**104**	75	382	293	0	1	4	5
Poland	22	162	**97**	65	347	263	1	5	2	8
France	25	176	**88**	88	334	333	0	4	2	6
Czechoslovakia	16	119	**77**	42	267	172	3	4	0	7
Romania	16	120	**73**	47	256	202	1	2	2	5
Netherlands	22	156	**70**	86	279	298	1	2	2	5
Russia	10	69	**51**	18	171	87	0	3	3	6
GDR	10	81	**48**	33	165	124	0	0	0	0
Yugoslavia	14	112	**48**	64	191	227	0	0	2	2
Hungary	11	85	**41**	44	153	167	0	1	1	2
Finland	14	100	**36**	64	158	220	0	0	0	0
Greece	14	85	**31**	54	124	189	0	0	1	1
Serbia and Montenegro	6	40	**29**	11	100	45	1	1	3	5
Belgium	12	82	**27**	55	116	180	0	0	0	0
Germany	9	53	**24**	29	91	110	0	0	0	0
Turkey	7	48	**19**	29	79	101	0	0	0	0
Czech Republic	8	41	**16**	25	63	91	0	0	0	0
Sweden	7	48	**16**	32	64	112	0	1	0	1
Spain	8	54	**16**	38	75	133	1	0	0	1
Serbia	3	20	**15**	5	51	26	1	0	1	2
Albania	3	29	**14**	15	48	57	0	0	0	0
Slovakia	6	33	**10**	23	46	80	0	0	0	0
FRG	6	45	**10**	35	48	113	0	0	0	0
Israel	3	23	**9**	14	34	46	0	0	0	0
Ukraine	4	24	**8**	16	31	56	0	0	0	0
Portugal	4	19	**7**	12	27	43	0	0	0	0
Austria	7	47	**6**	41	27	127	0	0	0	0
Switzerland	1	7	**3**	4	9	13	0	0	0	0
Egypt	2	19	**3**	16	18	49	0	0	0	0
Croatia	2	8	**2**	6	13	20	0	0	0	0
Tunisia	1	11	**2**	9	8	29	0	0	0	0
Slovenia	4	15	**2**	13	15	41	0	0	0	0
Denmark	3	24	**2**	22	7	68	0	0	0	0
Estonia	2	7	**1**	6	5	18	0	0	0	0
Latvia	1	5	**0**	5	1	15	0	0	0	0
Scotland	1	7	**0**	7	1	21	0	0	0	0

Notes: Serbia and Montenegro competed as Yugoslavia between the 1995 and 2001 European Championships. The following geographically non-European countries have participated in the European Championships: Egypt (1955, 1958) and Tunisia (1958) from Africa, Israel (1951, 1967, 1971) from Asia.

European Championships in women's volleyball (all-time table)

Country	App.	G	W	L	SW	SL	GM	SM	BM	TM
USSR	17	116	**111**	5	341	44	13	4	0	17
Poland	26	173	**108**	65	368	265	2	4	5	11
Italy	21	143	**84**	59	293	215	2	2	2	6
Bulgaria	25	164	**83**	81	307	303	1	0	2	3
Czechoslovakia	17	120	**80**	40	267	163	1	4	3	8
Netherlands	24	155	**76**	79	284	285	1	2	1	4
Romania	23	149	**72**	77	259	273	0	0	1	1
GDR	12	89	**59**	30	193	116	2	4	1	7
Russia	10	65	**54**	11	170	52	4	0	3	7
Hungary	14	99	**45**	54	171	182	0	1	3	4
Germany	11	68	**39**	29	132	115	0	1	2	3
FRG	12	82	**31**	51	120	174	0	0	0	0
France	14	83	**30**	53	120	182	0	0	0	0
Turkey	10	66	**27**	39	98	132	0	1	1	2
Croatia	9	47	**24**	23	85	83	0	3	0	3
Yugoslavia	10	69	**21**	48	85	154	0	0	1	1
Ukraine	6	36	**18**	18	62	70	0	0	1	1
Serbia	3	21	**14**	7	48	31	1	1	0	2
Czech Republic	7	39	**12**	27	49	89	0	0	1	1
Azerbaijan	4	23	**7**	16	28	53	0	0	0	0
Belarus	5	25	**5**	20	25	65	0	0	0	0
Belgium	6	41	**5**	36	34	111	0	0	0	0
Serbia and Montenegro	2	12	**4**	8	17	27	0	0	0	0
Israel	3	19	**4**	15	15	46	0	0	0	0
Switzerland	2	15	**3**	12	11	40	0	0	0	0
Latvia	3	17	**3**	14	15	46	0	0	0	0
Spain	4	18	**3**	15	17	49	0	0	0	0
Sweden	3	22	**3**	19	13	59	0	0	0	0
Slovakia	3	11	**2**	9	10	31	0	0	0	0
Denmark	2	13	**2**	11	9	33	0	0	0	0
Austria	3	18	**2**	16	9	50	0	0	0	0
Greece	4	24	**2**	22	19	69	0	0	0	0
Finland	2	14	**1**	13	8	41	0	0	0	0
Albania	1	5	**0**	5	2	15	0	0	0	0
England	1	7	**0**	7	0	21	0	0	0	0

Notes: In the 1993 European Championship, two countries: the Czech Republic and Slovakia were represented by one team, Czechoslovakia. The following geographically non-European countries have participated in the European Championships: Israel (1967, 1971, 2011) from Africa and Azerbaijan (2005, 2007, 2009, 2011) from Asia.

Men's European Championships

Date	Winner–Loser	Final Score	(Partial Scores)
24 Sep.	Italy–Belgium	3–0	(15–8, 15–5, 15–6)
24 Sep.	Czechoslovakia–Netherlands	3–0	(15–1, 15–5, 15–7)
24 Sep.	France–Portugal	3–1	(15–11, 15–9, 10–15, 15–10)
24 Sep.	Italy–Netherlands	3–0	(15–4, 15–5, 15–13)
24 Sep.	Czechoslovakia–Portugal	3–0	(15–3, 15–8, 15–6)
24 Sep.	France–Belgium	3–0	(15–8, 15–7, 15–7)
25 Sep.	Italy–Portugal	3–0	(15–8, 15–9, 15–10)
25 Sep.	Czechoslovakia–France	3–0	(15–7, 15–5, 15–5)
25 Sep.	Belgium–Netherlands	3–1	(15–11, 15–8, 7–15, 15–6)
26 Sep.	Czechoslovakia–Belgium	3–0	(15–4, 15–5, 15–5)
26 Sep.	France–Italy	3–2	(15–8, 8–15, 15–9, 15–17, 15–13)
26 Sep.	Portugal–Netherlands	3–0	(15–1, 15–2, 15–6)
26 Sep.	Czechoslovakia–Italy	3–0	(15–1, 15–5, 15–5)
26 Sep.	France–Netherlands	3–0	(15–11, 15–10, 15–4)
26 Sep.	Portugal–Belgium	3–0	(15–1, 15–?, 15–13)

	G	W/L	SW/SL	Pts.
1. Czechoslovakia	5	5/0	15/0	10
2. France	5	4/1	12/7	9
3. Italy	5	3/2	11/6	8
4. Portugal	5	2/3	6/11	7
5. Belgium	5	1/4	5/13	6
6. Netherlands	5	0/5	3/15	5

Final standings

	G	W/L	SW/SL
1. Czechoslovakia	5	5/0	15/0
2. France	5	4/1	12/7
3. Italy	5	3/2	11/6
4. Portugal	5	2/3	6/13
5. Belgium	5	1/4	7/13
6. Netherlands	5	0/5	3/15

Total: 6 teams, 15 games

Rosters of the medalists

Czechoslovakia–Josef Brož, Karel Brož, Josef Češpiva, Jaroslav Fučík, Stanislav Linke, František Mikota, Josef Reicho, Josef Tesař, Josef Votava; head coach: Josef Češpiva

France–Alphonse Claparede, Michel Constantin, Roger Delousteau, René Demotte, André Dulon, André Henry, Jacques Liou, Jean Pogenberg, Robert Recoque, Igor Stepanoff, Jacques Vabre; head coach: Marcel Mathore

Italy–Ermanno Baccarini, Francesco Cattaneo, Riccardo Ceppile, Bruno De Bernardi, Bruno Estasi, Mario Fanesi, Bruno Lollis, Orfeo Montanari, Mario Saragoni, Lino Schenal, Carlo Sforzini, Roberto Tazzari; head coach: Angelo Costa

II EUROPEAN CHAMPIONSHIP
14–22 October 1950, Sofia (Bulgaria)

14 Oct.	USSR–Romania	3–0	(15–5, 15–6, 15–6)
15 Oct.	Czechoslovakia–Poland	3–1	(15–12, 15–9, 14–16, 15–7)
15 Oct.	Hungary–Bulgaria	3–2	(8–15, 10–15, 17–15, 16–14, 17–15)
17 Oct.	USSR–Poland	3–0	(15–4, 15–5, 15–7)
17 Oct.	Hungary–Romania	3–0	(15–10, 15–7, 15–2)
18 Oct.	USSR–Hungary	3–0	(15–5, 15–4, 15–6)
19 Oct.	Czechoslovakia–Romania	3–0	(15–12, 15–12, 15–9)

19 Oct.	Bulgaria–Poland	3–0	(15–7, 15–7, 16–14)
20 Oct.	Bulgaria–Romania	3–1	(18–16, 15–12, 10–15, 17–15)
20 Oct.	USSR–Czechoslovakia	3–0	(15–9, 15–7, 15–7)
21 Oct.	Hungary–Poland	3–1	(15–6, 15–17, 15–7, 15–8)
21 Oct.	Czechoslovakia–Bulgaria	3–2	(12–15, 15–10, 15–11, 14–16, 15–10)*
22 Oct.	Romania–Poland	3–1	(11–15, 16–14, 15–7, 15–6)
22 Oct.	Czechoslovakia–Hungary	3–0	(15–12, 15–9, 15–4)
22 Oct.	USSR–Bulgaria	3–0	(15–6, 15–8, 15–4)

*The game between these two teams was initially played on 16 October, but with Czechoslovakia leading 2–0 (16–14, 15–12) in sets and 11–7 in the third set, the game was interrupted due to darkness and a new game had to be played five days later.

	G	W/L	SW/SL	Pts.
1. USSR	5	5/0	15/0	10
2. Czechoslovakia	5	4/1	12/6	9
3. Hungary	5	3/2	9/9	8
4. Bulgaria	5	2/3	10/10	7
5. Romania	5	1/4	4/13	6
6. Poland	5	0/5	3/15	5

Final standings

	G	W/L	SW/SL
1. USSR	5	5/0	15/0
2. Czechoslovakia	5	4/1	12/6
3. Hungary	5	3/2	9/9
4. Bulgaria	5	2/3	10/10
5. Romania	5	1/4	4/13
6. Poland	5	0/5	3/15

Total: 6 teams, 15 games

Rosters of the medalists

USSR–Vladimir Gaylit, Valentin Kitaev, Viktor Maltsman, Sergey Nefyodov, Mikhail Pimenov, Konstantin Reva, Anatoliy Sedov, Vladimir Shchagin, Vladimir Ulyanov, Porfiriy Voronin, Aleksey Yakushev, Arkadiy Zhavoronkov; head coach: Anatoliy Chinilin

Czechoslovakia–Josef Brož, Karel Brož, Jaroslav Fučík, Jiří Jonáš, Evžen Krob, Václav Matiášek, František Mikota, Antonín Nogol, Jaromír Paldus, Václav Raban, Josef Tesař, Josef Votava; head coach: Jan Fiedler

Hungary–Tibor Antalpéter, Attila Benke, László Bizik, Tibor Borsovszky, Gyula Havasi, Ernõ Hennig, László Imte, László Moss, Zoltán Németh, Lõrinc Szabó; head coach: Abad Árpád

III EUROPEAN CHAMPIONSHIP
15–22 September 1951, Paris (France)

Preliminary round

Group A

15 Sep.	Belgium–Italy	3–0	(15–6, 15–12, 15–13)
16 Sep.	USSR–Italy	3–0	(15–4, 15–7, 15–2)
17 Sep.	USSR–Belgium	3–0	(15–2, 15–1, 15–1)

	G	W/L	SW/SL	Pts.
1. USSR	2	2/0	6/0	4
2. Belgium	2	1/1	3/3	3
3. Italy	2	0/2	0/6	2

Group B

15 Sep.	Yugoslavia–Portugal	3–0	(15–12, 15–7, 16–14)
16 Sep.	Bulgaria–Yugoslavia	3–1	(15–10, 15–8, 14–16, 15–13)
16 Sep.	Portugal–Netherlands	3–1	(11–15, 15–12, 16–14, 15–6)
17 Sep.	Yugoslavia–Netherlands	3–0	(15–3, 15–8, 15–12)
17 Sep.	Bulgaria–Portugal	3–0	(15–5, 15–10, 15–1)
18 Sep.	Bulgaria–Netherlands	3–0	(15–1, 15–3, 15–2)

	G	W/L	SW/SL	Pts.
1. Bulgaria	3	3/0	9/1	6
2. Yugoslavia	3	2/1	7/3	5
3. Portugal	3	1/2	3/7	4
4. Netherlands	3	0/3	1/9	3

Group C

15 Sep.	France–Israel	3–0	(15–10, 15–7, 15–6)
16 Sep.	Romania–France	3–1	(13–15, 15–9, 16–14, 15–12)
17 Sep.	Romania–Israel	3–0	(15–3, 15–5, 15–6)

	G	W/L	SW/SL	Pts.
1. Romania	2	2/0	6/2	4
2. France	2	1/1	5/3	3
3. Israel	2	0/2	0/6	2

Final round

Final group for 7–10 places

19 Sep.	Portugal–Italy	3–2	(9–15, 15–12, 7–15, 15–13, 15–11)
19 Sep.	Netherlands–Israel	3–2	(13–15, 18–16, 15–8, 6–15, 15–5)
20 Sep.	Italy–Israel	3–0	(15–9, 15–6, 18–16)
20 Sep.	Portugal–Netherlands	3–0	(15–9, 15–7, 15–11)
21 Sep.	Italy–Netherlands	3–0	(15–10, 15–13, 15–13)
22 Sep.	Portugal–Israel	3–0	(15–9, 15–6, 15–13)

	G	W/L	SW/SL	Pts.
1. Portugal	3	3/0	9/2	6
2. Italy	3	2/1	8/3	5
3. Netherlands	3	1/2	3/8	4
4. Israel	3	0/3	2/9	3

Final group for 1–6 places

18 Sep.	USSR–Yugoslavia	3–0	(15–12, 15–2, 15–11)
18 Sep.	France–Bulgaria	3–2	(15–12, 15–9, 5–15, 10–15, 15–12)
18 Sep.	Romania–Belgium	3–0	(15–8, 15–3, 15–5)
19 Sep.	Yugoslavia–Romania	3–2	(11–15, 15–9, 5–15, 15–10, 17–15)
19 Sep.	USSR–France	3–0	(15–2, 15–6, 15–7)
19 Sep.	Bulgaria–Belgium	3–0	(15–2, 15–8, 15–7)
20 Sep.	Bulgaria–Yugoslavia	3–0	(15–5, 15–6, 15–8)
20 Sep.	USSR–Romania	3–0	(15–9, 15–9, 15–7)
20 Sep.	France–Belgium	3–0	(15–8, 15–10, 15–5)
21 Sep.	France–Yugoslavia	3–2	(7–15, 15–6, 15–12, 12–15, 15–10)
21 Sep.	USSR–Belgium	3–0	(15–4, 15–3, 15–3)
21 Sep.	Bulgaria–Romania	3–2	(15–1, 15–8, 8–15, 13–15, 15–7)
22 Sep.	Yugoslavia–Belgium	3–0	(16–14, 15–11, 15–6)
22 Sep.	USSR–Bulgaria	3–0	(15–8, 15–3, 15–4)
22 Sep.	Romania–France	3–0	(17–15, 15–11, 17–15)

	G	W/L	SW/SL	Pts.
1. USSR	5	5/0	15/0	10
2. Bulgaria	5	3/2	11/8	8
3. France	5	3/2	9/10	8
4. Romania	5	2/3	10/9	7
5. Yugoslavia	5	2/3	8/11	7
6. Belgium	5	0/5	0/15	5

Final standings

	G	W/L	SW/SL
1. USSR	7	7/0	21/0
2. Bulgaria	8	6/2	20/9
3. France	7	4/3	13/13
4. Romania	7	4/3	16/10
5. Yugoslavia	8	4/4	15/14
6. Belgium	7	1/6	3/18
7. Portugal	6	4/2	12/9
8. Italy	5	2/3	8/9
9. Netherlands	6	1/5	4/17
10. Israel	5	0/5	2/15

Total: 10 teams, 33 games

Rosters of the medalists

USSR–Givi Akhvlediani, Vladimir Andreev, Vladimir Gaylit, Valentin Kitaev, Sergey Nefyodov, Mikhail Pimenov, Konstantin Reva, Vladimir Savvin, Vladimir Shchagin, Vladimir Ulyanov, Porfiriy Voronin, Aleksey Yakushev; head coach: Anatoliy Chinilin

Bulgaria–Kosta Badzhakov, Botyu Danailov, Deno Denev, Boris Gyuderov, Stoycho Kardzhiev, Ivan Konarev, Petar Lozanov, Peyo Parlev, Gencho Petkov, Panayot Pondalov, Kostadin Shopov, Dragomir Stoyanov; head coach: Dimitar Elenkov

France–Igor Boulatsel, René Brockly, Igor Chichkine, Alphonse Claparede, Michel Constantin, René Demotte, François Dujardin, Henry Pasqualini, Robert Poujol, Jacques Vabre, René van Branteghem, Jacques Willemin; head coach: Marcel Mathore

IV EUROPEAN CHAMPIONSHIP
15–25 June 1955, Bucharest (Romania)

Preliminary round

Group A

15 Jun.	USSR–Albania	3–0	(15–8, 15–4, 15–5)
15 Jun.	France–Finland	3–0	(15–5, 15–6, 15–5)
16 Jun.	USSR–Finland	3–0	(15–4, 15–3, 15–8)
16 Jun.	France–Albania	3–0	(15–7, 15–4, 15–2)
17 Jun.	Albania–Finland	3–1	(15–13, 15–10, 4–15, 15–11)
17 Jun.	USSR–France	3–0	(15–10, 15–9, 15–9)

	G	W/L	SW/SL	Pts.
1. USSR	3	3/0	9/0	6
2. France	3	2/1	6/3	5
3. Albania	3	1/2	3/7	4
4. Finland	3	0/3	1/9	3

Group B

15 Jun.	Yugoslavia–Egypt	3–0	(15–3, 15–3, 15–5)
15 Jun.	Czechoslovakia–Austria	3–0	(15–2, 15–1, 15–0)
16 Jun.	Czechoslovakia–Yugoslavia	3–0	(15–13, 15–1, 15–4)
16 Jun.	Egypt–Austria	3–1	(9–15, 15–8, 15–10, 17–15)
17 Jun.	Yugoslavia–Austria	3–0	(15–6, 15–2, 15–7)
17 Jun.	Czechoslovakia–Egypt	3–0	(15–0, 15–0, 15–7)

	G	W/L	SW/SL	Pts.
1. Czechoslovakia	3	3/0	9/0	6
2. Yugoslavia	3	2/1	6/3	5
3. Egypt	3	1/2	3/7	4
4. Austria	3	0/3	1/9	3

Group C

15 Jun.	Hungary–Belgium	3–0	(15–10, 15–7, 15–4)
16 Jun.	Hungary–Bulgaria	3–2	(15–8, 13–15, 7–15, 15–7, 16–14)
17 Jun.	Bulgaria–Belgium	3–0	(15–6, 15–10, 15–10)

	G	W/L	SW/SL	Pts.
1. Hungary	2	2/0	6/2	4
2. Bulgaria	2	1/1	5/3	3
3. Belgium	2	0/2	0/6	2

Group D

15 Jun.	Romania–Italy	3–0	(15–9, 15–4, 15–10)
16 Jun.	Poland–Italy	3–0	(15–7, 15–9, 15–9)
17 Jun.	Romania–Poland	3–2	(15–12, 15–11, 2–15, 8–15, 15–11)

	G	W/L	SW/SL	Pts.
1. Romania	2	2/0	6/2	4
2. Poland	2	1/1	5/3	3
3. Italy	2	0/2	0/6	2

Final round

Final group for 9–14 places

20 Jun.	Belgium–Austria	3–1	(15–5, 15–9, 13–15, 15–9)
20 Jun.	Finland–Albania	3–2	(15–17, 10–15, 15–8, 15–9, 15–9)
20 Jun.	Italy–Egypt	3–0	(15–11, 15–1, 15–4)
21 Jun.	Italy–Austria	3–2	(15–10, 15–7, 12–15, 10–15, 15–6)
21 Jun.	Albania–Egypt	3–0	(15–12, 15–9, 16–14)
21 Jun.	Belgium–Finland	3–2	(15–1, 14–16, 15–8, 6–15, 15–4)
22 Jun.	Albania–Austria	3–0	(15–7, 15–7, 15–1)
22 Jun.	Italy–Belgium	3–0	(15–4, 15–4, 15–6)
22 Jun.	Finland–Egypt	3–0	(15–10, 16–14, 15–6)
24 Jun.	Italy–Finland	3–1	(15–11, 15–7, 15–17, 15–9)
24 Jun.	Albania–Belgium	3–2	(8–15, 15–13, 14–16, 15–11, 17–15)
24 Jun.	Austria–Egypt	3–2	(15–13, 8–15, 15–13, 6–15, 15–12)
25 Jun.	Finland–Austria	3–0	(15–1, 15–5, 15–10)
25 Jun.	Belgium–Egypt	3–0	(15–3, 15–9, 15–4)
25 Jun.	Italy–Albania	3–2	(15–8, 9–15, 16–14, 9–15, 15–13)

	G	W/L	SW/SL	Pts.
1. Italy	5	5/0	15/5	10
2. Albania	5	3/2	13/8	8
3. Finland	5	3/2	12/8	8
4. Belgium	5	3/2	11/9	8
5. Austria	5	1/4	6/14	6
6. Egypt	5	0/5	2/15	5

Final group for 1–8 places

19 Jun.	Yugoslavia–Romania	3–2	(15–11, 5–15, 15–10, 11–15, 17–15)
19 Jun.	USSR–Hungary	3–0	(16–14, 16–14, 15–6)
19 Jun.	Bulgaria–France	3–0	(15–6, 15–5, 15–7)
19 Jun.	Czechoslovakia–Poland	3–0	(15–7, 15–4, 15–5)
20 Jun.	Bulgaria–Yugoslavia	3–2	(15–12, 15–11, 2–15, 12–15, 15–13)
20 Jun.	USSR–France	3–1	(15–6, 14–16, 15–8, 19–17)
20 Jun.	Czechoslovakia–Hungary	3–0	(15–11, 15–5, 15–11)
20 Jun.	Romania–Poland	3–1	(15–9, 11–15, 15–13, 15–11)
21 Jun.	Hungary–Yugoslavia	3–2	(10–15, 12–15, 15–6, 15–10, 15–5)
21 Jun.	Romania–France	3–0	(15–10, 15–7, 15–11)
21 Jun.	Bulgaria–Poland	3–2	(15–12, 6–15, 15–11, 12–15, 15–6)
21 Jun.	USSR–Czechoslovakia	3–2	(15–3, 15–12, 6–15, 7–15, 15–12)
22 Jun.	Yugoslavia–USSR	3–1	(15–11, 15–10, 15–17, 18–16)
22 Jun.	Poland–Hungary	3–1	(15–12, 13–15, 15–10, 15–9)
22 Jun.	Czechoslovakia–France	3–0	(15–13, 15–8, 15–10)

(continued)

Final group for 1–8 places (continued)

22 Jun.	Romania–Bulgaria	3–1	(11–15, 15–6, 15–11, 15–10)
24 Jun.	Yugoslavia–France	3–1	(9–15, 15–3, 15–10, 15–9)
24 Jun.	Bulgaria–Hungary	3–0	(15–4, 16–14, 15–6)
24 Jun.	USSR–Poland	3–0	(15–13, 15–8, 15–4)
24 Jun.	Czechoslovakia–Romania	3–1	(15–11, 15–8, 8–15, 15–6)
25 Jun.	Czechoslovakia–Yugoslavia	3–1	(14–16, 17–15, 15–8, 15–7)
25 Jun.	Poland–France	3–1	(8–15, 15–2, 15–5, 15–8)
25 Jun.	Romania–Hungary	3–2	(15–10, 15–12, 12–15, 10–15, 15–2)
25 Jun.	Bulgaria–USSR	3–2	(11–15, 15–13, 15–12, 7–15, 15–10)
26 Jun.	Poland–Yugoslavia	3–1	(10–15, 15–13, 15–5, 16–14)
26 Jun.	Hungary–France	3–2	(6–15, 15–11, 12–15, 15–7, 15–10)
26 Jun.	Czechoslovakia–Bulgaria	3–0	(15–8, 15–5, 15–11)
26 Jun.	Romania–USSR	3–1	(9–15, 15–13, 15–6, 15–13)

	G	W/L	SW/SL	Pts.
1. Czechoslovakia	7	6/1	20/5	13
2. Romania	7	5/2	18/11	12
3. Bulgaria	7	5/2	16/12	12
4. USSR	7	4/3	16/12	11
5. Yugoslavia	7	3/4	15/16	10
6. Poland	7	3/4	12/15	10
7. Hungary	7	2/5	9/19	9
8. France	7	0/7	5/21	7

Final standings

	G	W/L	SW/SL
1. Czechoslovakia	10	9/1	29/5
2. Romania	9	7/2	24/13
3. Bulgaria	9	6/3	21/15
4. USSR	10	7/3	25/12
5. Yugoslavia	10	5/5	21/19
6. Poland	9	4/5	17/18
7. Hungary	9	4/5	15/21
8. France	10	2/8	11/24
9. Italy	7	5/2	15/11
10. Albania	8	4/4	16/15
11. Finland	8	3/5	13/17
12. Belgium	7	3/4	11/15
13. Austria	8	1/7	7/23
14. Egypt	8	1/7	5/22

Total: 14 teams, 61 games

Rosters of the medalists

Czechoslovakia–Karel Brož, Zdeněk Humhal, Jiří Jonáš, Karel Láznička, Zdeněk Malý, Josef Musil, Jaromír Paldus, Karel Paulus, Milan Purnoch, František Schwarzkopf, Ladislav Synovec, Josef Tesař; head coach: Josef Kozák

Romania–Sebastian Apostol, Ioan Mihaiu Chezan, Emil Claici, Ion Crivăţ, Dumitru Medianu, Sebastian Mihăilescu, Constantin Mitroi, Horaţiu Nicolau, Jean Ponova, Nicolae Răducanu, Ştefan Roman, Marcel Rusescu; head coach: Gheorghe Petrescu

Bulgaria–Nikola Chalashkanov, Deno Denev, Gencho Genchev, Boris Gyuderov, Lyudmil Gyuderov, Nikola Lechev, Boyan Moshelov, Yanko Otashliyski, Panayot Pondalov, Todor Simov, Nikola Taskov, Todor Vutov; head coach: Georgi Krastev

V EUROPEAN CHAMPIONSHIP
30 August–11 September 1958, Pardubice, Plzeň, and Prague
(Czechoslovakia)

Preliminary round

Group A (Prague)

30 Aug.	GDR–FRG	3–0	(15–2, 15–6, 15–3)
30 Aug.	France–Tunisia	3–0	(15–6, 15–0, 15–5)
31 Aug.	GDR–Tunisia	3–0	(15–3, 17–15, 15–0)
31 Aug.	Czechoslovakia–France	3–0	(15–8, 15–5, 15–11)
1 Sep.	Tunisia–FRG	3–0	(15–8, 15–12, 15–6)
1 Sep.	Czechoslovakia–GDR	3–0	(15–2, 15–4, 15–2)
2 Sep.	Czechoslovakia–FRG	3–0	(15–1, 15–1, 15–0)
2 Sep.	France–GDR	3–0	(15–10, 15–11, 15–10)
3 Sep.	France–FRG	3–0	(15–2, 15–3, 15–5)
3 Sep.	Czechoslovakia–Tunisia	3–0	(15–2, 15–2, 15–3)

	G	W/L	SW/SL	Pts.
1. Czechoslovakia	4	4/0	12/0	8
2. France	4	3/1	9/3	7
3. GDR	4	2/2	6/6	6
4. Tunisia	4	1/3	3/9	5
5. FRG	4	0/4	0/12	4

Group B (Prague)

30 Aug.	Netherlands–Belgium	3–2	(15–10, 6–15, 15–13, 13–15, 15–12)
30 Aug.	Hungary–Italy	3–0	(15–5, 15–4, 15–11)
31 Aug.	Italy–Belgium	3–2	(11–15, 15–5, 15–9, 11–15, 15–9)
31 Aug.	Romania–Hungary	3–0	(15–12, 15–13, 15–11)
1 Sep.	Italy–Netherlands	3–2	(16–18, 15–12, 9–15, 15–1, 15–1)

(continued)

Group B (Prague) (continued)

1 Sep.	Romania–Belgium	3–0	(15–8, 15–4, 15–7)
2 Sep.	Romania–Netherlands	3–0	(15–7, 15–10, 15–8)
2 Sep.	Hungary–Belgium	3–0	(15–12, 15–0, 15–6)
3 Sep.	Romania–Italy	3–0	(15–8, 15–10, 15–7)
3 Sep.	Hungary–Netherlands	3–2	(10–15, 12–15, 15–3, 15–4, 15–11)

	G	W/L	SW/SL	Pts.
1. Romania	4	4/0	12/0	8
2. Hungary	4	3/1	9/5	7
3. Italy	4	2/2	6/10	6
4. Netherlands	4	1/3	7/11	5
5. Belgium	4	0/4	4/12	4

Group C (Plzeň)

30 Aug.	Egypt–Denmark	3–0	(15–5, 15–4, 15–3)
30 Aug.	Poland–Finland	3–1	(12–15, 15–2, 15–1, 15–6)
31 Aug.	Finland–Denmark	3–0	(15–11, 15–4, 15–1)
31 Aug.	Poland–Bulgaria	3–1	(15–10, 15–10, 8–15, 15–7)
1 Sep.	Finland–Egypt	3–1	(16–14, 12–15, 15–8, 15–13)
1 Sep.	Bulgaria–Denmark	3–0	(15–0, 15–2, 15–5)
2 Sep.	Poland–Denmark	3–0	(15–1, 15–2, 15–2)
2 Sep.	Bulgaria–Egypt	3–1	(15–8, 15–9, 13–15, 15–3)
3 Sep.	Bulgaria–Finland	3–0	(15–0, 15–8, 15–4)
3 Sep.	Poland–Egypt	3–0	(15–7, 15–3, 15–6)

	G	W/L	SW/SL	Pts.
1. Poland	4	4/0	12/2	8
2. Bulgaria	4	3/1	10/4	7
3. Finland	4	2/2	7/7	6
4. Egypt	4	1/3	5/9	5
5. Denmark	4	0/4	0/12	4

Group D (Pardubice)

30 Aug.	Yugoslavia–Turkey	3–0	(15–8, 15–3, 15–13)
30 Aug.	Albania–Austria	3–0	(15–1, 15–2, 15–9)
31 Aug.	USSR–Yugoslavia	3–2	(15–10, 5–15, 15–7, 8–15, 15–8)
31 Aug.	Turkey–Albania	3–0	(17–15, 16–14, 15–8)
1 Sep.	Turkey–Austria	3–0	(15–5, 15–8, 17–15)
1 Sep.	USSR–Albania	3–0	(15–2, 15–10, 15–6)
2 Sep.	Yugoslavia–Albania	3–0	(15–4, 15–10, 15–9)
2 Sep.	USSR–Austria	3–0	(15–1, 15–7, 15–2)
3 Sep.	Yugoslavia–Austria	3–0	(15–1, 15–1, 15–6)
3 Sep.	USSR–Turkey	3–0	(15–4, 15–7, 15–8)

	G	W/L	SW/SL	Pts.
1. USSR	4	4/0	12/2	8
2. Yugoslavia	4	3/1	11/3	7
3. Turkey	4	2/2	6/6	6
4. Albania	4	1/3	3/9	5
5. Austria	4	0/4	0/12	4

Final round (Prague)

Final group for 17–20 places

6 Sep.	Belgium–Austria	3–0	(15–5, 15–9, 15–3)
7 Sep.	Austria–Denmark	3–0	(15–8, 15–2, 15–11)
7 Sep.	Belgium–FRG	3–0	(15–5, 15–11, 15–6)
9 Sep.	Belgium–Denmark	3–0	(15–7, 15–1, 15–9)
10 Sep.	FRG–Denmark	3–0	(15–9, 15–8, 15–10)*
11 Sep.	Austria–FRG	3–1	(14–16, 15–7, 15–13, 15–2)

*The game between these two teams was initially played earlier in the day, but after the FRG won 3–0 (15–8, 15–11, 15–13), the Danish team made an official protest and, as a consequence, the game was repeated.

	G	W/L	SW/SL	Pts.
1. Belgium	3	3/0	9/0	6
2. Austria	3	2/1	6/4	5
3. FRG	3	1/2	4/6	4
4. Denmark	3	0/3	0/9	3

Final group for 9–16 places

5 Sep.	Egypt–Tunisia	3–0	(15–4, 15–8, 15–10)
5 Sep.	GDR–Netherlands	3–0	(16–14, 17–15, 16–14)
5 Sep.	Albania–Turkey	3–1	(15–10, 15–11, 6–15, 15–7)
5 Sep.	Italy–Finland	3–1	(15–13, 10–15, 18–16, 15–9)
6 Sep.	Netherlands–Egypt	3–0	(15–6, 15–11, 15–13)
6 Sep.	Albania–Tunisia	3–1	(9–15, 15–6, 15–12, 15–11)
6 Sep.	GDR–Italy	3–2	(1–15, 16–14, 15–3, 12–15, 16–14)
6 Sep.	Turkey–Finland	3–1	(15–11, 1–15, 15–13, 15–6)
7 Sep.	Italy–Netherlands	3–2	(2–15, 17–15, 3–15, 15–11, 15–11)
7 Sep.	Tunisia–Finland	3–2	(13–15, 16–18, 16–14, 15–8, 15–4)
7 Sep.	GDR–Turkey	3–2	(13–15, 15–5, 12–15, 15–6, 15–7)
7 Sep.	Albania–Egypt	3–0	(15–9, 15–12, 15–10)
8 Sep.	Albania–Finland	3–1	(15–10, 15–12, 12–15, 15–8)
8 Sep.	GDR–Tunisia	3–0	(15–9, 15–4, 15–11)
8 Sep.	Turkey–Netherlands	3–2	(15–11, 12–15, 13–15, 15–13, 15–9)
8 Sep.	Italy–Egypt	3–2	(12–15, 15–8, 5–15, 15–6, 15–4)

(continued)

Final group for 9–16 places (continued)

9 Sep.	GDR–Albania	3–0	(17–15, 15–11, 15–10)
9 Sep.	Finland–Egypt	3–2	(15–13, 10–15, 15–5, 15–17, 15–6)
9 Sep.	Netherlands–Tunisia	3–1	(12–15, 15–5, 15–7, 15–12)
9 Sep.	Italy–Turkey	3–1	(15–6, 15–10, 9–15, 15–13)
10 Sep.	GDR–Finland	3–0	(15–7, 15–9, 15–4)
10 Sep.	Turkey–Egypt	3–1	(15–6, 10–15, 15–5, 15–7)
10 Sep.	Albania–Netherlands	3–2	(15–10, 12–15, 15–10, 7–15, 15–10)
10 Sep.	Italy–Tunisia	3–0	(15–8, 16–14, 15–13)
11 Sep.	Turkey–Tunisia	3–0	(15–6, 15–12, 15–11)
11 Sep.	Finland–Netherlands	3–2	(15–10, 15–7, 12–15, 7–15, 15–7)
11 Sep.	GDR–Egypt	3–0	(15–11, 15–11, 15–12)
11 Sep.	Italy–Albania	3–0	(15–9, 15–10, 15–7)

	G	W/L	SW/SL	Pts.
1. GDR	7	7/0	21/4	14
2. Italy	7	6/1	20/9	13
3. Albania	7	5/2	15/11	12
4. Turkey	7	4/3	16/13	11
5. Netherlands	7	2/5	14/16	9
6. Finland	7	2/5	11/19	9
7. Egypt	7	1/6	8/18	8
8. Tunisia	7	1/6	5/20	8

Final group for 1–8 places

5 Sep.	Poland–Yugoslavia	3–0	(15–9, 15–5, 17–15)
5 Sep.	Bulgaria–Romania	3–1	(15–7, 13–15, 15–11, 15–13)
5 Sep.	Hungary–Czechoslovakia	3–2	(15–17, 15–8, 15–10, 9–15, 16–14)
5 Sep.	USSR–France	3–0	(18–16, 15–5, 15–12)
6 Sep.	Bulgaria–Yugoslavia	3–2	(15–4, 11–15, 10–15, 15–11, 15–7)
6 Sep.	Hungary–Poland	3–1	(7–15, 15–4, 15–13, 15–10)
6 Sep.	Czechoslovakia–France	3–0	(15–4, 15–3, 15–12)
6 Sep.	Romania–USSR	3–2	(7–15, 15–12, 16–14, 5–15, 15–8)
7 Sep.	USSR–Yugoslavia	3–0	(15–4, 15–1, 15–5)
7 Sep.	Hungary–France	3–0	(15–8, 15–10, 15–9)
7 Sep.	Bulgaria–Poland	3–2	(15–13, 17–15, 3–15, 10–15, 15–8)
7 Sep.	Czechoslovakia–Romania	3–1	(6–15, 15–6, 15–9, 15–5)
8 Sep.	Czechoslovakia–Yugoslavia	3–0	(15–5, 15–4, 15–11)
8 Sep.	Hungary–Bulgaria	3–2	(8–15, 17–15, 15–17, 15–10, 17–15)
8 Sep.	Poland–USSR	3–1	(15–7, 9–15, 15–10, 15–9)
8 Sep.	Romania–France	3–2	(15–10, 15–8, 7–15, 12–15, 15–5)
9 Sep.	Yugoslavia–France	3–1	(15–11, 15–2, 11–15, 15–11)
9 Sep.	Romania–Hungary	3–2	(14–16, 15–9, 15–10, 9–15, 15–6)

(continued)

Final group for 1–8 places (continued)

9 Sep.	USSR–Bulgaria	3–2	(15–8, 14–16, 15–6, 11–15, 15–10)
9 Sep.	Czechoslovakia–Poland	3–1	(13–15, 15–12, 15–6, 15–13)
10 Sep.	Romania–Yugoslavia	3–2	(15–2, 13–15, 15–10, 11–15, 15–6)
10 Sep.	Poland–France	3–0	(15–10, 15–10, 15–6)
10 Sep.	Czechoslovakia–Bulgaria	3–0	(15–5, 15–6, 16–14)
10 Sep.	USSR–Hungary	3–0	(15–8, 15–13, 15–12)
11 Sep.	Yugoslavia–Hungary	3–2	(15–8, 10–15, 15–7, 11–15, 15–10)
11 Sep.	Bulgaria–France	3–0	(15–6, 15–4, 15–7)
11 Sep.	Romania–Poland	3–0	(15–13, 15–12, 16–14)
11 Sep.	Czechoslovakia–USSR	3–2	(15–7, 10–15, 15–10, 14–16, 15–9)

	G	W/L	SW/SL	Pts.
1. Czechoslovakia	7	6/1	20/7	13
2. Romania	7	5/2	17/14	12
3. USSR	7	4/3	17/11	11
4. Bulgaria	7	4/3	16/14	11
5. Hungary	7	4/3	16/14	11
6. Poland	7	3/4	13/13	10
7. Yugoslavia	7	2/5	10/18	9
8. France	7	0/7	3/21	7

Final standings

	G	W/L	SW/SL
1. Czechoslovakia	11	10/1	32/7
2. Romania	11	9/2	29/14
3. USSR	11	8/3	29/13
4. Bulgaria	11	7/4	26/18
5. Hungary	11	7/4	25/19
6. Poland	11	7/4	25/15
7. Yugoslavia	11	5/6	21/21
8. France	11	3/8	12/24
9. GDR	11	9/2	27/10
10. Italy	11	8/3	26/19
11. Albania	11	6/5	18/20
12. Turkey	11	6/5	22/19
13. Netherlands	11	3/8	21/27
14. Finland	11	4/7	18/26
15. Egypt	11	2/9	13/27
16. Tunisia	11	2/9	8/29
17. Belgium	7	3/4	13/12
18. Austria	7	2/5	6/16
19. FRG	7	1/6	4/18
20. Denmark	7	0/7	0/21

Total: 20 teams, 102 games

Rosters of the medalists

Czechoslovakia–Bohumil Golian, Zdeněk Humhal, Miloslav Kemel, Karel Láznička, Zdeněk Malý, Josef Musil, Jaromír Paldus, Karel Paulus, Milan Purnoch, Ladislav Synovec, Josef Tesař, Ladislav Toman; head coach: Josef Kozák

Romania–Gabriel Cherebeţiu, Eduard Derzsei, Aurel Drăgan, Gheorghe Ferariu, Constantin Ganciu, Caius Miculescu, Sebastian Mihăilescu, Horaţiu Nicolau, Petre Păunoiu, Ştefan Roman, Marcel Rusescu; head coach: Gheorghe Petrescu

USSR–Oktay Agaev, Vladimir Astafev, Nikolay Burobin, Nil Fasakhov, Gennadiy Gaykovoy, Yuriy Khudyakov, Eduards Lībiņš, Valentin Lityagin, Marat Shablygin, German Smolyaninov, Yuriy Vengerovskiy, Anatoliy Zakrzhevskiy; head coach: Anatoliy Eyngorn

VI EUROPEAN CHAMPIONSHIP
21 October–2 November 1963, Braşov, Bucharest, Cluj, and Târgu Mureş (Romania)

Preliminary round

Group A (Braşov)

22 Oct.	Czechoslovakia–Belgium	3–0	(15–9, 15–3, 15–5)
22 Oct.	Hungary–Italy	3–0	(15–11, 15–7, 15–13)
23 Oct.	Italy–Belgium	3–1	(15–10, 9–15, 15–10, 15–10)
23 Oct.	Hungary–Czechoslovakia	3–2	(15–13, 15–12, 10–15, 14–16, 15–8)
24 Oct.	Hungary–Belgium	3–0	(15–3, 15–4, 15–9)
24 Oct.	Czechoslovakia–Italy	3–0	(15–11, 15–12, 15–10)

	G	W/L	SW/SL	Pts.
1. Hungary	3	3/0	9/2	6
2. Czechoslovakia	3	2/1	8/3	5
3. Italy	3	1/2	3/7	4
4. Belgium	3	0/3	1/9	3

Group B (Bucharest)

22 Oct.	Poland–Netherlands	3–0	(15–12, 17–15, 15–9)
22 Oct.	Romania–Finland	3–0	(15–5, 15–0, 15–4)
23 Oct.	Netherlands–Finland	3–0	(15–2, 15–10, 15–9)
23 Oct.	Romania–Poland	3–0	(15–9, 15–9, 15–11)
24 Oct.	Romania–Netherlands	3–1	(16–14, 15–8, 8–15, 15–6)
24 Oct.	Poland–Finland	3–0	(15–5, 15–5, 15–6)

	G	W/L	SW/SL	Pts.
1. Romania	3	3/0	9/1	6
2. Poland	3	2/1	6/3	5
3. Netherlands	3	1/2	4/6	4
4. Finland	3	0/3	0/9	3

Group C (Cluj)

22 Oct.	Yugoslavia–GDR	3–1	(15–13, 15–12, 11–15, 15–7)
22 Oct.	USSR–Austria	3–0	(15–1, 15–5, 15–3)
23 Oct.	USSR–Yugoslavia	3–2	(15–8, 15–9, 10–15, 9–15, 15–11)
23 Oct.	GDR–Austria	3–0	(15–5, 15–2, 15–9)
24 Oct.	Yugoslavia–Austria	3–0	(15–3, 15–1, 15–0)
24 Oct.	GDR–USSR	3–2	(11–15, 11–15, 15–10, 15–8, 15–8)

	G	W/L	SW/SL	Pts.
1. Yugoslavia	3	2/1	8/4	5
2. USSR	3	2/1	8/5	5
3. GDR	3	2/1	7/5	5
4. Austria	3	0/3	0/9	3

Group D (Târgu Mureş)

21 Oct.	Bulgaria–FRG	3–0	(15–2, 15–6, 15–0)
21 Oct.	France–Turkey	3–2	(13–15, 15–8, 14–16, 15–5, 15–9)
22 Oct.	Turkey–Denmark	3–0	(15–5, 15–1, 15–5)
22 Oct.	Bulgaria–France	3–0	(15–8, 15–2, 15–5)
23 Oct.	FRG–Denmark	3–0	(15–10, 15–13, 15–11)
23 Oct.	Bulgaria–Turkey	3–0	(15–4, 15–10, 15–11)
24 Oct.	Bulgaria–Denmark	3–0	(15–3, 15–6, 15–2)
24 Oct.	France–FRG	3–0	(15–5, 15–7, 15–7)
25 Oct.	France–Denmark	3–0	(15–5, 15–11, 15–7)
25 Oct.	Turkey–FRG	3–0	(15–3, 15–8, 15–3)

	G	W/L	SW/SL	Pts.
1. Bulgaria	4	4/0	12/0	8
2. France	4	3/1	9/5	7
3. Turkey	4	2/2	8/6	6
4. FRG	4	1/3	3/9	5
5. Denmark	4	0/4	0/12	4

Final round (head-to-head games were carried over from the preliminary round)

Final group for 9–17 places (Cluj)

26 Oct.	Italy–Denmark	3–0	(15–2, 15–3, 15–5)
26 Oct.	Turkey–Austria	3–0	(15–5, 15–3, 15–0)
26 Oct.	GDR–Finland	3–0	(15–2, 15–3, 15–3)
26 Oct.	Netherlands–Belgium	3–0	(15–4, 15–12, 17–15)
27 Oct.	Belgium–FRG	3–0	(15–10, 15–5, 15–8)
27 Oct.	Finland–Austria	3–0	(15–3, 15–7, 15–6)
27 Oct.	GDR–Italy	3–0	(17–15, 15–4, 15–6)
28 Oct.	GDR–Denmark	3–0	(15–0, 15–1, 15–1)
28 Oct.	Italy–Netherlands	3–2	(13–15, 8–15, 15–13, 15–8, 15–11)
28 Oct.	Finland–FRG	3–1	(15–9, 9–15, 15–8, 15–12)
28 Oct.	Turkey–Belgium	3–1	(11–15, 15–12, 15–13, 17–15)
29 Oct.	GDR–Belgium	3–0	(15–5, 15–5, 15–1)
29 Oct.	Netherlands–Denmark	3–0	(15–4, 15–8, 15–3)
29 Oct.	Turkey–Finland	3–0	(15–9, 15–9, 15–8)
29 Oct.	FRG–Austria	3–1	(15–8, 7–15, 15–12, 15–7)
30 Oct.	Belgium–Austria	3–0	(15–5, 15–3, 15–2)
30 Oct.	Italy–Turkey	3–1	(15–17, 20–18, 16–14, 15–12)
30 Oct.	GDR–Netherlands	3–0	(15–11, 15–11, 15–10)
31 Oct.	Italy–FRG	3–0	(15–6, 15–5, 15–11)
31 Oct.	Turkey–Netherlands	3–1	(15–13, 16–14, 12–15, 17–15)
31 Oct.	Belgium–Finland	3–0	(15–5, 15–7, 15–10)
31 Oct.	Austria–Denmark	3–0	(15–3, 15–12, 16–14)
1 Nov.	Netherlands–FRG	3–0	(15–3, 15–6, 15–11)
1 Nov.	Italy–Austria	3–0	(15–4, 15–1, 15–7)
1 Nov.	GDR–Turkey	3–0	(15–5, 15–5, 16–14)
1 Nov.	Finland–Denmark	3–0	(15–4, 15–0, 15–12)
2 Nov.	Italy–Finland	3–1	(15–3, 15–13, 7–15, 15–7)
2 Nov.	GDR–FRG	3–0	(15–2, 15–0, 15–2)
2 Nov.	Belgium–Denmark	3–0	(15–8, 15–6, 15–7)
2 Nov.	Netherlands–Austria	3–0	(15–3, 15–1, 15–5)

	G	W/L	SW/SL	Pts.
1. GDR	8	8/0	24/0	16
2. Italy	8	7/1	21/8	15
3. Turkey	8	6/2	19/8	14
4. Netherlands	8	5/3	18/9	13
5. Belgium	8	4/4	14/12	12
6. Finland	8	3/5	10/16	11
7. FRG	8	2/6	7/19	10
8. Austria	8	1/7	4/21	9
9. Denmark	8	0/8	0/24	8

Final group for 1–8 places (Bucharest)

26 Oct.	Romania–Yugoslavia	3–0	(15–6, 15–11, 15–8)
26 Oct.	USSR–France	3–0	(15–6, 15–10, 15–12)
26 Oct.	Bulgaria–Poland	3–1	(15–3, 12–15, 15–13, 15–8)
27 Oct.	Bulgaria–Yugoslavia	3–0	(15–7, 15–6, 15–13)
27 Oct.	Poland–Czechoslovakia	3–2	(11–15, 15–11, 7–15, 15–8, 15–10)
27 Oct.	Romania–USSR	3–2	(8–15, 15–7, 15–13, 13–15, 15–8)
27 Oct.	Hungary–France	3–0	(16–14, 15–7, 15–5)
28 Oct.	Poland–Yugoslavia	3–1	(15–12, 15–9, 7–15, 15–12)
28 Oct.	USSR–Bulgaria	3–2	(6–15, 15–4, 4–15, 15–2, 15–7)
28 Oct.	Romania–Hungary	3–0	(15–11, 15–3, 15–7)
28 Oct.	Czechoslovakia–France	3–0	(15–10, 15–4, 15–11)
29 Oct.	Poland–France	3–1	(15–12, 10–15, 15–10, 15–5)
29 Oct.	Hungary–Bulgaria	3–1	(13–15, 15–4, 15–8, 15–6)
29 Oct.	Romania–Czechoslovakia	3–1	(15–9, 4–15, 15–5, 15–11)
31 Oct.	Hungary–Yugoslavia	3–1	(15–9, 15–7, 9–15, 15–7)
31 Oct.	Romania–France	3–0	(15–4, 15–5, 15–11)
31 Oct.	USSR–Poland	3–2	(8–15, 15–4, 15–6, 10–15, 15–8)
31 Oct.	Bulgaria–Czechoslovakia	3–2	(16–18, 15–9, 13–15, 15–12, 15–11)
1 Nov.	Czechoslovakia–Yugoslavia	3–0	(15–4, 15–12, 16–14)
1 Nov.	USSR–Hungary	3–1	(15–8, 7–15, 15–13, 15–3)
2 Nov.	Yugoslavia–France	3–2	(15–8, 12–15, 10–15, 15–13, 15–6)
2 Nov.	Romania–Bulgaria	3–1	(8–15, 15–11, 15–8, 15–11)
2 Nov.	Hungary–Poland	3–0	(15–7, 15–8, 15–12)
2 Nov.	Czechoslovakia–USSR	3–2	(11–15, 17–15, 12–15, 15–12, 15–13)

	G	W/L	SW/SL	Pts.
1. Romania	7	7/0	21/4	14
2. Hungary	7	5/2	16/10	12
3. USSR	7	5/2	19/13	12
4. Bulgaria	7	4/3	16/12	11
5. Czechoslovakia	7	3/4	16/14	10
6. Poland	7	3/4	12/16	10
7. Yugoslavia	7	1/6	7/20	8
8. France	7	0/7	3/21	7

Final standings

	G	W/L	SW/SL
1. Romania	9	9/0	27/5
2. Hungary	9	7/2	22/10
3. USSR	9	6/3	24/16
4. Bulgaria	10	7/3	25/12
5. Czechoslovakia	9	5/4	22/14
6. Poland	9	5/4	18/16
7. Yugoslavia	9	3/6	13/21
8. France	10	3/7	12/23
9. GDR	10	9/1	28/5
10. Italy	10	7/3	21/14
11. Turkey	10	6/4	21/14
12. Netherlands	10	5/5	19/15
13. Belgium	10	4/6	14/18
14. Finland	10	3/7	10/22
15. FRG	10	2/8	7/25
16. Austria	10	1/9	4/27
17. Denmark	10	0/10	0/30

Total: 17 teams, 82 games

Rosters of the medalists

Romania–Nicolae Bărbuţă, Ioan Mihaiu Chezan, Mihai Iuliu Coste, Eduard Derzsei, Aurel Drăgan, Gheorghe Ferariu, Constantin Ganciu, Mihai Grigorovici, Horaţiu Nicolau, Davila Plocon, Wiliam Schreiber, Iuliu Szöcs; head coach: Ştefan Roman

Hungary–Béla Czafik, József Farkas, Tibor Flórián, László Gálos, Vilmos Iváncsó, Ferenc Jánosi, Antal Kangyerka, Csaba Lantos, István Molnár, Ottó Prouza, Mihály Tatár, Ferenc Tüske; head coach: László Porubszky

USSR–Ivans Bugajenkovs, Nikolay Burobin, Yuriy Chesnokov, Gennadiy Gaykovoy, Vazha Kacharava, Valeriy Kalachikhin, Vitaliy Kovalenko, Veniamin Merkulov, Georgiy Mondzolevskiy, Yuriy Poyarkov, Eduard Sibiryakov, Dmitriy Voskoboynikov; head coach: Givi Akhvlediani

VII EUROPEAN CHAMPIONSHIP
26 October–8 November 1967, Adana, Ankara, Istanbul, and Izmir (Turkey)

Preliminary round

Group A (Adana)

27 Oct.	GDR–Netherlands	3–0	(15–4, 15–7, 15–1)
28 Oct.	GDR–Austria	3–0	(15–1, 15–1, 15–5)

(continued)

Group A (Adana) (continued)

28 Oct.	Netherlands–Sweden	3–0	(15–1, 15–1, 15–3)
29 Oct.	Sweden–Austria	3–2	(17–19, 15–5, 11–15, 15–10, 17–15)
29 Oct.	USSR–Netherlands	3–0	(15–9, 15–10, 15–3)
30 Oct.	USSR–Austria	3–0	(15–2, 15–0, 15–1)
30 Oct.	GDR–Sweden	3–0	(15–1, 15–0, 15–6)

	G	W/L	SW/SL	Pts.
1. USSR	4	4/0	12/2	8
2. GDR	4	3/1	11/3	7
3. Netherlands	4	2/2	6/6	6
4. Sweden	4	1/3	3/11	5
5. Austria	4	0/4	2/12	4

Group B (Izmir)

26 Oct.	Yugoslavia–France	3–1	(7–15, 15–10, 17–15, 15–12)
26 Oct.	Hungary–Greece	3–0	(15–2, 15–8, 15–4)
27 Oct.	Yugoslavia–Greece	3–0	(15–5, 15–6, 15–7)
27 Oct.	Hungary–Belgium	3–1	(7–15, 15–7, 15–12, 15–4)
28 Oct.	Yugoslavia–Belgium	3–0	(15–13, 15–6, 15–5)
28 Oct.	France–Greece	3–0	(15–7, 15–7, 15–8)
29 Oct.	Hungary–Yugoslavia	3–1	(13–15, 15–12, 15–10, 16–14)
29 Oct.	Belgium–France	3–1	(8–15, 15–12, 15–10, 15–10)
30 Oct.	Hungary–France	3–1	(6–15, 15–5, 15–7, 15–6)
30 Oct.	Belgium–Greece	3–0	(15–3, 15–9, 15–8)

	G	W/L	SW/SL	Pts.
1. Hungary	4	4/0	12/3	8
2. Yugoslavia	4	3/1	10/4	7
3. Belgium	4	2/2	7/7	6
4. France	4	1/3	6/9	5
5. Greece	4	0/4	0/12	4

Group C (Ankara)

26 Oct.	Czechoslovakia–Turkey	3–0	(15–4, 15–7, 15–5)
26 Oct.	Italy–Finland	3–1	(15–8, 8–15, 15–10, 19–17)
27 Oct.	Czechoslovakia–Israel	3–0	(15–5, 15–3, 17–15)
27 Oct.	Turkey–Finland	3–2	(15–7, 15–4, 14–16, 14–16, 15–10)
28 Oct.	Italy–Israel	3–2	(15–11, 8–15, 15–8, 11–15, 16–14)
28 Oct.	Czechoslovakia–Finland	3–0	(15–4, 15–1, 15–1)
29 Oct.	Italy–Turkey	3–1	(15–9, 9–15, 15–10, 15–10)

(continued)

Group C (Ankara) (continued)

29 Oct.	Israel–Finland	3–0	(15–9, 15–7, 15–9)
30 Oct.	Czechoslovakia–Italy	3–1	(15–8, 15–2, 14–16, 15–6)
30 Oct.	Israel–Turkey	3–0	(15–11, 15–12, 15–0)

	G	W/L	SW/SL	Pts.
1. Czechoslovakia	4	4/0	12/1	8
2. Italy	4	3/1	10/7	7
3. Israel	4	2/2	8/6	6
4. Turkey	4	1/3	4/11	5
5. Finland	4	0/4	3/12	4

Group D (Istanbul)

26 Oct.	Poland–Bulgaria	3–2	(15–13, 13–15, 15–13, 9–15, 15–6)
26 Oct.	Romania–Albania	3–0	(15–7, 15–7, 15–12)
27 Oct.	Bulgaria–Albania	3–1	(7–15, 15–11, 15–9, 15–10)
27 Oct.	Romania–FRG	3–0	(15–4, 15–6, 15–6)
28 Oct.	Poland–Albania	3–0	(15–2, 15–7, 15–10)
28 Oct.	Bulgaria–FRG	3–0	(15–7, 15–5, 15–5)
29 Oct.	Poland–FRG	3–0	(15–8, 15–6, 15–4)
29 Oct.	Romania–Bulgaria	3–2	(12–15, 15–10, 15–17, 15–6, 15–12)
30 Oct.	Poland–Romania	3–1	(15–8, 14–16, 19–17, 15–11)
30 Oct.	Albania–FRG	3–1	(15–17, 15–11, 15–8, 15–1)

	G	W/L	SW/SL	Pts.
1. Poland	4	4/0	12/3	8
2. Romania	4	3/1	10/5	7
3. Bulgaria	4	2/2	0/7	6
4. Albania	4	1/3	4/10	5
5. FRG	4	0/4	1/12	4

Final round (head-to-head games were carried over from the preliminary round)

Final group for 17–20 places (Ankara)

2 Nov.	Finland–Greece	3–0	(15–5, 15–12, 15–2)
2 Nov.	FRG–Austria	3–0	(15–9, 15–11, 15–8)
3 Nov.	Finland–FRG	3–2	(15–13, 8–15, 17–15, 14–16, 15–5)
3 Nov.	Austria–Greece	3–0	(15–11, 15–9, 15–9)
4 Nov.	Finland–Austria	3–0	(15–6, 15–4, 15–7)
4 Nov.	FRG–Greece	3–2	(7–15, 15–8, 9–15, 15–5, 15–9)

	G	W/L	SW/SL	Pts.
1. Finland	3	3/0	9/2	6
2. FRG	3	2/1	8/5	5
3. Austria	3	1/2	3/6	4
4. Greece	3	0/3	2/9	3

Final group for 9–16 places (Ankara)

2 Nov.	Belgium–Netherlands	3–2	(15–12, 7–15, 15–10, 10–15, 17–15)
2 Nov.	Turkey–Sweden	3–0	(15–3, 15–3, 15–10)
2 Nov.	France–Albania	3–1	(15–7, 14–16, 15–10, 15–10)
2 Nov.	Bulgaria–Israel	3–0	(15–6, 17–15, 15–9)
3 Nov.	Bulgaria–Turkey	3–1	(15–9, 15–2, 12–15, 15–3)
3 Nov.	Belgium–Albania	3–0	(15–7, 15–9, 15–7)
3 Nov.	France–Sweden	3–0	(15–6, 15–4, 15–5)
3 Nov.	Israel–Netherlands	3–1	(9–15, 15–10, 15–6, 15–6)
4 Nov.	Albania–Turkey	3–1	(15–13, 13–15, 15–9, 15–3)
4 Nov.	Bulgaria–Netherlands	3–0	(15–12, 15–12, 15–10)
4 Nov.	Belgium–Sweden	3–0	(15–3, 15–6, 15–4)
4 Nov.	France–Israel	3–1	(9–15, 16–14, 15–11, 15–5)
6 Nov.	Turkey–Netherlands	3–2	(9–15, 15–6, 9–15, 15–6, 16–14)
6 Nov.	Albania–Sweden	3–0	(15–1, 15–7, 15–6)
6 Nov.	France–Bulgaria	3–1	(15–8, 15–10, 8–15, 15–9)
6 Nov.	Israel–Belgium	3–2	(5–15, 15–9, 3–15, 15–12, 16–14)
7 Nov.	France–Turkey	3–1	(15–8, 15–6, 12–15, 15–8)
7 Nov.	Albania–Netherlands	3–2	(15–10, 5–15, 10–15, 15–6, 15–9)
7 Nov.	Israel–Sweden	3–0	(15–3, 15–3, 15–5)
7 Nov.	Bulgaria–Belgium	3–0	(15–5, 15–12, 15–9)
8 Nov.	Belgium–Turkey	3–2	(15–8, 14–16, 15–8, 12–15, 15–10)
8 Nov.	France–Netherlands	3–0	(15–4, 15–11, 15–9)
8 Nov.	Israel–Albania	3–0	(16–14, 17–15, 15–10)
8 Nov.	Bulgaria–Sweden	3–0	(15–4, 15–6, 15–4)

	G	W/L	SW/SL	Pts.
1. Bulgaria	7	6/1	19/5	13
2. France	7	6/1	19/7	13
3. Israel	7	5/2	16/9	12
4. Belgium	7	5/2	17/11	12
5. Albania	7	3/4	11/15	10
6. Turkey	7	2/5	11/17	9
7. Netherlands	7	1/6	10/18	8
8. Sweden	7	0/7	0/21	7

Final group for 1–8 places (Istanbul)

2 Nov.	Czechoslovakia–Yugoslavia	3–0	(15–12, 15–2, 16–14)
2 Nov.	GDR–Italy	3–0	(15–5, 15–5, 15–9)
2 Nov.	USSR–Romania	3–1	(15–6, 15–8, 5–15, 15–7)
2 Nov.	Poland–Hungary	3–1	(10–15, 15–13, 15–9, 15–9)
3 Nov.	GDR–Yugoslavia	3–1	(9–15, 15–13, 15–11, 15–10)
3 Nov.	Hungary–Italy	3–1	(16–14, 13–15, 15–8, 15–11)
3 Nov.	USSR–Poland	3–1	(15–6, 15–6, 5–15, 15–11)
3 Nov.	Czechoslovakia–Romania	3–1	(17–15, 12–15, 15–3, 15–9)
4 Nov.	Romania–Yugoslavia	3–0	(15–11, 15–6, 16–14)
4 Nov.	USSR–Italy	3–0	(15–8, 15–8, 15–3)
4 Nov.	Hungary–GDR	3–2	(15–11, 4–15, 8–15, 16–14, 16–14)
4 Nov.	Czechoslovakia–Poland	3–2	(7–15, 16–14, 10–15, 15–9, 15–6)
6 Nov.	Romania–Italy	3–0	(15–7, 15–5, 15–8)
6 Nov.	Poland–Yugoslavia	3–0	(15–7, 15–13, 15–12)
6 Nov.	USSR–Hungary	3–0	(15–8, 15–8, 15–6)
6 Nov.	Czechoslovakia–GDR	3–0	(15–13, 15–8, 15–11)
7 Nov.	Poland–Italy	3–0	(15–10, 16–14, 15–6)
7 Nov.	USSR–Yugoslavia	3–0	(15–1, 15–9, 15–8)
7 Nov.	Czechoslovakia–Hungary	3–2	(15–5, 6–15, 15–5, 12–15, 15–5)
7 Nov.	GDR–Romania	3–1	(15–12, 10–15, 15–10, 15–2)
8 Nov.	Yugoslavia–Italy	3–0	(15–12, 15–7, 15–11)
8 Nov.	GDR–Poland	3–1	(15–9, 5–15, 15–7, 17–15)
8 Nov.	Romania–Hungary	3–1	(15–5, 11–15, 15–13, 15–8)
8 Nov.	USSR–Czechoslovakia	3–2	(15–7, 15–13, 13–15, 10–15, 15–10)

	G	W/L	SW/SL	Pts.
1. USSR	7	7/0	21/6	14
2. Czechoslovakia	7	6/1	20/9	13
3. Poland	7	4/3	16/11	11
4. GDR	7	4/3	16/12	11
5. Romania	7	3/4	13/13	10
6. Hungary	7	3/4	13/16	10
7. Yugoslavia	7	1/6	5/18	8
8. Italy	7	0/7	2/21	7

Final standings

	G	W/L	SW/SL
1. USSR	10	10/0	30/6
2. Czechoslovakia	10	9/1	29/9
3. Poland	10	7/3	25/13
4. GDR	10	7/3	25/12
5. Romania	10	6/4	22/15

(continued)

	G	W/L	SW/SL
6. Hungary	10	6/4	22/18
7. Yugoslavia	10	4/6	14/19
8. Italy	10	3/7	11/25
9. Bulgaria	10	7/3	26/11
10. France	10	7/3	24/13
11. Israel	10	6/4	21/15
12. Belgium	10	6/4	21/17
13. Albania	10	4/6	14/22
14. Turkey	10	3/7	15/25
15. Netherlands	10	2/8	13/24
16. Sweden	10	1/9	3/29
17. Finland	7	3/4	12/14
18. FRG	7	2/5	9/17
19. Austria	7	1/6	5/18
20. Greece	7	0/7	2/21

Total: 20 teams, 94 games

Rosters of the medalists

USSR–Vladimir Belyaev, Ivans Bugajenkovs, Vladimir Ivanov, Vazha Kacharava, Valeriy Kravchenko, Evgeniy Lapinskiy, Viktor Mikhalchuk, Georgiy Mondzolevskiy, Vadim Penteshkin, Yuriy Poyarkov, Zhanbek Saurambaev, Eduard Sibiryakov; head coach: Yuriy Kleshchyov

Czechoslovakia–Bohumil Golian, Zdeněk Groessl, Petr Kop, Drahomír Koudelka, Antonín Mozr, Josef Musil, Vladimír Petlák, Antonín Procházka, Pavel Schenk, Václav Šmídl, Josef Smolka, Jiří Svoboda; head coach: Václav Matiášek

Poland–Zdzisław Ambroziak, Stanisław Gościniak, Zbigniew Jasiukiewicz, Romuald Paszkiewicz, Wojciech Rutkowski, Ryszard Sierszulski, Tadeusz Siwek, Aleksander Skiba, Edward Skorek, Jerzy Szymczyk, Hubert Wagner, Stanisław Zduńczyk; head coach: Tadeusz Szlagor

VIII EUROPEAN CHAMPIONSHIP
23 September–1 October 1971, Ancona, Bergamo, Bologna, Imola, Milan, Modena, and Turin (Italy)

Preliminary round

Group A (Imola)

25 Sep.   USSR–Belgium   3–0   (15–1, 15–11, 15–12)

	G	W/L	SW/SL	Pts.
1. USSR	1	1/0	3/0	2
2. Belgium	1	0/1	0/3	1

Group B (Bergamo)

23 Sep.	Israel–Turkey	3–0	(15–10, 15–13, 15–2)
23 Sep.	Czechoslovakia–Scotland	3–0	(15–0, 15–6, 15–2)
24 Sep.	Turkey–Scotland	3–0	(15–5, 15–11, 15–9)
24 Sep.	Czechoslovakia–Israel	3–0	(15–5, 15–12, 15–0)
25 Sep.	Israel–Scotland	3–0	(15–8, 15–5, 15–3)
25 Sep.	Czechoslovakia–Turkey	3–0	(15–9, 15–6, 15–7)

	G	W/L	SW/SL	Pts.
1. Czechoslovakia	3	3/0	9/0	6
2. Israel	3	2/1	6/3	5
3. Turkey	3	1/2	3/6	4
4. Scotland	3	0/3	0/9	3

Group C (Ancona)

23 Sep.	Poland–Denmark	3–0	(15–2, 15–3, 15–5)
23 Sep.	Netherlands–France	3–2	(10–15, 15–8, 13–15, 15–7, 16–14)
24 Sep.	France–Denmark	3–0	(15–8, 15–12, 18–16)
24 Sep.	Poland–Netherlands	3–0	(15–4, 15–11, 15–12)
25 Sep.	Netherlands–Denmark	3–0	(16–14, 15–5, 15–5)
25 Sep.	Poland–France	3–1	(15–4, 14–16, 15–11, 15–12)

	G	W/L	SW/SL	Pts.
1. Poland	3	3/0	9/1	6
2. Netherlands	3	2/1	6/5	5
3. France	3	1/2	6/6	4
4. Denmark	3	0/3	0/9	3

Group D (Milan)

23 Sep.	GDR–Sweden	3–0	(15–0, 15–1, 15–4)
23 Sep.	Bulgaria–Switzerland	3–0	(15–5, 15–6, 15–1)
24 Sep.	GDR–Switzerland	3–0	(15–3, 15–3, 15–5)
24 Sep.	Bulgaria–Sweden	3–0	(15–1, 15–8, 15–6)
25 Sep.	Sweden–Switzerland	3–0	(16–14, 15–8, 15–10)
25 Sep.	GDR–Bulgaria	3–2	(15–5, 10–15, 15–5, 11–15, 15–7)

	G	W/L	SW/SL	Pts.
1. GDR	3	3/0	9/2	6
2. Bulgaria	3	2/1	8/3	5
3. Sweden	3	1/2	3/6	4
4. Switzerland	3	0/3	0/9	3

Group E (Turin)

23 Sep.	Romania–Italy	3–2	(15–7, 8–15, 15–13, 9–15, 15–8)
23 Sep.	Finland–Greece	3–0	(15–5, 15–10, 15–6)
24 Sep.	Italy–Finland	3–0	(15–6, 15–8, 15–13)
24 Sep.	Romania–Greece	3–0	(15–3, 15–10, 15–13)
25 Sep.	Italy–Greece	3–0	(15–11, 15–4, 15–12)
25 Sep.	Romania–Finland	3–1	(22–24, 15–12, 15–10, 15–1)

	G	W/L	SW/SL	Pts.
1. Romania	3	3/0	9/3	6
2. Italy	3	2/1	8/3	5
3. Finland	3	1/2	4/6	4
4. Greece	3	0/3	0/9	3

Group F (Modena)

23 Sep.	Yugoslavia–FRG	3–0	(15–13, 15–3, 15–8)
23 Sep.	Hungary–Austria	3–0	(15–3, 15–4, 15–6)
24 Sep.	Hungary–Yugoslavia	3–1	(15–5, 15–6, 13–15, 15–9)
24 Sep.	FRG–Austria	3–0	(15–5, 15–5, 15–6)
25 Sep.	Yugoslavia–Austria	3–0	(15–9, 15–1, 15–3)
25 Sep.	Hungary–FRG	3–0	(15–2, 17–15, 15–7)

	G	W/L	SW/SL	Pts.
1. Hungary	3	3/0	9/1	6
2. Yugoslavia	3	2/1	7/3	5
3. FRG	3	1/2	3/6	4
4. Austria	3	0/3	0/9	3

Final round

Final group for 18–22 places (Milan)

27 Sep.	Greece–Scotland	3–0	(15–2, 16–14, 15–3)
27 Sep.	Switzerland–Denmark	3–1	(10–15, 19–17, 15–7, 17–15)
28 Sep.	Greece–Switzerland	3–0	(15–11, 15–8, 15–7)
28 Sep.	Austria–Scotland	3–1	(15–10, 13–15, 15–3, 15–7)
29 Sep.	Switzerland–Austria	3–0	(15–6, 16–14, 15–11)
29 Sep.	Greece–Denmark	3–0	(15–11, 15–12, 15–5)
30 Sep.	Denmark–Scotland	3–0	(15–0, 15–5, 15–6)
30 Sep.	Greece–Austria	3–0	(15–3, 15–5, 15–12)
1 Oct.	Denmark–Austria	3–2	(15–11, 15–11, 12–15, 2–15, 15–8)
1 Oct.	Switzerland–Scotland	3–0	(15–7, 15–5, 15–13)

	G	W/L	SW/SL	Pts.
1. Greece	4	4/0	12/0	8
2. Switzerland	4	3/1	9/4	7
3. Denmark	4	2/2	7/8	6
4. Austria	4	1/3	5/10	5
5. Scotland	4	0/4	1/12	4

Final group for 13–17 places (Imola)

27 Sep.	Finland–Sweden	3–1	(14–16, 15–8, 15–10, 15–13)
27 Sep.	France–FRG	3–2	(15–8, 12–15, 12–15, 15–11, 15–13)
28 Sep.	France–Turkey	3–1	(10–15, 15–7, 15–3, 15–9)
28 Sep.	Finland–FRG	3–1	(15–12, 15–13, 13–15, 15–11)
29 Sep.	Finland–Turkey	3–0	(15–10, 15–6, 15–12)
29 Sep.	FRG–Sweden	3–1	(15–11, 13–15, 15–7, 15–9)
30 Sep.	Turkey–Sweden	3–2	(15–1, 9–15, 12–15, 15–8, 15–7)
30 Sep.	Finland–France	3–1	(15–9, 9–15, 15–9, 15–6)
1 Oct.	France–Sweden	3–0	(15–2, 15–11, 15–8)
1 Oct.	Turkey–FRG	3–2	(13–15, 13–15, 15–12, 15–13, 15–5)

	G	W/L	SW/SL	Pts.
1. Finland	4	4/0	12/3	8
2. France	4	3/1	10/6	7
3. Turkey	4	2/2	7/10	6
4. FRG	4	1/3	8/10	5
5. Sweden	4	0/4	4/12	4

Final group for 7–12 places (Bologna)

27 Sep.	Bulgaria–Belgium	3–0	(15–11, 15–11, 15–8)
27 Sep.	Italy–Israel	3–1	(13–15, 15–2, 15–11, 15–7)
27 Sep.	Netherlands–Yugoslavia	3–1	(7–15, 15–9, 15–10, 15–11)
28 Sep.	Belgium–Yugoslavia	3–1	(12–15, 15–8, 15–8, 15–8)
28 Sep.	Bulgaria–Israel	3–0	(15–1, 15–3, 15–6)
28 Sep.	Italy–Netherlands	3–1	(15–7, 15–9, 11–15, 15–13)
29 Sep.	Italy–Yugoslavia	3–1	(15–8, 15–9, 3–15, 15–6)
29 Sep.	Belgium–Israel	3–1	(5–15, 15–12, 15–11, 15–13)
29 Sep.	Bulgaria–Netherlands	3–0	(15–5, 15–6, 15–12)
30 Sep.	Bulgaria–Yugoslavia	3–1	(15–9, 16–14, 10–15, 15–13)
30 Sep.	Israel–Netherlands	3–1	(10–15, 15–8, 15–12, 15–12)
30 Sep.	Italy–Belgium	3–1	(16–14, 15–7, 8–15, 15–6)
1 Oct.	Netherlands–Belgium	3–0	(15–11, 15–4, 15–9)
1 Oct.	Yugoslavia–Israel	3–0	(15–2, 15–6, 15–6)
1 Oct.	Bulgaria–Italy	3–1	(7–15, 15–12, 15–9, 15–11)

	G	W/L	SW/SL	Pts.
1. Bulgaria	5	5/0	15/2	10
2. Italy	5	4/1	13/7	9
3. Netherlands	5	2/3	8/10	7
4. Belgium	5	2/3	7/11	7
5. Yugoslavia	5	1/4	7/12	6
6. Israel	5	1/4	5/13	6

Final group for 1–6 places (Milan)

27 Sep.	USSR–Hungary	3–0	(15–8, 15–8, 15–3)
27 Sep.	Romania–Poland	3–2	(9–15, 15–3, 9–15, 15–8, 15–7)
27 Sep.	Czechoslovakia–GDR	3–0	(15–11, 15–9, 15–9)
28 Sep.	Czechoslovakia–Hungary	3–0	(15–8, 15–6, 15–8)
28 Sep.	USSR–Romania	3–0	(15–11, 15–9, 15–11)
28 Sep.	GDR–Poland	3–0	(15–9, 15–6, 15–4)
29 Sep.	GDR–Hungary	3–0	(15–5, 15–12, 15–6)
29 Sep.	USSR–Poland	3–1	(15–8, 15–11, 13–15, 15–3)
29 Sep.	Romania–Czechoslovakia	3–0	(15–13, 16–14, 15–5)
30 Sep.	Czechoslovakia–Poland	3–2	(7–15, 15–6, 14–16, 15–9, 15–8)
30 Sep.	Romania–Hungary	3–1	(15–7, 13–15, 15–7, 15–1)
30 Sep.	USSR–GDR	3–0	(15–10, 15–6, 15–11)
1 Oct.	Romania–GDR	3–0	(16–14, 15–13, 15–12)
1 Oct.	Hungary–Poland	3–0	(15–9, 15–13, 15–13)
1 Oct.	Czechoslovakia–USSR	3–0	(15–10, 15–11, 15–4)

	G	W/L	SW/SL	Pts.
1. USSR	5	4/1	12/4	9
2. Czechoslovakia	5	4/1	12/5	9
3. Romania	5	4/1	12/6	9
4. GDR	5	2/3	6/9	7
5. Hungary	5	1/4	4/12	6
6. Poland	5	0/5	5/15	5

Final standings

	G	W/L	SW/SL
1. USSR	6	5/1	15/4
2. Czechoslovakia	8	7/1	21/5
3. Romania	8	7/1	21/9
4. GDR	8	5/3	15/11
5. Hungary	8	4/4	13/13
6. Poland	8	3/5	14/16
7. Bulgaria	8	7/1	23/5

(continued)

	G	W/L	SW/SL
8. Italy	8	6/2	21/10
9. Netherlands	8	4/4	14/15
10. Belgium	6	2/4	7/14
11. Yugoslavia	8	3/5	14/15
12. Israel	8	3/5	11/16
13. Finland	7	5/2	16/9
14. France	7	4/3	16/12
15. Turkey	7	3/4	10/16
16. FRG	7	2/5	11/16
17. Sweden	7	1/6	7/18
18. Greece	7	4/3	12/9
19. Switzerland	7	3/4	9/13
20. Denmark	7	2/5	7/17
21. Austria	7	1/6	5/19
22. Scotland	7	0/7	1/21

Total: 22 teams, 81 games

Rosters of the medalists

USSR–Efim Chulak, Vyacheslav Domani, Vladimir Kondra, Valeriy Kravchenko, Evgeniy Lapinskiy, Vladimir Patkin, Yuriy Poyarkov, Aleksandr Saprykin, Yuriy Starunskiy, Boris Tereshchuk, Oleg Zaporozhets, Leonid Zayko; head coach: Yuriy Chesnokov

Czechoslovakia Zdeněk Groessl, Drahomír Koudelka, Miroslav Nekola, Ludvík Němec, Petr Pavlík, Vladimír Petlák, Štefan Pipa, Pavel Schenk, Jaroslav Stančo, Jaroslav Tomáš, Milan Vápenka, Lubomír Zajíček; head coach: Karel Láznička

Romania–Viorel Bălaş, Gyula Bartha, Laurenţiu Dumănoiu, Romeo Enescu, Cristian Ion, Stelian Moculescu, Corneliu Oros, Corneliu Păduraru, Wiliam Schreiber, Marian Stamate, Mircea Tutovan-Codoi, Gabriel Udişteanu; head coach: Nicolae Sotir

IX EUROPEAN CHAMPIONSHIP
18–25 October 1975, Belgrade, Kraljevo, Skopje, and Subotica (Yugoslavia)

Preliminary round

Group A (Skopje)

18 Oct.	Yugoslavia–Italy	3–1	(12–15, 15–3, 15–10, 15–12)
18 Oct.	Poland–Hungary	3–0	(15–7, 15–12, 15–7)
19 Oct.	Yugoslavia–Hungary	3–1	(15–3, 11–15, 15–10, 15–7)
19 Oct.	Poland–Italy	3–0	(15–3, 15–7, 15–13)
20 Oct.	Poland–Yugoslavia	3–0	(15–7, 15–8, 15–8)
20 Oct.	Italy–Hungary	3–0	(16–14, 17–15, 15–5)

	G	W/L	SW/SL	Pts.
1. Poland	3	3/0	9/0	6
2. Yugoslavia	3	2/1	6/5	5
3. Italy	3	1/2	4/6	4
4. Hungary	3	0/3	1/9	3

Group B (Subotica)

18 Oct.	GDR–France	3–0	(15–3, 15–11, 15–4)
18 Oct.	USSR–Bulgaria	3–1	(8–15, 15–8, 15–7, 15–10)
19 Oct.	USSR–France	3–0	(15–4, 15–10, 15–7)
19 Oct.	Bulgaria–GDR	3–1	(15–12, 15–17, 15–12, 15–7)
20 Oct.	Bulgaria–France	3–0	(16–14, 15–11, 15–11)
20 Oct.	USSR–GDR	3–0	(15–6, 15–12, 15–5)

	G	W/L	SW/SL	Pts.
1. USSR	3	3/0	9/1	6
2. Bulgaria	3	2/1	7/4	5
3. GDR	3	1/2	4/6	4
4. France	3	0/3	0/9	3

Group C (Krajlevo)

18 Oct.	Czechoslovakia–Belgium	3–0	(15–8, 15–10, 15–7)
18 Oct.	Romania–Netherlands	3–2	(11–15, 16–18, 15–9, 15–1, 15–7)
19 Oct.	Czechoslovakia–Romania	3–2	(15–4, 11–15, 11–15, 15–11, 15–13)
19 Oct.	Netherlands–Belgium	3–2	(9–15, 15–7, 13–15, 16–14, 15–13)
20 Oct.	Romania–Belgium	3–0	(15–2, 15–9, 15–7)
20 Oct.	Czechoslovakia–Netherlands	3–0	(15–4, 15–7, 15–0)

	G	W/L	SW/SL	Pts.
1. Czechoslovakia	3	3/0	9/2	6
2. Romania	3	2/1	8/5	5
3. Netherlands	3	1/2	5/8	4
4. Belgium	3	0/3	2/9	3

Final round (head-to-head games were carried over from the preliminary round)

Final group for 7–12 places (Belgrade)

22 Oct.	France–Hungary	3–2	(9–15, 8–15, 16–14, 15–12, 16–14)
22 Oct.	GDR–Belgium	3–0	(15–13, 15–3, 15–6)
22 Oct.	Netherlands–Italy	3–0	(16–14, 15–7, 15–8)
23 Oct.	France–Belgium	3–2	(17–15, 15–8, 4–15, 11–15, 15–10)
23 Oct.	GDR–Italy	3–0	(15–5, 15–4, 15–11)
23 Oct.	Netherlands–Hungary	3–2	(8–15, 13–15, 15–8, 15–7, 15–13)
24 Oct.	Hungary–Belgium	3–1	(6–15, 15–13, 15–4, 15–11)
24 Oct.	France–Italy	3–1	(16–14, 11–15, 15–6, 15–11)
24 Oct.	GDR–Netherlands	3–0	(15–9, 15–7, 15–13)
25 Oct.	France–Netherlands	3–0	(15–7, 15–9, 15–7)
25 Oct.	GDR–Hungary	3–1	(15–4, 15–8, 13–15, 15–10)
25 Oct.	Italy–Belgium	3–2	(9–15, 9–15, 15–11, 15–6, 16–14)

	G	W/L	SW/SL	Pts.
1. GDR	5	5/0	15/1	10
2. France	5	4/1	12/8	9
3. Netherlands	5	3/2	9/10	8
4. Italy	5	2/3	7/11	7
5. Hungary	5	1/4	8/13	6
6. Belgium	5	0/5	7/15	5

Final group for 1–6 places (Belgrade)

22 Oct.	USSR–Poland	3–0	(15–12, 15–10, 15–7)
22 Oct.	Yugoslavia–Romania	3–2	(11–15, 15–10, 15–13, 8–15, 15–9)
22 Oct.	Bulgaria–Czechoslovakia	3–0	(15–12, 15–8, 15–7)
23 Oct.	Yugoslavia–Czechoslovakia	3–2	(15–6, 11–15, 12–15, 15–9, 15–13)
23 Oct.	Poland–Bulgaria	3–2	(9–15, 15–5, 15–6, 9–15, 15–3)
23 Oct.	USSR–Romania	3–0	(15–2, 15–8, 15–10)
24 Oct.	Romania–Bulgaria	3–0	(15–11, 15–10, 15–11)
24 Oct.	USSR–Yugoslavia	3–2	(13–15, 7–15, 15–0, 15–5, 15–8)
24 Oct.	Poland–Czechoslovakia	3–1	(15–8, 15–6, 11–15, 15–8)
25 Oct.	Yugoslavia–Bulgaria	3–0	(16–14, 16–14, 17–15)
25 Oct.	Romania–Poland	3–2	(13–15, 15–9, 6–15, 15–13, 15–12)
25 Oct.	USSR–Czechoslovakia	3–0	(15–8, 15–13, 15–3)

	G	W/L	SW/SL	Pts.
1. USSR	5	5/0	15/3	10
2. Poland	5	3/2	11/9	8
3. Yugoslavia	5	3/2	11/10	8
4. Romania	5	2/3	10/11	7
5. Bulgaria	5	1/4	6/12	6
6. Czechoslovakia	5	1/4	6/14	6

Final standings

	G	W/L	SW/SL
1. USSR	7	7/0	21/3
2. Poland	7	5/2	17/9
3. Yugoslavia	7	5/2	17/12
4. Romania	7	4/3	16/13
5. Bulgaria	7	3/4	12/13
6. Czechoslovakia	7	3/4	12/14
7. GDR	7	5/2	16/7
8. France	7	4/3	12/14
9. Netherlands	7	3/4	11/16
10. Italy	7	2/5	8/17
11. Hungary	7	1/6	9/19
12. Belgium	7	0/7	7/21

Total: 12 teams, 42 games

Rosters of the medalists

USSR–Vladimir Chernyshyov, Efim Chulak, Vladimir Dorokhov, Aleksandr Ermilov, Vladimir Kondra, Viljar Loor, Anatoliy Polishchuk, Aleksandr Savin, Pāvels Seļivanovs, Yuriy Starunskiy, Vladimir Ulanov, Vyacheslav Zaytsev; head coach: Yuriy Chesnokov

Poland–Ryszard Bosek, Wiesław Czaja, Wiesław Gawłowski, Stanisław Iwaniak, Zbigniew Jasiukiewicz, Władysław Kustra, Zbigniew Lubiejewski, Lech Łasko, Mirosław Rybaczewski, Włodzimierz Sadalski, Włodzimierz Stefański, Tomasz Wójtowicz; head coach: Hubert Wagner

Yugoslavia–Vladimir Bogoevski, Aleksandar Boričić, Vladimir Bošnjak, Vinko Dobrić, Mirsad Elezović, Miloš Grbić, Miodrag Gvozdenović, Ivica Jelić, Slobodan Lozančić, Laslo Lukač, Nikola Matijašević, Živojin Vračarić; head coach: Lazar Grozdanović

X EUROPEAN CHAMPIONSHIP
25 September–2 October 1977, Helsinki, Oulu, Tampere, and Turku (Finland)

Preliminary round

Group A (Helsinki)

25 Sep.	Finland–Hungary	3–1	(15–13, 11–15, 15–4, 15–11)
25 Sep.	Italy–Romania	3–2	(14–16, 15–12, 8–15, 15–8, 15–11)
25 Sep.	Yugoslavia–France	3–1	(14–16, 15–10, 15–4, 15–7)
26 Sep.	Romania–France	3–0	(15–8, 15–7, 15–3)

(continued)

Group A (Helsinki) (continued)

26 Sep.	Hungary–Yugoslavia	3–0	(15–7, 16–14, 15–6)
26 Sep.	Italy–Finland	3–2	(15–13, 10–15, 15–13, 9–15, 15–8)
27 Sep.	Romania–Yugoslavia	3–1	(15–13, 14–16, 15–10, 15–4)
27 Sep.	France–Finland	3–2	(15–7, 10–15, 21–19, 12–15, 15–11)
27 Sep.	Hungary–Italy	3–2	(5–15, 15–8, 10–15, 15–1, 15–10)
28 Sep.	France–Italy	3–1	(11–15, 15–9, 15–12, 15–7)
28 Sep.	Yugoslavia–Finland	3–0	(15–13, 15–6, 15–13)
28 Sep.	Romania–Hungary	3–1	(15–5, 15–9, 10–15, 15–7)
29 Sep.	Italy–Yugoslavia	3–0	(15–8, 15–4, 15–6)
29 Sep.	Hungary–France	3–0	(15–13, 15–11, 15–8)
29 Sep.	Romania–Finland	3–0	(15–9, 15–8, 15–13)

	G	W/L	SW/SL	Pts.
1. Romania	5	4/1	14/5	9
2. Hungary	5	3/2	11/8	8
3. Italy	5	3/2	12/10	8
4. Yugoslavia	5	2/3	7/10	7
5. France	5	2/3	7/12	7
6. Finland	5	1/4	7/13	6

Group B (Tampere)

25 Sep.	Poland–USSR	3–1	(16–14, 15–11, 6–15, 15–13)
25 Sep.	Czechoslovakia–GDR	3–1	(15–10, 4–15, 16–14, 15–6)
25 Sep.	Bulgaria–Netherlands	3–0	(15–12, 15–11, 15–8)
26 Sep.	Czechoslovakia–Netherlands	3–1	(15–13, 15–3, 14–16, 15–7)
26 Sep.	USSR–Bulgaria	3–0	(15–10, 15–7, 15–11)
26 Sep.	GDR–Poland	3–2	(15–11, 15–3, 13–15, 14–16, 15–11)
27 Sep.	Czechoslovakia–Bulgaria	3–2	(16–14, 12–15, 11–15, 18–16, 15–13)
27 Sep.	Poland–Netherlands	3–0	(15–10, 15–0, 15–10)
27 Sep.	USSR–GDR	3–0	(15–2, 15–3, 15–11)
28 Sep.	GDR–Netherlands	3–1	(10–15, 15–10, 15–5, 15–2)
28 Sep.	Poland–Bulgaria	3–0	(15–2, 15–5, 15–9)
28 Sep.	USSR–Czechoslovakia	3–1	(13–15, 15–6, 16–14, 15–5)
29 Sep.	Bulgaria–GDR	3–0	(21–19, 15–11, 15–8)
29 Sep.	USSR–Netherlands	3–0	(15–10, 15–5, 15–5)
29 Sep.	Poland–Czechoslovakia	3–1	(12–15, 15–7, 15–5, 15–3)

	G	W/L	SW/SL	Pts.
1. USSR	5	4/1	13/4	9
2. Poland	5	4/1	14/5	9
3. Czechoslovakia	5	3/2	11/10	8
4. Bulgaria	5	2/3	8/9	7
5. GDR	5	2/3	7/12	7
6. Netherlands	5	0/5	2/15	5

Final round

Semifinals (9–12 places)

| 1 Oct. | France–Netherlands | 3–0 | (15–4, 15–10, 15–8) | Turku |
| 1 Oct. | GDR–Finland | 3–0 | (15–9, 15–8, 15–6) | Turku |

Game for 11th place

| 2 Oct. | Finland–Netherlands | 3–1 | (15–1, 15–4, 8–15, 16–14) | Turku |

Game for 9th place

| 2 Oct. | GDR–France | 3–1 | (15–7, 9–15, 15–9, 15–5) | Turku |

Semifinals (5–8 places)

| 1 Oct. | Bulgaria–Italy | 3–0 | (15–7, 15–11, 15–6) | Oulu |
| 1 Oct. | Czechoslovakia–Yugoslavia | 3–0 | (15–5, 16–14, 16–14) | Oulu |

Game for 7th place

| 2 Oct. | Yugoslavia–Italy | 3–0 | (15–11, 15–13, 15–10) | Oulu |

Game for 5th place

| 2 Oct. | Bulgaria–Czechoslovakia | 3–0 | (15–13, 15–5, 16–14) | Oulu |

Semifinals (1–4 places)

| 1 Oct. | Poland–Romania | 3–1 | (15–8, 16–18, 15–8, 15–5) | Helsinki |
| 1 Oct. | USSR–Hungary | 3–0 | (15–0, 15–12, 15–6) | Helsinki |

Game for 3rd place

| 2 Oct. | Romania–Hungary | 3–0 | (15–9, 15–13, 15–9) | Helsinki |

Final

| 2 Oct. | USSR–Poland | 3–1 | (8–15, 15–9, 15–13, 15–9) | Helsinki |

Final standings

	G	W/L	SW/SL
1. USSR	7	6/1	19/5
2. Poland	7	5/2	18/9
3. Romania	7	5/2	18/8
4. Hungary	7	3/4	11/14
5. Bulgaria	7	4/3	14/9
6. Czechoslovakia	7	4/3	14/13
7. Yugoslavia	7	3/4	10/13
8. Italy	7	3/4	12/16
9. GDR	7	4/3	13/13
10. France	7	3/4	11/15
11. Finland	7	2/5	10/17
12. Netherlands	7	0/7	3/21

Total: 12 teams, 42 games

Rosters of the medalists

USSR–Vladimir Chernyshyov, Vladimir Dorokhov, Aleksandr Ermilov, Vladimir Kondra, Valeriy Krivov, Fyodor Lashchyonov, Viljar Loor, Oleg Moliboga, Anatoliy Polishchuk, Aleksandr Savin, Pāvels Seļivanovs, Vyacheslav Zaytsev; head coach: Vyacheslav Platonov

Poland–Bronisław Bebel, Ryszard Bosek, Marek Ciaszkiewicz, Wiesław Czaja, Wiesław Gawłowski, Maciej Jarosz, Marek Karbarz, Władysław Kustra, Leszek Molenda, Włodzimierz Sadalski, Włodzimierz Stefański, Tomasz Wójtowicz; head coach: Jerzy Welcz

Romania–Adrian Arbuzov, Valter Chifu, Teofil Chiş, Laurenţiu Dumănoiu, Dan Gîrleanu, Petre Ionescu, Sorin Macavei, Vasile Măşcăşan, Nicolae Pop, Ion Ţerbea, Mircea Tutovan-Codoi, Gabriel Udişteanu; head coach: George Eremia

XI EUROPEAN CHAMPIONSHIP
5–12 October 1979, Nancy, Nantes, Paris, Saint-Quentin, and Toulouse (France)

Preliminary round

Group A (Nantes)

5 Oct.	USSR–Yugoslavia	3–2	(15–6, 11–15, 16–14, 10–15, 15–13)
5 Oct.	Hungary–Greece	3–1	(11–15, 15–4, 15–6, 18–16)
6 Oct.	USSR–Hungary	3–0	(15–6, 15–10, 15–7)
6 Oct.	Yugoslavia–Greece	3–1	(15–9, 16–18, 15–10, 15–12)
7 Oct.	USSR–Greece	3–0	(15–11, 15–4, 15–2)
7 Oct.	Yugoslavia–Hungary	3–0	(15–12, 15–9, 15–3)

	G	W/L	SW/SL	Pts.
1. USSR	3	3/0	9/2	6
2. Yugoslavia	3	2/1	8/4	5
3. Hungary	3	1/2	3/7	4
4. Greece	3	0/3	2/9	3

Group B (Saint-Quentin)

5 Oct.	Italy–Belgium	3–1	(15–9, 15–8, 13–15, 15–9)
5 Oct.	Poland–Bulgaria	3–1	(15–12, 12–15, 15–12, 15–12)
6 Oct.	Bulgaria–Belgium	3–2	(15–11, 11–15, 11–15, 15–6, 15–13)
6 Oct.	Poland–Italy	3–1	(12–15, 15–11, 15–9, 15–7)
7 Oct.	Poland–Belgium	3–1	(12–15, 15–4, 15–3, 15–9)
7 Oct.	Italy–Bulgaria	3–1	(15–10, 15–12, 10–15, 15–12)

	G	W/L	SW/SL	Pts.
1. Poland	3	3/0	9/3	6
2. Italy	3	2/1	7/5	5
3. Bulgaria	3	1/2	5/8	4
4. Belgium	3	0/3	4/9	3

Group C (Toulouse)

5 Oct.	Romania–GDR	3–0	(15–3, 15–12, 15–10)
5 Oct.	France–Czechoslovakia	3–2	(10–15, 16–14, 5–15, 15–5, 15–13)
6 Oct.	France–GDR	3–0	(15–2, 17–15, 15–11)
6 Oct.	Czechoslovakia–Romania	3–1	(15–13, 15–11, 12–15, 15–5)
7 Oct.	Czechoslovakia–GDR	3–1	(14–16, 15–7, 15–6, 15–4)
7 Oct.	Romania–France	3–2	(9–15, 15–5, 15–13, 5–15, 15–8)

	G	W/L	SW/SL	Pts.
1. Czechoslovakia	3	2/1	8/5	5
2. France	3	2/1	8/5	5
3. Romania	3	2/1	7/5	5
4. GDR	3	0/3	1/9	3

Final round (head-to-head games were carried over from the preliminary round)

Final group for 7–12 places (Nancy)

10 Oct.	Romania–Greece	3–1	(13–15, 16–14, 15–1, 15–5)
10 Oct.	Bulgaria–GDR	3–2	(10–15, 12–15, 15–12, 15–7, 15–6)
10 Oct.	Hungary–Belgium	3–1	(15–11, 15–9, 7–15, 15–9)
11 Oct.	GDR–Greece	3–0	(15–10, 15–12, 15–8)
11 Oct.	Romania–Belgium	3–0	(15–8, 15–10, 15–13)
11 Oct.	Hungary–Bulgaria	3–2	(4–15, 15–10, 15–10, 16–18, 16–14)
12 Oct.	Greece–Bulgaria	3–1	(15–8, 15–11, 12–15, 16–14)
12 Oct.	GDR–Belgium	3–0	(15–7, 15–6, 15–4)
12 Oct.	Romania–Hungary	3–1	(15–10, 13–15, 15–5, 15–10)
13 Oct.	Hungary–GDR	3–0	(15–11, 15–11, 15–10)
13 Oct.	Belgium–Greece	3–0	(15–12, 15–9, 15–13)
13 Oct.	Romania–Bulgaria	3–0	(15–2, 16–14, 15–11)

	G	W/L	SW/SL	Pts.
1. Romania	5	5/0	15/2	10
2. Hungary	5	4/1	13/7	9
3. GDR	5	2/3	8/9	7
4. Bulgaria	5	2/3	9/13	7
5. Greece	5	1/4	5/13	6
6. Belgium	5	1/4	6/12	6

Final group for 1–6 places (Paris)

10 Oct.	USSR–Poland	3–0	(16–14, 15–9, 15–12)
10 Oct.	France–Italy	3–1	(7–15, 15–10, 15–12, 15–8)
10 Oct.	Yugoslavia–Czechoslovakia	3–1	(15–10, 7–15, 15–7, 15–13)
11 Oct.	Yugoslavia–France	3–0	(15–4, 15–11, 15–10)
11 Oct.	Poland–Czechoslovakia	3–0	(15–11, 15–5, 15–5)
11 Oct.	USSR–Italy	3–0	(15–9, 15–13, 15–12)
12 Oct.	USSR–Czechoslovakia	3–0	(15–13, 15–7, 15–5)
12 Oct.	Yugoslavia–Italy	3–2	(15–13, 7–15, 14–16, 15–9, 15–3)
12 Oct.	Poland–France	3–2	(9–15, 15–7, 4–15, 15–4, 15–5)
13 Oct.	USSR–France	3–1	(15–10, 15–11, 8–15, 15–8)
13 Oct.	Poland–Yugoslavia	3–0	(15–8, 15–6, 15–8)
13 Oct.	Italy–Czechoslovakia	3–0	(15–6, 15–12, 15–11)

	G	W/L	SW/SL	Pts.
1. USSR	5	5/0	15/3	10
2. Poland	5	4/1	12/6	9
3. Yugoslavia	5	3/2	11/9	8
4. France	5	2/3	9/12	7
5. Italy	5	1/4	7/12	6
6. Czechoslovakia	5	0/5	3/15	5

Final standings

	G	W/L	SW/SL
1. USSR	7	7/0	21/3
2. Poland	7	6/1	18/8
3. Yugoslavia	7	5/2	17/10
4. France	7	3/4	14/15
5. Italy	7	3/4	13/14
6. Czechoslovakia	7	2/5	9/17
7. Romania	7	6/1	19/7
8. Hungary	7	4/3	13/13
9. GDR	7	2/5	9/15
10. Bulgaria	7	2/5	11/19
11. Belgium	7	1/6	8/18
12. Greece	7	1/6	6/19

Total: 12 teams, 42 games

Rosters of the medalists

USSR–Vladimir Chernyshyov, Vladimir Dorokhov, Aleksandr Ermilov, Vladimir Kondra, Yuriy Kuznetsov, Fyodor Lashchyonov, Viljar Loor, Oleg Moliboga, Yuriy Panchenko, Aleksandr Savin, Pāvels Seļivanovs, Vyacheslav Zaytsev; head coach: Vyacheslav Platonov

Poland–Ryszard Bosek, Wiesław Czaja, Wojciech Drzyzga, Wiesław Gawłowski, Maciej Jarosz, Ireneusz Kłos, Władysław Kustra, Lech Łasko, Robert Malinowski, Leszek Molenda, Włodzimierz Nalazek, Tomasz Wójtowicz; head coach: Aleksander Skiba

Yugoslavia–Vladimir Bogoevski, Vinko Dobrić, Boro Jović, Zdravko Kuljić, Slobodan Lozančić, Radovan Malević, Miodrag Mitić, Dragan Nišić, Goran Srbinovski, Aleksandar Tasevski, Ljubomir Travica, Vladimir Trifunović; head coach: Drago Tomić

XII EUROPEAN CHAMPIONSHIP
19–27 September 1981, Burgas, Pazardzhik, and Varna (Bulgaria)

Preliminary round

Group A (Pazardzhik)

19 Sep.	GDR–FRG	3–0	(15–11, 15–9, 15–8)
19 Sep.	USSR–France	3–1	(10–15, 15–12, 15–7, 15–10)
20 Sep.	USSR–FRG	3–0	(15–7, 15–3, 15–5)
20 Sep.	GDR–France	3–2	(13–15, 15–10, 15–11, 9–15, 15–8)
21 Sep.	France–FRG	3–2	(15–11, 13–15, 15–3, 7–15, 15–10)
21 Sep.	USSR–GDR	3–0	(15–3, 15–5, 15–7)

	G	W/L	SW/SL	Pts.
1. USSR	3	3/0	9/1	6
2. GDR	3	2/1	6/5	5
3. France	3	1/2	6/8	4
4. FRG	3	0/3	2/9	3

Group B (Burgas)

19 Sep.	Poland–Spain	3–0	(15–2, 15–4, 15–6)
19 Sep.	Czechoslovakia–Italy	3–0	(15–7, 15–11, 16–14)
20 Sep.	Italy–Spain	3–0	(15–4, 15–2, 15–6)
20 Sep.	Poland–Czechoslovakia	3–1	(15–10, 11–15, 15–8, 15–8)
21 Sep.	Czechoslovakia–Spain	3–1	(15–8, 15–9, 9–15, 15–1)
21 Sep.	Poland–Italy	3–0	(15–3, 15–8, 15–12)

	G	W/L	SW/SL	Pts.
1. Poland	3	3/0	9/1	6
2. Czechoslovakia	3	2/1	7/4	5
3. Italy	3	1/2	3/6	4
4. Spain	3	0/3	1/9	3

Group C (Varna)

19 Sep.	Romania–Finland	3–2	(15–11, 12–15, 10–15, 15–5, 16–14)
19 Sep.	Bulgaria–Yugoslavia	3–2	(15–9, 8–15, 15–6, 12–15, 15–10)
20 Sep.	Romania–Yugoslavia	3–2	(5–15, 13–15, 15–13, 15–9, 16–14)
20 Sep.	Bulgaria–Finland	3–0	(15–13, 16–14, 15–9)
21 Sep.	Finland–Yugoslavia	3–0	(16–14, 15–13, 15–5)
21 Sep.	Romania–Bulgaria	3–2	(8–15, 15–7, 15–11, 12–15, 16–14)

	G	W/L	SW/SL	Pts.
1. Romania	3	3/0	9/6	6
2. Bulgaria	3	2/1	8/5	5
3. Finland	3	1/2	5/6	4
4. Yugoslavia	3	0/3	4/9	3

Final round (head-to-head games were carried over from the preliminary round)

Final group for 7–12 places (Pazardzhik)

24 Sep.	Italy–Yugoslavia	3–0	(15–6, 15–9, 15–5)
24 Sep.	France–Spain	3–1	(15–5, 15–10, 18–20, 15–11)
24 Sep.	Finland–FRG	3–1	(15–5, 3–15, 15–11, 15–1)
25 Sep.	Spain–Finland	3–2	(15–11, 15–10, 13–15, 11–15, 15–4)

(continued)

Final group for 7–12 places (Pazardzhik) (continued)

25 Sep.	Italy–France	3–0	(15–8, 15–6, 15–10)
25 Sep.	Yugoslavia–FRG	3–0	(15–9, 17–15, 15–6)
26 Sep.	FRG–Spain	3–1	(12–15, 15–10, 15–5, 15–3)
26 Sep.	France–Yugoslavia	3–0	(15–11, 15–3, 15–11)
26 Sep.	Italy–Finland	3–1	(15–13, 15–4, 9–15, 15–8)
27 Sep.	Yugoslavia–Spain	3–0	(15–3, 15–5, 15–3)
27 Sep.	Italy–FRG	3–2	(15–10, 6–15, 17–15, 11–15, 15–7)
27 Sep.	France–Finland	3–2	(15–10, 15–17, 12–15, 15–12, 15–13)

	G	W/L	SW/SL	Pts.
1. Italy	5	5/0	15/3	10
2. France	5	4/1	12/8	9
3. Finland	5	2/3	11/10	7
4. Yugoslavia	5	2/3	6/9	7
5. FRG	5	1/4	8/13	6
6. Spain	5	1/4	5/14	6

Final group for 1–6 places (Varna)

24 Sep.	Poland–GDR	3–0	(15–8, 15–10, 15–7)
24 Sep.	Bulgaria–Czechoslovakia	3–1	(15–10, 15–10, 10–15, 16–14)
24 Sep.	USSR–Romania	3–0	(15–2, 15–7, 15–3)
25 Sep.	USSR–Czechoslovakia	3–2	(13–15, 12–15, 15–4, 15–13, 15–10)
25 Sep.	Poland–Bulgaria	3–1	(15–6, 15–6, 14–16, 15–9)
25 Sep.	Romania–GDR	3–2	(12–15, 8–15, 15–6, 15–8, 15–7)
26 Sep.	Czechoslovakia–Romania	3–2	(10–15, 15–8, 3–15, 17–15, 15–13)
26 Sep.	Bulgaria–GDR	3–1	(15–9, 13–15, 17–15, 15–6)
26 Sep.	USSR–Poland	3–0	(15–12, 15–12, 15–12)
27 Sep.	Czechoslovakia–GDR	3–2	(13–15, 15–7, 9–15, 15–10, 15–12)
27 Sep.	Poland–Romania	3–0	(15–8, 15–6, 15–12)
27 Sep.	USSR–Bulgaria	3–0	(15–3, 15–6, 15–2)

	G	W/L	SW/SL	Pts.
1. USSR	5	5/0	15/2	10
2. Poland	5	4/1	12/5	9
3. Bulgaria	5	2/3	9/11	7
4. Czechoslovakia	5	2/3	10/13	7
5. Romania	5	2/3	8/13	7
6. GDR	5	0/5	5/15	5

Final standings

	G	W/L	SW/SL
1. USSR	7	7/0	21/3
2. Poland	7	6/1	18/5
3. Bulgaria	7	4/3	15/13
4. Czechoslovakia	7	4/3	16/14
5. Romania	7	4/3	14/17
6. GDR	7	2/5	11/17
7. Italy	7	5/2	15/9
8. France	7	4/3	15/14
9. Finland	7	2/5	13/16
10. Yugoslavia	7	2/5	10/15
11. FRG	7	1/6	8/19
12. Spain	7	1/6	6/20

Total: 12 teams, 42 games

Rosters of the medalists

USSR–Vladimir Chernyshyov, Vladimir Dorokhov, Vladimir Kondra, Yuriy Kuznetsov, Viljar Loor, Oleg Moliboga, Yuriy Panchenko, Aleksandr Sapega, Aleksandr Savin, Vladimir Shkurikhin, Pavel Voronkov, Vyacheslav Zaytsev; head coach: Vyacheslav Platonov

Poland–Wojciech Drzyzga, Maciej Jarosz, Ryszard Jurek, Ireneusz Kłos, Lech Łasko, Robert Malinowski, Andrzej Martyniuk, Ireneusz Nalazek, Włodzimierz Nalazek, Krzysztof Olszewski, Sławomir Skup, Marek Szydlik; head coach: Aleksander Skiba

Bulgaria–Yordan Angelov, Dimitar Dimitrov, Asen Galabinov, Borislav Kosev, Milcho Natov, Valentin Nenov, Ivan Nikolov, Petko Petkov, Stefan Petrov, Khristo Stoyanov, Mitko Todorov, Georgi Vasilev; head coach: Tsvetan Pavlov

XIII EUROPEAN CHAMPIONSHIP
17–25 September 1983, East Berlin, Erfurt, and Suhl (GDR)

Preliminary round

Group A (Erfurt)

17 Sep.	USSR–Netherlands	3–0	(15–9, 15–13, 15–8)
17 Sep.	Czechoslovakia–Finland	3–0	(15–12, 15–9, 15–11)
18 Sep.	Czechoslovakia–Netherlands	3–2	(15–8, 15–8, 17–19, 15–17, 15–8)
18 Sep.	USSR–Finland	3–1	(15–17, 15–7, 15–8, 15–11)
19 Sep.	Finland–Netherlands	3–0	(15–13, 15–10, 15–6)
19 Sep.	USSR–Czechoslovakia	3–0	(15–12, 15–7, 15–10)

	G	W/L	SW/SL	Pts.
1. USSR	3	3/0	9/1	6
2. Czechoslovakia	3	2/1	6/5	5
3. Finland	3	1/2	4/6	4
4. Netherlands	3	0/3	2/9	3

Group B (Suhl)

17 Sep.	Poland–France	3–0	(15–0, 15–0, 15–0)*
17 Sep.	Italy–Romania	3–2	(15–12, 15–11, 5–15, 12–15, 15–11)
18 Sep.	Romania–France	3–2	(9–15, 15–13, 11–15, 15–11, 15–12)
18 Sep.	Poland–Italy	3–1	(15–13, 16–14, 2–15, 16–14)
19 Sep.	Italy–France	3–1	(14–16, 15–9, 15–7, 15–2)
19 Sep.	Poland–Romania	3–2	(13–15, 15–11, 18–20, 15–10, 15–10)

*Poland won the match 3–2 (15–9, 15–4, 13–15, 11–15, 15–13), but because a French player, Alain Clévenot, tested positive for doping after the game, the results of the game were changed and the French team did not get 1 point for a loss, but 0 instead.

	G	W/L	SW/SL	Pts.
1. Poland	3	3/0	9/3	6
2. Italy	3	2/1	7/6	5
3. Romania	3	1/2	7/8	4
4. France	3	0/3	3/9	2

Group C (East Berlin)

17 Sep.	GDR–Hungary	3–0	(15–6, 15–11, 15–9)
17 Sep.	Bulgaria–Greece	3–0	(16–14, 15–6, 15–8)
18 Sep.	Bulgaria–Hungary	3–1	(15–6, 15–5, 8–15, 15–0)
18 Sep.	GDR–Greece	3–1	(15–11, 15–10, 8–15, 15–9)
19 Sep.	Hungary–Greece	3–1	(15–10, 15–13, 15–17, 15–10)
19 Sep.	Bulgaria–GDR	3–0	(15–11, 15–3, 15–8)

	G	W/L	SW/SL	Pts.
1. Bulgaria	3	3/0	9/1	6
2. GDR	3	2/1	6/4	5
3. Hungary	3	1/2	4/7	4
4. Greece	3	0/3	2/9	3

Final round (head-to-head games were carried over from the preliminary round)

Final group for 7–12 places (Suhl)

22 Sep.	Greece–Romania	3–0	(15–12, 15–10, 15–13)
22 Sep.	Netherlands–Hungary	3–0	(15–9, 15–6, 15–3)
22 Sep.	Finland–France	3–1	(15–10, 4–15, 15–6, 15–12)
23 Sep.	Romania–Hungary	3–2	(15–13, 13–15, 15–11, 9–15, 15–11)
23 Sep.	Finland–Greece	3–1	(12–15, 15–8, 15–9, 15–8)
23 Sep.	Netherlands–France	3–0	(15–12, 15–12, 15–2)
24 Sep.	Finland–Hungary	3–1	(15–5, 14–16, 15–5, 15–7)
24 Sep.	Greece–France	3–1	(15–11, 9–15, 15–11, 15–10)
24 Sep.	Romania–Netherlands	3–1	(15–13, 11–15, 15–7, 15–12)
25 Sep.	France–Hungary	3–2	(8–15, 15–12, 15–7, 10–15, 15–12)
25 Sep.	Greece–Netherlands	3–0	(15–7, 15–11, 15–11)
25 Sep.	Romania–Finland	3–0	(15–5, 15–11, 15–11)

	G	W/L	SW/SL	Pts.
1. Finland	5	4/1	12/6	9
2. Romania	5	4/1	12/8	9
3. Greece	5	3/2	11/7	8
4. Netherlands	5	2/3	7/9	7
5. Hungary	5	1/4	8/13	6
6. France	5	1/4	7/14	6

Final group for 1–6 places (East Berlin)

22 Sep.	Italy–Czechoslovakia	3–2	(11–15, 13–15, 17–15, 15–12, 15–12)
22 Sep.	Poland–GDR	3–1	(15–11, 15–8, 10–15, 16–14)
22 Sep.	USSR–Bulgaria	3–0	(15–7, 18–16, 15–12)
23 Sep.	Poland–Bulgaria	3–2	(9–15, 6–15, 15–5, 15–8, 15–12)
23 Sep.	USSR–Italy	3–1	(10–15, 15–5, 15–13, 15–5)
23 Sep.	Czechoslovakia–GDR	3–0	(15–13, 15–13, 15–6)
24 Sep.	USSR–GDR	3–0	(15–4, 15–9, 15–11)
24 Sep.	Italy–Bulgaria	3–2	(14–16, 15–12, 13–15, 15–6, 15–9)
24 Sep.	Poland–Czechoslovakia	3–0	(15–10, 15–9, 15–10)
25 Sep.	Bulgaria–Czechoslovakia	3–0	(16–14, 15–3, 15–13)
25 Sep.	GDR–Italy	3–2	(15–10, 6–15, 8–15, 16–14, 15–13)
25 Sep.	USSR–Poland	3–1	(15–3, 15–11, 11–15, 15–9)

	G	W/L	SW/SL	Pts.
1. USSR	5	5/0	15/2	10
2. Poland	5	4/1	13/7	9
3. Bulgaria	5	2/3	10/9	7
4. Italy	5	2/3	10/13	7
5. Czechoslovakia	5	1/4	5/12	6
6. GDR	5	1/4	4/14	6

Final standings

	G	W/L	SW/SL
1. USSR	7	7/0	21/3
2. Poland	7	6/1	19/9
3. Bulgaria	7	4/3	16/10
4. Italy	7	4/3	16/16
5. Czechoslovakia	7	3/4	11/14
6. GDR	7	3/4	10/15
7. Finland	7	4/3	13/12
8. Romania	7	4/3	16/14
9. Greece	7	3/4	12/13
10. Netherlands	7	2/5	9/15
11. Hungary	7	1/6	9/19
12. France	7	1/6	8/20

Total: 12 teams, 42 games

Rosters of the medalists

USSR–Aleksandr Belevich, Albert Dillenburg, Viljar Loor, Oleg Moliboga, Yuriy Panchenko, Aleksandr Sapega, Aleksandr Savin, Pāvels Seļivanovs, Vladimir Shkurikhin, Viktor Sidelnikov, Aleksandr Sorokolet, Vyacheslav Zaytsev; head coach: Vyacheslav Platonov

Poland–Wojciech Drzyzga, Wacław Golec, Ireneusz Kłos, Piotr Koczan, Lech Łasko, Andrzej Martyniuk, Włodzimierz Nalazek, Jacek Rychlicki, Krzysztof Stefanowicz, Janusz Wojdyga, Tomasz Wójtowicz, Zbigniew Zieliński; head coach: Hubert Wagner

Bulgaria–Dimitur Dimitrov, Peto Dragiev, Asen Galabinov, Stoyan Gunchev, Plamen Khristov, Borislav Kosev, Valeri Milanov, Milcho Natov, Ivan Nikolov, Petko Petkov, Stefan Sokolov, Mitko Todorov; head coach: Vasil Simov

XIV EUROPEAN CHAMPIONSHIP
29 September–6 October 1985, Amsterdam, Den Bosch, Groningen, Voorburg, and Zwolle (Netherlands)

Preliminary round

Group A (Voorburg)

29 Sep.	Italy–Greece	3–0	(15–7, 15–9, 15–12)
29 Sep.	USSR–Sweden	3–0	(15–6, 15–7, 15–1)
30 Sep.	Greece–Sweden	3–2	(15–6, 20–18, 9–15, 11–15, 15–9)
30 Sep.	USSR–Italy	3–1	(16–14, 15–13, 13–15, 15–12)
1 Oct.	USSR–Greece	3–0	(15–10, 15–5, 15–7)
1 Oct.	Sweden–Italy	3–2	(14–16, 15–8, 15–6, 5–15, 15–13)

	G	W/L	SW/SL	Pts.
1. USSR	3	3/0	9/1	6
2. Italy	3	1/2	6/6	4
3. Sweden	3	1/2	5/8	4
4. Greece	3	1/2	3/8	4

Group B (Zwolle)

29 Sep.	Poland–Romania	3–0	(15–12, 15–11, 15–6)
29 Sep.	Czechoslovakia–Spain	3–0	(15–9, 15–7, 15–7)
30 Sep.	Romania–Spain	3–1	(15–5, 4–15, 15–9, 15–8)
30 Sep.	Czechoslovakia–Poland	3–1	(12–15, 15–13, 15–9, 15–10)
1 Oct.	Poland–Spain	3–0	(15–9, 15–10, 15–10)
1 Oct.	Czechoslovakia–Romania	3–1	(15–8, 10–15, 15–12, 15–2)

	G	W/L	SW/SL	Pts.
1. Czechoslovakia	3	3/0	9/2	6
2. Poland	3	2/1	7/3	5
3. Romania	3	1/2	4/7	4
4. Spain	3	0/3	1/9	3

Group C (Den Bosch)

29 Sep.	France–Bulgaria	3–0	(15–11, 15–8, 15–1)
29 Sep.	Netherlands–Yugoslavia	3–1	(16–14, 15–10, 13–15, 15–12)
30 Sep.	Bulgaria–Yugoslavia	3–0	(15–9, 15–7, 15–4)
30 Sep.	France–Netherlands	3–0	(15–4, 15–5, 15–2)
1 Oct.	France–Yugoslavia	3–1	(15–9, 16–14, 9–15, 15–13)
1 Oct.	Bulgaria–Netherlands	3–2	(15–13, 6–15, 6–15, 15–10, 15–13)

	G	W/L	SW/SL	Pts.
1. France	3	3/0	9/1	6
2. Bulgaria	3	2/1	6/5	5
3. Netherlands	3	1/2	5/7	4
4. Yugoslavia	3	0/3	2/9	3

Final round (head-to-head games were carried over from the preliminary round)

Final group for 7–12 places (Groningen)

3 Oct.	Greece–Romania	3–1	(15–7, 10–15, 16–14, 19–17)
3 Oct.	Sweden–Yugoslavia	3–0	(15–8, 15–7, 15–7)
3 Oct.	Netherlands–Spain	3–2	(5–15, 15–9, 15–9, 9–15, 15–4)
4 Oct.	Greece–Spain	3–0	(15–11, 15–4, 15–13)
4 Oct.	Romania–Yugoslavia	3–0	(15–4, 15–7, 15–1)
4 Oct.	Sweden–Netherlands	3–0	(15–8, 15–12, 15–10)
5 Oct.	Netherlands–Greece	3–0	(15–11, 15–7, 15–6)
5 Oct.	Romania–Sweden	3–2	(3–15, 10–15, 15–9, 15–10, 15–10)
5 Oct.	Yugoslavia–Spain	3–1	(17–15, 15–13, 13–15, 15–10)
6 Oct.	Greece–Yugoslavia	3–0	(15–12, 15–7, 15–5)
6 Oct.	Sweden–Spain	3–1	(15–13, 15–6, 11–15, 15–11)
6 Oct.	Romania–Netherlands	3–1	(15–5, 5–15, 15–13, 15–6)

	G	W/L	SW/SL	Pts.
1. Greece	5	4/1	12/6	9
2. Romania	5	4/1	13/7	9
3. Sweden	5	3/2	13/7	8
4. Netherlands	5	3/2	10/9	8
5. Yugoslavia	5	1/4	4/13	6
6. Spain	5	0/5	5/15	5

Final group for 1–6 places (Amsterdam)

3 Oct.	USSR–Czechoslovakia	3–0	(15–8, 15–10, 16–14)
3 Oct.	France–Poland	3–1	(15–10, 16–14, 7–15, 15–6)
3 Oct.	Bulgaria–Italy	3–2	(15–8, 13–15, 15–11, 13–15, 15–8)
4 Oct.	Czechoslovakia–France	3–1	(16–14, 18–16, 15–17, 16–14)
4 Oct.	USSR–Bulgaria	3–1	(15–9, 15–6, 13–15, 15–1)
4 Oct.	Poland–Italy	3–0	(15–12, 15–12, 15–8)
5 Oct.	Czechoslovakia–Bulgaria	3–0	(15–7, 15–6, 15–3)
5 Oct.	USSR–Poland	3–0	(15–6, 15–8, 15–7)
5 Oct.	France–Italy	3–1	(15–4, 15–5, 12–15, 15–10)
6 Oct.	Poland–Bulgaria	3–2	(15–9, 15–12, 14–16, 8–15, 15–8)
6 Oct.	Czechoslovakia–Italy	3–1	(15–11, 15–17, 15–11, 15–11)
6 Oct.	USSR–France	3–0	(15–4, 15–6, 15–12)

	G	W/L	SW/SL	Pts.
1. USSR	5	5/0	15/2	10
2. Czechoslovakia	5	4/1	12/6	9
3. France	5	3/2	10/8	8
4. Poland	5	2/3	8/11	7
5. Bulgaria	5	1/4	6/14	6
6. Italy	5	0/5	5/15	5

Final standings

	G	W/L	SW/SL
1. USSR	7	7/0	21/2
2. Czechoslovakia	7	6/1	18/7
3. France	7	5/2	16/9
4. Poland	7	4/3	14/11
5. Bulgaria	7	3/4	12/16
6. Italy	7	1/6	10/18
7. Greece	7	4/3	12/12
8. Romania	7	4/3	14/13
9. Sweden	7	4/3	16/12
10. Netherlands	7	3/4	12/15
11. Yugoslavia	7	1/6	5/19
12. Spain	7	0/7	5/21

Total: 12 teams, 42 games

Rosters of the medalists

USSR–Yaroslav Antonov, Albert Dillenburg, Sergey Gribov, Aleksandr Ivanov, Valeriy Losev, Yuriy Panchenko, Aleksandr Savin, Vladimir Shkurikhin, Oleg Smugilyov, Aleksandr Sorokolet, Raimonds Vilde, Vyacheslav Zaytsev; head coach: Vyacheslav Platonov

Czechoslovakia–Pavel Barborka, Přemysl Bláha, Milan Černoušek, Štefan Chrtianský, Helmut Jamka, Zdeněk Kaláb, Cyril Krejčí, Bronislav Mikyska, Josef Novotný, Igor Prieložný, Jaroslav Šmíd, Ivan Strumienský; head coach: Karel Láznička

France–Pierre Bezault, Philippe Blain, Eric Bouvier, Lionel Devos, Alain Fabiani, Bertrand Faitg, Stéphane Faure, Jean Hornain, Jean–Marc Jurkovitz, Jean-Baptiste Martzluff, Hervé Mazzon, Laurent Tillie; head coach: Jean-Marc Buchel

XV EUROPEAN CHAMPIONSHIP
25 September–4 October 1987, Auderghem, Genk, and Gent (Belgium)

Preliminary round

Group A (Auderghem)

25 Sep.	USSR–Romania	3–0	(15–1, 15–5, 15–3)
25 Sep.	France–Italy	3–1	(10–15, 15–5, 15–5, 16–14)
25 Sep.	Netherlands–Yugoslavia	3–0	(15–6, 15–10, 15–1)
26 Sep.	France–Yugoslavia	3–0	(15–3, 15–11, 15–11)
26 Sep.	Italy–Romania	3–1	(15–3, 9–15, 15–8, 15–12)
26 Sep.	USSR–Netherlands	3–1	(15–10, 15–2, 4–15, 15–13)
27 Sep.	USSR–Yugoslavia	3–0	(15–6, 15–7, 15–6)
27 Sep.	France–Romania	3–0	(15–8, 15–5, 15–5)
27 Sep.	Netherlands–Italy	3–0	(15–5, 15–11, 15–10)
29 Sep.	USSR–Italy	3–2	(15–13, 9–15, 7–15, 15–10, 15–3)
29 Sep.	France–Netherlands	3–0	(15–7, 16–14, 15–6)
29 Sep.	Yugoslavia–Romania	3–0	(15–6, 15–9, 15–9)
30 Sep.	USSR–France	3–1	(15–9, 15–12, 12–15, 16–14)
30 Sep.	Yugoslavia–Italy	3–2	(7–15, 15–12, 17–15, 14–16, 15–13)
30 Sep.	Romania–Netherlands	3–2	(15–13, 9–15, 6–15, 15–9, 16–14)

		G	W/L	SW/SL	Pts.
1.	USSR	5	5/0	15/4	10
2.	France	5	4/1	13/4	9
3.	Netherlands	5	2/3	9/9	7
4.	Yugoslavia	5	2/3	6/11	7
5.	Italy	5	1/4	8/13	6
6.	Romania	5	1/4	4/14	6

Group B (Genk)

25 Sep.	Greece–Czechoslovakia	3–2	(13–15, 15–8, 15–6, 4–15, 15–5)
25 Sep.	Belgium–Spain	3–0	(16–14, 15–9, 15–13)
25 Sep.	Sweden–Bulgaria	3–1	(15–8, 9–15, 15–13, 15–10)
26 Sep.	Czechoslovakia–Spain	3–0	(15–4, 15–5, 15–12)
26 Sep.	Belgium–Sweden	3–0	(15–0, 15–0, 15–0)*
26 Sep.	Greece–Bulgaria	3–1	(7–15, 15–8, 15–8, 15–8)
27 Sep.	Sweden–Czechoslovakia	3–2	(16–14, 5–15, 7–15, 15–6, 15–11)
27 Sep.	Bulgaria–Belgium	3–0	(15–11, 15–7, 15–13)
27 Sep.	Greece–Spain	3–0	(15–7, 15–9, 15–12)
29 Sep.	Sweden–Spain	3–0	(15–5, 15–4, 15–13)
29 Sep.	Greece–Belgium	3–2	(15–7, 10–15, 15–7, 12–15, 15–8)
29 Sep.	Czechoslovakia–Bulgaria	3–1	(5–15, 15–11, 17–15, 15–11)

(continued)

Group B (Genk) (continued)

30 Sep.	Sweden–Greece	3–1	(15–8, 10–15, 15–10, 15–12)
30 Sep.	Bulgaria–Spain	3–1	(11–15, 15–6, 15–7, 15–7)
30 Sep.	Czechoslovakia–Belgium	3–2	(15–12, 4–15, 7–15, 15–6, 15–12)

*Sweden won the match 3–1 (14–16, 15–4, 15–8, 15–6), but because its player, Hakan Björne, tested positive for doping after the game, the results of the game were changed (Sweden received 1 point for a loss).

	G	W/L	SW/SL	Pts.
1. Sweden	5	4/1	12/7	9
2. Greece	5	4/1	13/8	9
3. Czechoslovakia	5	3/2	13/9	8
4. Belgium	5	2/3	10/9	7
5. Bulgaria	5	2/3	9/10	7
6. Spain	5	0/5	1/15	5

Final round

Semifinals (9–12 places)

2 Oct.	Italy–Spain	3–1	(15–10, 12–15, 15–7, 15–9)	Genk
2 Oct.	Romania–Bulgaria	3–0	(15–11, 15–8, 15–3)	Genk

Game for 11th place

3 Oct.	Bulgaria–Spain	3–0	(16–14, 15–10, 15–9)	Genk

Game for 9th place

3 Oct.	Italy–Romania	3–0	(15–5, 15–4, 16–14)	Genk

Semifinals (5–8 places)

2 Oct.	Czechoslovakia–Yugoslavia	3–2	(15–11, 10–15, 15–4, 4–15, 15–13)	Genk
2 Oct.	Netherlands–Belgium	3–2	(10–15, 10–15, 15–10, 15–9, 15–9)	Genk

Game for 7th place

3 Oct.	Belgium–Yugoslavia	3–0	(15–2, 15–13, 15–13)	Genk

Game for 5th place

3 Oct.	Netherlands–Czechoslovakia	3–0	(17–15, 15–12, 15–10)	Genk

Semifinals (1–4 places)

| 2 Oct. | France–Sweden | 3–0 | (15–10, 15–9, 15–5) | Gent |
| 2 Oct. | USSR–Greece | 3–0 | (15–5, 15–5, 15–12) | Gent |

Game for 3rd place

| 4 Oct. | Greece–Sweden | 3–2 | (14–16, 15–9, 6–15, 15–10, 16–14) | Gent |

Final

| 4 Oct. | USSR–France | 3–1 | (15–7, 15–6, 7–15, 15–9) | Gent |

Final standings

	G	W/L	SW/SL
1. USSR	7	7/0	21/5
2. France	7	5/2	17/7
3. Greece	7	5/2	16/13
4. Sweden	7	4/3	14/13
5. Netherlands	7	4/3	15/11
6. Czechoslovakia	7	4/3	16/14
7. Belgium	7	3/4	15/12
8. Yugoslavia	7	2/5	8/17
9. Italy	7	3/4	14/14
10. Romania	7	2/5	7/17
11. Bulgaria	7	3/4	12/13
12. Spain	7	0/7	2/21

Total: 12 teams, 42 games

Rosters of the medalists

USSR–Yaroslav Antonov, Gennadiy Cheremisov, Aleksandr Chyornyy, Aleksandr Gordienko, Andrey Kuznetsov, Jaanus Lillepuu, Valeriy Losev, Pavel Moiseenko, Yuriy Panchenko, Igor Runov, Vladimir Shkurikhin, Aleksandr Sorokolet; head coach: Gennadiy Parshin

France–Philippe Blain, Eric Bouvier, Patrick Duflos, Alain Fabiani, Stéphane Faure, Luc Garlenc, Jean-Marc Jurkovitz, Hervé Mazzon, Christophe Meneau, Eric N'Gapeth, Olivier Rossard, Laurent Tillie; head coach: Eric Daniel

Greece–Sotiris Amarianakis, Makis Dimitriadis, Georgios Dragovits, Dimitris Gontikas, Dimitris Kazazis, Stelios Kazazis, Vangelis Koutsonikas, Kostas Margaronis, Sakis Moustakidis, Yannis Nikolaidis, Tassos Tentzeris, Michalis Triantafyllidis; head coach: Thanassis Margaritis

XVI EUROPEAN CHAMPIONSHIP
23 September–1 October 1989, Örebro and Stockholm (Sweden)

Preliminary round

Group A (Stockholm)

23 Sep.	Italy–Bulgaria	3–1	(10–15, 15–9, 15–5, 15–6)
23 Sep.	Sweden–FRG	3–2	(15–9, 12–15, 15–4, 7–15, 15–8)
23 Sep.	France–GDR	3–1	(9–15, 15–5, 15–4, 15–3)
24 Sep.	Italy–FRG	3–1	(15–2, 15–9, 13–15, 15–2)
24 Sep.	Bulgaria–France	3–0	(15–9, 15–11, 15–8)
24 Sep.	Sweden–GDR	3–0	(15–9, 15–4, 15–7)
25 Sep.	Bulgaria–FRG	3–0	(15–7, 15–1, 15–6)
25 Sep.	Sweden–France	3–1	(15–11, 8–15, 15–12, 15–11)
25 Sep.	Italy–GDR	3–1	(11–15, 15–5, 15–1, 15–13)
27 Sep.	France–FRG	3–0	(15–9, 15–6, 15–12)
27 Sep.	Italy–Sweden	3–0	(15–8, 15–9, 15–8)
27 Sep.	Bulgaria–GDR	3–2	(14–16, 15–5, 15–11, 11–15, 15–10)
28 Sep.	France–Italy	3–2	(15–5, 15–13, 4–15, 15–17, 15–13)
28 Sep.	FRG–GDR	3–1	(15–3, 11–15, 15–10, 15–4)
28 Sep.	Sweden–Bulgaria	3–2	(10–15, 15–13, 15–12, 13–15, 15–10)

	G	W/L	SW/SL	Pts.
1. Italy	5	4/1	14/6	9
2. Sweden	5	4/1	12/8	9
3. Bulgaria	5	3/2	12/8	8
4. France	5	3/2	10/9	8
5. FRG	5	1/4	6/13	6
6. GDR	5	0/5	5/15	5

Group B (Örebro)

23 Sep.	Poland–Greece	3–0	(15–11, 15–8, 15–12)
23 Sep.	USSR–Netherlands	3–1	(6–15, 15–12, 15–10, 15–12)
23 Sep.	Yugoslavia–Romania	3–2	(13–15, 15–12, 5–15, 15–11, 15–6)
24 Sep.	USSR–Yugoslavia	3–1	(9–15, 15–13, 16–14, 15–6)
24 Sep.	Poland–Romania	3–0	(15–4, 15–3, 15–10)
24 Sep.	Netherlands–Greece	3–1	(15–4, 15–17, 15–8, 15–7)
25 Sep.	USSR–Greece	3–1	(15–12, 15–8, 11–15, 15–5)
25 Sep.	Netherlands–Romania	3–0	(15–6, 15–7, 15–6)
25 Sep.	Poland–Yugoslavia	3–1	(14–16, 15–6, 15–11, 15–8)
27 Sep.	USSR–Poland	3–1	(6–15, 15–5, 15–9, 15–4)
27 Sep.	Yugoslavia–Netherlands	3–1	(2–15, 15–13, 15–12, 15–10)
27 Sep.	Romania–Greece	3–1	(15–9, 15–10, 4–15, 15–10)

(continued)

Group B (Örebro) (continued)

28 Sep.	USSR–Romania	3–0	(15–5, 15–9, 15–6)
28 Sep.	Netherlands–Poland	3–0	(15–3, 15–7, 15–6)
28 Sep.	Yugoslavia–Greece	3–2	(8–15, 15–10, 10–15, 15–12, 16–14)

	G	W/L	SW/SL	Pts.
1. USSR	5	5/0	15/4	10
2. Netherlands	5	3/2	11/7	8
3. Poland	5	3/2	10/7	8
4. Yugoslavia	5	3/2	11/11	8
5. Romania	5	1/4	5/13	6
6. Greece	5	0/5	5/15	5

Final round (Stockholm)

Semifinals (9–12 places)

| 30 Sep. | GDR–Romania | 3–2 | (13–15, 15–12, 13–15, 15–10, 15–8) |
| 30 Sep. | Greece–FRG | 3–0 | (15–10, 15–10, 15–13) |

Game for 11th place

| 1 Oct. | FRG–Romania | 3–2 | (12–15, 2–15, 15–12, 15–7, 15–13) |

Game for 9th place

| 1 Oct. | GDR–Greece | 3–2 | (15–13, 12–15, 15–12, 14–16, 17–15) |

Semifinals (5–8 places)

| 30 Sep. | France–Poland | 3–2 | (13–15, 12–15, 15–9, 17–15, 15–12) |
| 30 Sep. | Bulgaria–Yugoslavia | 3–0 | (15–7, 15–7, 15–11) |

Game for 7th place

| 1 Oct. | Poland–Yugoslavia | 3–1 | (15–5, 14–16, 15–6, 15–3) |

Game for 5th place

| 1 Oct. | France–Bulgaria | 3–1 | (6–15, 15–13, 15–4, 15–13) |

Semifinals (1–4 places)

| 30 Sep. | Sweden–USSR | 3–2 | (12–15, 15–10, 15–10, 9–15, 17–15) |
| 30 Sep. | Italy–Netherlands | 3–0 | (15–7, 15–3, 15–2) |

Game for 3rd place

| 1 Oct. | Netherlands–USSR | 3–0 | (15–11, 15–8, 15–7) |

Final

1 Oct.	Italy–Sweden	3–1	(14–16, 15–7, 15–13, 15–7)

Final standings

	G	W/L	SW/SL
1. Italy	7	6/1	20/7
2. Sweden	7	5/2	16/13
3. Netherlands	7	4/3	14/10
4. USSR	7	5/2	17/10
5. France	7	5/2	16/12
6. Bulgaria	7	4/3	16/11
7. Poland	7	4/3	15/11
8. Yugoslavia	7	3/4	12/17
9. GDR	7	2/5	11/19
10. Greece	7	1/6	10/18
11. FRG	7	2/5	9/18
12. Romania	7	1/6	9/19

Total: 12 teams, 42 games

Rosters of the medalists

Italy–Andrea Anastasi, Lorenzo Bernardi, Marco Bracci, Luca Cantagalli, Ferdinando De Giorgi, Andrea Gardini, Andrea Lucchetta, Stefano Margutti, Roberto Masciarelli, Gilberto Passani, Paolo Tofoli, Andrea Zorzi; head coach: Julio Velasco

Sweden–Hakan Björne, Bengt Gustafson, Jan Hedengard, Jan Holmqvist, Johan Isacsson, Jannis Kalmazidis, Mats Karlsson, Urban Lennartsson, Lars Nilsson, Per-Anders Sääf, Bo Strand, Peter Tholse; head coach: Anders Kristiansson

Netherlands–Edwin Benne, Peter Blangé, Ron Boudrie, Marco Brouwers, Teun Buijs, Rob Grabert, Jan Posthuma, Avital Selinger, Martin Teffer, Martin van der Horst, Ronald Zoodsma, Ron Zwerver; head coach: Arie "Harry" Brokking

XVII EUROPEAN CHAMPIONSHIP
7–15 September 1991, Berlin, Hamburg, and Karlsruhe (Germany)

Preliminary round

Group A (Karlsruhe)

7 Sep.	Germany–Finland	3–1	(8–15, 15–6, 15–3, 15–10)
7 Sep.	USSR–Sweden	3–0	(15–5, 15–13, 15–13)
7 Sep.	Greece–Poland	3–1	(7–15, 15–9, 15–8, 15–11)

(continued)

Group A (Karlsruhe) (continued)

8 Sep.	Germany–Sweden	3–1	(12–15, 15–9, 17–15, 15–12)
8 Sep.	USSR–Poland	3–0	(16–14, 15–11, 15–6)
8 Sep.	Finland–Greece	3–2	(13–15, 15–11, 8–15, 15–13, 15–13)
9 Sep.	Poland–Sweden	3–1	(15–8, 9–15, 17–16, 15–6)
9 Sep.	Germany–Greece	3–0	(15–7, 15–4, 15–5)
9 Sep.	USSR–Finland	3–0	(15–12, 15–7, 15–11)
11 Sep.	Poland–Germany	3–2	(10–15, 15–7, 16–14, 10–15, 17–15)
11 Sep.	Finland–Sweden	3–2	(12–15, 6–15, 15–11, 15–8, 16–14)
11 Sep.	USSR–Greece	3–1	(10–15, 15–9, 15–2, 15–6)
12 Sep.	Poland–Finland	3–2	(15–9, 15–11, 9–15, 15–17, 15–10)
12 Sep.	Sweden–Greece	3–0	(16–14, 15–7, 15–7)
12 Sep.	USSR–Germany	3–0	(15–13, 15–11, 15–13)

	G	W/L	SW/SL	Pts.
1. USSR	5	5/0	15/1	10
2. Germany	5	3/2	11/8	8
3. Poland	5	3/2	10/11	8
4. Finland	5	2/3	9/13	7
5. Sweden	5	1/4	7/12	6
6. Greece	5	1/4	6/13	6

Group B (Hamburg)

7 Sep.	Italy–Netherlands	3–0	(15–8, 15–6, 15–8)
7 Sep.	Bulgaria–Yugoslavia	3–1	(14–16, 17–15, 17–16, 15–13)
7 Sep.	France–Czechoslovakia	3–0	(17–16, 15–13, 15–12)
8 Sep.	Italy–France	3–0	(15–4, 15–6, 15–6)
8 Sep.	Netherlands–Yugoslavia	3–2	(9–15, 8–15, 15–7, 15–13, 15–9)
8 Sep.	Bulgaria–Czechoslovakia	3–0	(17–16, 15–7, 15–8)
9 Sep.	Netherlands–Bulgaria	3–1	(7–15, 15–8, 15–7, 15–10)
9 Sep.	Italy–Czechoslovakia	3–0	(15–11, 15–4, 15–12)
9 Sep.	Yugoslavia–France	3–1	(15–8, 15–9, 9–15, 15–11)
11 Sep.	Italy–Yugoslavia	3–1	(15–17, 15–6, 17–15, 15–10)
11 Sep.	France–Bulgaria	3–1	(16–14, 15–11, 14–16, 15–11)
11 Sep.	Netherlands–Czechoslovakia	3–0	(15–11, 15–6, 15–9)
12 Sep.	Netherlands–France	3–0	(15–4, 15–1, 15–6)
12 Sep.	Italy–Bulgaria	3–2	(7–15, 7–15, 15–12, 15–10, 15–13)
12 Sep.	Yugoslavia–Czechoslovakia	3–1	(15–13, 7–15, 15–10, 15–6)

	G	W/L	SW/SL	Pts.
1. Italy	5	5/0	15/3	10
2. Netherlands	5	4/1	12/6	9
3. Bulgaria	5	2/3	10/10	7

(continued)

	G	W/L	SW/SL	Pts.
4. Yugoslavia	5	2/3	10/11	7
5. France	5	2/3	7/10	7
6. Czechoslovakia	5	0/5	1/15	5

Final round for 1–8 places (Berlin)

Semifinals (5–8 places)

14 Sep.	Yugoslavia–Poland	3–1	(6–15, 16–14, 16–14, 15–3)
14 Sep.	Bulgaria–Finland	3–0	(16–14, 15–4, 17–16)

Game for 7th place

15 Sep.	Poland–Finland	3–1	(15–5, 15–12, 5–15, 15–12)

Game for 5th place

15 Sep.	Bulgaria–Yugoslavia	3–1	(15–10, 4–15, 15–6, 15–9)

Semifinals (1–4 places)

14 Sep.	Italy–Germany	3–1	(15–12, 15–4, 11–15, 15–6)
14 Sep.	USSR–Netherlands	3–0	(15–8, 15–8, 15–8)

Game for 3rd place

15 Sep.	Netherlands–Germany	3–0	(15–11, 15–9, 15–1)

Final

15 Sep.	USSR–Italy	3–0	(15–11, 17–16, 15–9)

Final standings

	G	W/L	SW/SL
1. USSR	7	7/0	21/1
2. Italy	7	6/1	18/7
3. Netherlands	7	5/2	15/9
4. Germany	7	3/4	12/14
5. Bulgaria	7	4/3	16/11
6. Yugoslavia	7	3/4	14/15
7. Poland	7	4/3	14/15
8. Finland	7	2/5	10/19
9. France	5	2/3	7/10
9. Sweden	5	1/4	7/12
11. Greece	5	1/4	6/13
11. Czechoslovakia	5	0/5	1/15

Total: 12 teams, 38 games

Rosters of the medalists

USSR–Yuriy Cherednik, Dmitriy Fomin, Sergey Gorbunov, Yuriy Korovyanskiy, Evgeniy Krasilnikov, Andrey Kuznetsov, Ruslan Olikhver, Igor Runov, Yuriy Sapega, Aleksandr Shadchin, Oleg Shatunov, Konstantin Ushakov; head coach: Vyacheslav Platonov

Italy–Lorenzo Bernardi, Luca Cantagalli, Ferdinando De Giorgi, Claudio Galli, Andrea Gardini, Andrea Giani, Andrea Lucchetta, Stefano Margutti, Marco Martinelli, Roberto Masciarelli, Paolo Tofoli, Andrea Zorzi; head coach: Julio Velasco

Netherlands–Edwin Benne, Ron Boudrie, Patrick de Reus, Henk-Jan Held, Marko Klok, Bas Koek, Avital Selinger, Martin Teffer, Martin van der Horst, Olof van der Meulen, Arnold van Ree, Ron Zwerver; head coach: Arie "Harry" Brokking

XVIII EUROPEAN CHAMPIONSHIP
4–12 September 1993, Oulu and Turku (Finland)

Preliminary round

Group A (Oulu)

4 Sep.	Italy–Bulgaria	3–1	(15–6, 15–8, 13–15, 15–8)
4 Sep.	Netherlands–France	3–0	(15–7, 15–10, 15–3)
4 Sep.	Czechoslovakia–Sweden	3–1	(7–15, 15–13, 15–13, 15–10)
5 Sep.	Italy–France	3–1	(15–4, 16–14, 15–17, 16–14)
5 Sep.	Netherlands–Czechoslovakia	3–1	(15–3, 5–15, 15–13, 15–3)
5 Sep.	Bulgaria–Sweden	3–0	(15–12, 15–3, 15–8)
6 Sep.	Italy–Czechoslovakia	3–0	(15–3, 15–6, 15–2)
6 Sep.	Bulgaria–France	3–1	(15–11, 15–13, 13–15, 15–11)
6 Sep.	Netherlands–Sweden	3–0	(15–8, 15–13, 15–7)
8 Sep.	France–Czechoslovakia	3–2	(12–15, 15–6, 15–8, 7–15, 15–13)
8 Sep.	Netherlands–Bulgaria	3–0	(15–10, 15–3, 15–10)
8 Sep.	Italy–Sweden	3–0	(15–4, 15–7, 15–5)
9 Sep.	Czechoslovakia–Bulgaria	3–2	(7–15, 17–15, 15–12, 13–15, 15–10)
9 Sep.	Italy–Netherlands	3–1	(15–4, 15–10, 11–15, 15–11)
9 Sep.	France–Sweden	3–0	(15–11, 15–8, 15–10)

	G	W/L	SW/SL	Pts.
1. Italy	5	5/0	15/3	10
2. Netherlands	5	4/1	13/4	9
3. Bulgaria	5	2/3	9/10	7
4. Czechoslovakia	5	2/3	9/12	7
5. France	5	2/3	8/11	7
6. Sweden	5	0/5	1/15	5

Group B (Turku)

4 Sep.	Finland–Spain	3–1	(14–16, 15–13, 15–12, 16–14)
4 Sep.	Russia–Ukraine	3–0	(15–2, 15–4, 15–5)
4 Sep.	Germany–Poland	3–2	(12–15, 6–15, 15–12, 15–12, 15–6)
5 Sep.	Russia–Finland	3–0	(15–7, 15–5, 15–13)
5 Sep.	Poland–Spain	3–0	(15–12, 15–13, 15–13)
5 Sep.	Germany–Ukraine	3–0	(15–6, 15–5, 16–14)
6 Sep.	Russia–Spain	3–1	(9–15, 15–2, 15–9, 15–8)
6 Sep.	Germany–Finland	3–2	(15–10, 15–17, 8–15, 15–7, 15–12)
6 Sep.	Ukraine–Poland	3–1	(15–9, 5–15, 15–12, 15–9)
8 Sep.	Russia–Germany	3–0	(15–8, 15–9, 15–5)
8 Sep.	Poland–Finland	3–1	(15–2, 12–15, 15–7, 15–9)
8 Sep.	Ukraine–Spain	3–1	(15–5, 8–15, 15–6, 15–7)
9 Sep.	Russia–Poland	3–1	(12–15, 15–9, 15–8, 15–5)
9 Sep.	Ukraine–Finland	3–2	(15–10, 14–16, 15–6, 13–15, 15–12)
9 Sep.	Germany–Spain	3–2	(15–6, 15–8, 11–15, 10–15, 15–7)

	G	W/L	SW/SL	Pts.
1. Russia	5	5/0	15/2	10
2. Germany	5	4/1	12/9	9
3. Ukraine	5	3/2	9/10	8
4. Poland	5	2/3	10/10	7
5. Finland	5	1/4	8/13	6
6. Spain	5	0/5	5/15	5

Final round for 1–8 places (Turku)

Semifinals (5–8 places)

11 Sep.	Bulgaria–Poland	3–1	(10–15, 15–10, 15–1, 15–11)
11 Sep.	Ukraine–Czechoslovakia	3–0	(15–7, 15–13, 15–6)

Game for 7th place

12 Sep.	Poland–Czechoslovakia	3–1	(15–10, 12–15, 16–14, 15–7)

Game for 5th place

12 Sep.	Bulgaria–Ukraine	3–2	(8–15, 15–5, 15–3, 12–15, 15–11)

Semifinals (1–4 places)

11 Sep.	Italy–Germany	3–0	(15–1, 15–6, 15–11)
11 Sep.	Netherlands–Russia	3–0	(15–11, 15–8, 15–2)

Game for 3rd place

12 Sep.	Russia–Germany	3–1	(15–3, 9–15, 15–8, 15–5)

Final

12 Sep.   Italy–Netherlands   3–2   (15–6, 15–5, 13–15, 8–15, 15–9)

Final standings

	G	W/L	SW/SL
1. Italy	7	7/0	21/5
2. Netherlands	7	5/2	18/7
3. Russia	7	6/1	18/6
4. Germany	7	4/3	13/15
5. Bulgaria	7	4/3	15/13
6. Ukraine	7	4/3	14/13
7. Poland	7	3/4	14/14
8. Czechoslovakia	7	2/5	10/18
9. France	5	2/3	8/11
9. Finland	5	1/4	8/13
11. Spain	5	0/5	5/15
11. Sweden	5	0/5	1/15

Total: 12 teams, 38 games

Rosters of the medalists

Italy–Davide Bellini, Marco Bracci, Luca Cantagalli, Claudio Galli, Andrea Gardini, Andrea Giani, Pasquale Gravina, Marco Martinelli, Michele Pasinato, Damiano Pippi, Paolo Tofoli, Andrea Zorzi; head coach: Julio Velasco

Netherlands–Edwin Benne, Jeroen Bijl, Peter Blangé, Rob Grabert, Henk-Jan Held, Marko Klok, Brecht Rodenburg, Bas van der Goor, Martin van der Horst, Olof van der Meulen, Ronald Zoodsma, Ron Zwerver; head coach: Joop Alberda

Russia–Ruslan Chigrin, Dmitriy Fomin, Evgeniy Krasilnikov, Andrey Kuznetsov, Evgeniy Mitkov, Ruslan Olikhver, Sergey Orlenko, Ilya Savelev, Oleg Shatunov, Pavel Shishkin, Oleg Sogrin, Konstantin Ushakov; head coach: Viktor Radin

XIX EUROPEAN CHAMPIONSHIP
8–16 September 1995, Athens and Patras (Greece)

Preliminary round

Group A (Athens)

8 Sep.	Netherlands–Yugoslavia	3–0	(15–5, 15–2, 15–9)
8 Sep.	Greece–Latvia	3–0	(16–14, 15–13, 15–7)
8 Sep.	Germany–Ukraine	3–0	(15–9, 15–8, 15–12)
9 Sep.	Netherlands–Latvia	3–0	(15–4, 15–2, 15–2)
9 Sep.	Greece–Germany	3–1	(9–15, 15–9, 15–8, 15–6)
9 Sep.	Yugoslavia–Ukraine	3–0	(15–4, 15–13, 15–6)

(continued)

Group A (Athens) (continued)

10 Sep.	Germany–Latvia	3–1	(15–2, 15–9, 13–15, 15–12)
10 Sep.	Yugoslavia–Greece	3–1	(16–14, 15–10, 7–15, 15–7)
10 Sep.	Netherlands–Ukraine	3–0	(15–5, 15–5, 17–15)
12 Sep.	Yugoslavia–Latvia	3–0	(17–15, 15–9, 15–4)
12 Sep.	Greece–Ukraine	3–0	(15–5, 15–12, 15–9)
12 Sep.	Netherlands–Germany	3–0	(15–8, 16–14, 15–6)
13 Sep.	Ukraine–Latvia	3–0	(15–9, 15–8, 15–5)
13 Sep.	Netherlands–Greece	3–0	(15–13, 15–4, 15–4)
13 Sep.	Yugoslavia–Germany	3–0	(15–2, 15–4, 15–7)

	G	W/L	SW/SL	Pts.
1. Netherlands	5	5/0	15/0	10
2. Yugoslavia	5	4/1	12/4	9
3. Greece	5	3/2	10/7	8
4. Germany	5	2/3	7/10	7
5. Ukraine	5	1/4	3/12	6
6. Latvia	5	0/5	1/15	5

Group B (Patras)

8 Sep.	Czech Republic–Russia	3–2	(3–15, 15–13, 15–13, 14–16, 15–12)
8 Sep.	Italy–Romania	3–0	(15–7, 15–2, 15–5)
8 Sep.	Bulgaria–Poland	3–0	(15–12, 16–14, 15–7)
9 Sep.	Czech Republic–Romania	3–0	(15–4, 15–5, 15–4)
9 Sep.	Italy–Bulgaria	3–0	(15–6, 15–10, 15–12)
9 Sep.	Russia–Poland	3–1	(15–12, 10–15, 15–5, 15–2)
10 Sep.	Bulgaria–Czech Republic	3–1	(12–15, 15–7, 15–8, 15–9)
10 Sep.	Italy–Poland	3–0	(15–8, 15–6, 16–14)
10 Sep.	Russia–Romania	3–0	(15–3, 15–4, 15–9)
12 Sep.	Italy–Czech Republic	3–0	(15–8, 17–15, 15–11)
12 Sep.	Poland–Romania	3–0	(15–13, 15–3, 15–5)
12 Sep.	Bulgaria–Russia	3–1	(13–15, 15–10, 15–13, 17–16)
13 Sep.	Poland–Czech Republic	3–0	(15–10, 17–15, 15–10)
13 Sep.	Russia–Italy	3–1	(15–10, 15–12, 4–15, 15–10)
13 Sep.	Bulgaria–Romania	3–0	(15–7, 15–7, 15–7)

	G	W/L	SW/SL	Pts.
1. Italy	5	4/1	13/3	9
2. Bulgaria	5	4/1	12/5	9
3. Russia	5	3/2	12/8	8
4. Poland	5	2/3	7/9	7
5. Czech Republic	5	2/3	7/11	7
6. Romania	5	0/5	0/15	5

Final round for 1–8 places (Athens)

Semifinals (5–8 places)

15 Sep.	Russia–Germany	3–0	(15–13, 15–7, 15–11)
15 Sep.	Poland–Greece	3–0	(15–11, 16–14, 17–15)

Game for 7th place

16 Sep.	Greece–Germany	3–2	(15–11, 15–4, 13–15, 10–15, 15–10)

Game for 5th place

16 Sep.	Russia–Poland	3–0	(15–5, 15–9, 15–1)

Semifinals (1–4 places)

15 Sep.	Italy–Yugoslavia	3–1	(15–11, 10–15, 15–6, 15–9)
15 Sep.	Netherlands–Bulgaria	3–0	(15–6, 15–5, 15–8)

Game for 3rd place

16 Sep.	Yugoslavia–Bulgaria	3–0	(15–4, 15–4, 15–6)

Final

16 Sep.	Italy–Netherlands	3–2	(13–15, 15–10, 11–15, 15–12, 15–11)

Final standings

	G	W/L	SW/SL
1. Italy	7	6/1	19/6
2. Netherlands	7	6/1	20/3
3. Yugoslavia	7	5/2	16/7
4. Bulgaria	7	4/3	12/11
5. Russia	7	5/2	18/8
6. Poland	7	3/4	10/12
7. Greece	7	4/3	13/12
8. Germany	7	2/5	9/16
9. Czech Republic	5	2/3	7/11
9. Ukraine	5	1/4	3/12
11. Latvia	5	0/5	1/15
11. Romania	5	0/5	0/15

Total: 12 teams, 38 games

Rosters of the medalists

Italy–Lorenzo Bernardi, Vigor Bovolenta, Marco Bracci, Luca Cantagalli, Andrea Gardini, Andrea Giani, Pasquale Gravina, Marco Meoni, Samuele Papi, Michele Pasinato, Paolo Tofoli, Andrea Zorzi; head coach: Julio Velasco

Netherlands–Peter Blangé, Guido Görtzen, Henk-Jan Held, Misha Latuhihin, Reinder Nummerdor, Brecht Rodenburg, Richard Schuil, Bas van der Goor, Martin van der Horst, Olof van der Meulen, Robert van Es, Ron Zwerver; head coach: Joop Alberda

Yugoslavia–Slobodan Boškan, Dejan Brđović, Đorđe Đurić, Andrija Gerić, Nikola Grbić, Vladimir Grbić, Rajko Jokanović, Slobodan Kovač, Đula Mešter, Žarko Petrović, Željko Tanasković, Goran Vujević; head coach: Zoran Gajić

XX EUROPEAN CHAMPIONSHIP
6–14 September 1997, Den Bosch and Eindhoven (Netherlands)

Preliminary round

Group A (Den Bosch)

6 Sep.	Italy–Greece	3–0	(16–14, 15–4, 15–3)
6 Sep.	Slovakia–Germany	3–1	(13–15, 15–12, 15–9, 15–10)
6 Sep.	Russia–Yugoslavia	3–0	(16–14, 15–11, 15–13)
7 Sep.	Germany–Greece	3–1	(17–15, 15–9, 7–15, 15–8)
7 Sep.	Slovakia–Russia	3–2	(6–15, 15–10, 16–14, 10–15, 15–12)
7 Sep.	Yugoslavia–Italy	3–0	(15–13, 15–9, 15–5)
8 Sep.	Germany–Russia	3–2	(15–9, 15–10, 6–15, 4–15, 16–14)
8 Sep.	Italy–Slovakia	3–1	(15–13, 12–15, 15–11, 15–5)
8 Sep.	Yugoslavia–Greece	3–1	(15–5, 14–16, 15–6, 15–6)
10 Sep.	Italy–Germany	3–0	(15–10, 15–9, 15–4)
10 Sep.	Russia–Greece	3–0	(15–5, 15–9, 15–12)
10 Sep.	Yugoslavia–Slovakia	3–0	(15–7, 15–4, 15–8)
11 Sep.	Italy–Russia	3–0	(15–6, 15–10, 15–12)
11 Sep.	Slovakia–Greece	3–1	(15–10, 15–11, 2–15, 15–13)
11 Sep.	Yugoslavia–Germany	3–0	(15–8, 16–14, 15–7)

	G	W/L	SW/SL	Pts.
1. Yugoslavia	5	4/1	12/4	9
2. Italy	5	4/1	12/4	9
3. Slovakia	5	3/2	10/10	8
4. Russia	5	2/3	10/9	7
5. Germany	5	2/3	7/12	7
6. Greece	5	0/5	3/15	5

Group B (Eindhoven)

6 Sep.	Netherlands–Finland	3–0	(15–3, 15–7, 15–2)
6 Sep.	Czech Republic–France	3–1	(16–14, 7–15, 15–1, 15–12)
6 Sep.	Ukraine–Bulgaria	3–2	(8–15, 15–7, 11–15, 15–10, 15–9)
7 Sep.	France–Finland	3–0	(15–5, 15–13, 15–7)
7 Sep.	Netherlands–Ukraine	3–0	(15–6, 15–10, 15–1)
7 Sep.	Bulgaria–Czech Republic	3–2	(5–15, 15–10, 15–11, 10–15, 15–11)
8 Sep.	Ukraine–Finland	3–0	(15–12, 15–1, 15–9)
8 Sep.	France–Bulgaria	3–0	(15–10, 17–15, 15–2)
8 Sep.	Netherlands–Czech Republic	3–0	(15–7, 15–2, 15–6)
10 Sep.	Bulgaria–Finland	3–1	(15–12, 9–15, 15–7, 15–11)
10 Sep.	Ukraine–Czech Republic	3–2	(11–15, 15–9, 10–15, 15–13, 15–11)
10 Sep.	Netherlands–France	3–0	(16–14, 15–6, 15–5)
11 Sep.	Czech Republic–Finland	3–2	(12–15, 15–11, 15–11, 10–15, 15–11)
11 Sep.	France–Ukraine	3–2	(15–13, 15–8, 10–15, 3–15, 19–17)
11 Sep.	Netherlands–Bulgaria	3–0	(15–3, 15–9, 15–11)

	G	W/L	SW/SL	Pts.
1. Netherlands	5	5/0	15/0	10
2. France	5	3/2	10/8	8
3. Ukraine	5	3/2	11/10	8
4. Czech Republic	5	2/3	10/12	7
5. Bulgaria	5	2/3	8/12	7
6. Finland	5	0/5	3/15	5

Final round for 1–8 places (Eindhoven)

Semifinals (5–8 places)

13 Sep.	Czech Republic–Slovakia	3–0	(15–5, 15–11, 15–11)
13 Sep.	Russia–Ukraine	3–0	(15–10, 15–4, 15–12)

Game for 7th place

14 Sep.	Slovakia–Ukraine	3–0	(15–3, 15–13, 15–3)

Game for 5th place

14 Sep.	Russia–Czech Republic	3–0	(15–10, 15–9, 15–9)

Semifinals (1–4 places)

13 Sep.	Yugoslavia–France	3–0	(15–6, 17–15, 15–11)
13 Sep.	Netherlands–Italy	3–0	(15–9, 15–6, 15–13)

Game for 3rd place

14 Sep.	Italy–France	3–1	(15–2, 15–6, 10–15, 15–8)

Final

14 Sep.   Netherlands–Yugoslavia   3–1   (15–11, 10–15, 15–10, 15–9)

Final standings

	G	W/L	SW/SL
1. Netherlands	7	7/0	21/1
2. Yugoslavia	7	5/2	16/7
3. Italy	7	5/2	15/8
4. France	7	3/4	11/14
5. Russia	7	4/3	16/9
6. Czech Republic	7	3/4	13/15
7. Ukraine	7	3/4	11/16
8. Slovakia	7	4/3	13/13
9. Bulgaria	5	2/3	8/12
9. Germany	5	2/3	7/12
11. Finland	5	0/5	3/15
11. Greece	5	0/5	3/15

Total: 12 teams, 38 games

Rosters of the medalists

Netherlands–Peter Blangé, Albert Cristina, Jochem de Gruijter, Guido Görtzen, Henk-Jan Held, Misha Latuhihin, Reinder Nummerdor, Richard Schuil, Bas van de Goor, Mike van de Goor, Olof van der Meulen, Robert van Es; head coach: Toon Gerbrands

Yugoslavia–Vladimir Batez, Slobodan Boškan, Đorđe Đurić, Andrija Gerić, Nikola Grbić, Vladimir Grbić, Rajko Jokanović, Slobodan Kovač, Đula Mešter, Željko Tanasković, Goran Vujević, Igor Vušurović; head coach: Zoran Gajić

Italy–Alberto Bachi, Davide Bellini, Claudio Bonati, Vigor Bovolenta, Andrea Gardini, Andrea Giani, Pasquale Gravina, Marco Meoni, Michele Pasinato, Damiano Pippi, Simone Rosalba, Andrea Sartoretti; head coach: Paulo Roberto de Freitas "Bebeto"

XXI EUROPEAN CHAMPIONSHIP
7–12 September 1999, Vienna and Wiener Neustadt (Austria)

Preliminary round

Group A (Vienna)

7 Sep.   Italy–Austria   3–0   (25–12, 25–16, 25–19)
7 Sep.   Russia–Bulgaria   3–1   (27–25, 17–25, 25–13, 25–16)

(continued)

Group A (Vienna) (continued)

8 Sep.	Italy–Bulgaria	3–0	(25–21, 25–21, 25–23)
8 Sep.	Russia–Austria	3–0	(25–19, 25–13, 25–22)
9 Sep.	Bulgaria–Austria	3–0	(25–22, 25–23, 25–15)
9 Sep.	Russia–Italy	3–1	(25–20, 22–25, 25–18, 25–20)

	G	W/L	SW/SL	Pts.
1. Russia	3	3/0	9/2	6
2. Italy	3	2/1	7/3	5
3. Bulgaria	3	1/2	4/6	4
4. Austria	3	0/3	0/9	3

Group B (Wiener Neustadt)

7 Sep.	Yugoslavia–Czech Republic	3–1	(25–20, 25–14, 24–26, 25–22)
7 Sep.	France–Netherlands	3–0	(26–24, 27–25, 30–28)
8 Sep.	Yugoslavia–France	3–1	(25–12, 25–17, 25–27, 25–17)
8 Sep.	Czech Republic–Netherlands	3–2	(19–25, 25–20, 17–25, 25–23, 18–16)
9 Sep.	Czech Republic–France	3–2	(26–24, 25–19, 20–25, 23–25, 15–13)
9 Sep.	Netherlands–Yugoslavia	3–1	(17–25, 25–21, 25–21, 25–22)

	G	W/L	SW/SL	Pts.
1. Yugoslavia	3	2/1	7/5	5
2. Czech Republic	3	2/1	7/7	5
3. France	3	1/2	6/6	4
4. Netherlands	3	1/2	5/7	4

Final round (Vienna)

Semifinals (5–8 places)

11 Sep.	Netherlands–Bulgaria	3–0	(25–17, 25–19, 25–18)
11 Sep.	France–Austria	3–0	(25–15, 25–23, 27–25)

Game for 7th place

12 Sep.	Bulgaria–Austria	3–0	(25–23, 25–19, 25–15)

Game for 5th place

12 Sep.	Netherlands–France	3–2	(25–21, 23–25, 22–25, 25–23, 15–12)

Semifinals (1–4 places)

11 Sep.	Italy–Yugoslavia	3–1	(25–17, 25–22, 24–26, 25–22)
11 Sep.	Russia–Czech Republic	3–0	(25–21, 25–15, 25–13)

Game for 3rd place

12 Sep.	Yugoslavia–Czech Republic	3–0	(25–17, 25–19, 25–23)

Final

12 Sep.	Italy–Russia	3–1	(19–25, 25–17, 25–22, 30–28)

Final standings

	G	W/L	SW/SL
1. Italy	5	4/1	13/5
2. Russia	5	4/1	13/5
3. Yugoslavia	5	3/2	11/8
4. Czech Republic	5	2/3	7/13
5. Netherlands	5	3/2	11/9
6. France	5	2/3	11/9
7. Bulgaria	5	2/3	7/9
8. Austria	5	0/5	0/15

Total: 8 teams, 20 games

Rosters of the medalists

Italy–Marco Bracci, Mirko Corsano, Andrea Gardini, Andrea Giani, Leondino Giombini, Pasquale Gravina, Luigi Mastrangelo, Marco Meoni, Samuele Papi, Simone Rosalba, Andrea Sartoretti, Paolo Tofoli; head coach: Andrea Anastasi

Russia–Stanislav Dineykin, Aleksandr Gerasimov, Valeriy Goryushev, Aleksey Kazakov, Vadim Khamuttskikh, Evgeniy Mitkov, Ruslan Olikhver, Sergey Orlenko, Igor Shulepov, Sergey Tetyukhin, Konstantin Ushakov, Roman Yakovlev; head coach: Gennadiy Shipulin

Yugoslavia–Vladimir Batez, Slobodan Boškan, Đorđe Đurić, Andrija Gerić, Nikola Grbić, Vladimir Grbić, Đula Mešter, Vasa Mijić, Ivan Miljković, Veljko Petković, Željko Tanasković, Goran Vujević; head coach: Zoran Gajić

XXII EUROPEAN CHAMPIONSHIP
8–16 September 2001, Ostrava (Czech Republic)

Preliminary round

Group A

8 Sep.	Netherlands–Slovakia	3–0	(25–20, 25–21, 31–29)
8 Sep.	Czech Republic–Slovenia	3–1	(25–15, 21–25, 25–17, 25–12)
8 Sep.	Russia–Bulgaria	3–1	(25–13, 25–13, 20–25, 25–18)
9 Sep.	Netherlands–Czech Republic	3–1	(25–15, 25–17, 19–25, 25–20)
9 Sep.	Russia–Slovakia	3–1	(20–25, 25–19, 25–20, 25–17)
9 Sep.	Bulgaria–Slovenia	3–0	(25–21, 25–15, 25–20)
10 Sep.	Russia–Netherlands	3–1	(24–26, 25–22, 25–20, 25–17)
10 Sep.	Czech Republic–Bulgaria	3–1	(25–22, 25–20, 20–25, 25–20)
10 Sep.	Slovakia–Slovenia	3–2	(20–25, 25–21, 25–22, 22–25, 15–13)
12 Sep.	Bulgaria–Netherlands	3–2	(25–22, 23–25, 17–25, 25–23, 15–13)
12 Sep.	Czech Republic–Slovakia	3–0	(25–19, 25–23, 25–12)
12 Sep.	Russia–Slovenia	3–0	(25–17, 25–14, 25–21)
13 Sep.	Bulgaria–Slovakia	3–1	(20–25, 25–15, 25–21, 25–20)
13 Sep.	Czech Republic–Russia	3–0	(25–19, 25–21, 25–23)
13 Sep.	Netherlands–Slovenia	3–0	(25–20, 25–16, 25–20)

	G	W/L	SW/SL	Pts.
1. Czech Republic	5	4/1	13/5	9
2. Russia	5	4/1	12/6	9
3. Netherlands	5	3/2	12/7	8
4. Bulgaria	5	3/2	11/9	8
5. Slovakia	5	1/4	5/14	6
6. Slovenia	5	0/5	3/15	5

Group B

8 Sep.	Yugoslavia–France	3–2	(25–18, 25–21, 25–27, 23–25, 15–13)
8 Sep.	Italy–Hungary	3–0	(25–23, 25–14, 25–13)
8 Sep.	Poland–Germany	3–1	(21–25, 31–29, 25–15, 25–14)
9 Sep.	France–Hungary	3–0	(27–25, 25–18, 25–21)
9 Sep.	Italy–Germany	3–1	(25–14, 25–16, 23–25, 25–16)
9 Sep.	Yugoslavia–Poland	3–0	(25–19, 25–14, 25–22)
10 Sep.	France–Germany	3–1	(25–20, 20–25, 25–16, 26–24)
10 Sep.	Italy–Poland	3–0	(25–21, 34–32, 25–21)
10 Sep.	Yugoslavia–Hungary	3–1	(27–29, 25–18, 25–17, 25–19)
12 Sep.	Hungary–Germany	3–0	(26–24, 25–21, 25–22)

(continued)

Group B (continued)

12 Sep.	Yugoslavia–Italy	3–0	(25–21, 25–23, 27–25)
12 Sep.	Poland–France	3–2	(23–25, 25–17, 19–25, 27–25, 15–12)
13 Sep.	Germany–Yugoslavia	3–2	(19–25, 25–21, 17–25, 25–23, 15–12)
13 Sep.	France–Italy	3–2	(25–21, 21–25, 25–22, 21–25, 19–17)
13 Sep.	Poland–Hungary	3–1	(25–15, 20–25, 27–25, 25–23)

	G	W/L	SW/SL	Pts.
1. Yugoslavia	5	4/1	14/6	9
2. Italy	5	3/2	11/7	8
3. France	5	3/2	13/9	8
4. Poland	5	3/2	9/10	8
5. Hungary	5	1/4	5/12	6
6. Germany	5	1/4	6/14	6

Final round for 1–8 places

Semifinals (5–8 places)

15 Sep.	Poland–Netherlands	3–1	(25–21, 21–25, 25–21, 27–25)
15 Sep.	Bulgaria–France	3–1	(24–26, 26–24, 30–28, 25–16)

Game for 7th place

16 Sep.	France–Netherlands	3–1	(25–18, 18–25, 25–22, 26–24)

Game for 5th place

16 Sep.	Poland–Bulgaria	3–2	(25–27, 27–25, 25–21, 22–25, 15–11)

Semifinals (1–4 places)

15 Sep.	Italy–Czech Republic	3–0	(25–22, 29–27, 25–9)
15 Sep.	Yugoslavia–Russia	3–0	(25–20, 25–17, 29–27)

Game for 3rd place

16 Sep.	Russia–Czech Republic	3–2	(18–25, 25–15, 21–25, 25–22, 15–12)

Final

16 Sep.	Yugoslavia–Italy	3–0	(25–21, 25–18, 25–20)

Final standings

	G	W/L	SW/SL
1. Yugoslavia	7	6/1	20/6
2. Italy	7	4/3	14/10
3. Russia	7	5/2	15/11
4. Czech Republic	7	4/3	15/11
5. Poland	7	5/2	15/13
6. Bulgaria	7	4/3	16/13
7. France	7	4/3	17/13
8. Netherlands	7	3/4	14/13
9. Germany	5	1/4	6/14
9. Slovakia	5	1/4	5/14
11. Hungary	5	1/4	5/12
11. Slovenia	5	0/5	3/15

Total: 12 teams, 38 games

Rosters of the medalists

Yugoslavia–Slobodan Boškan, Andrija Gerić, Nikola Grbić, Vladimir Grbić, Rajko Jokanović, Goran Marić, Đula Mešter, Vasa Mijić, Ivan Miljković, Edin Škorić, Goran Vujević, Igor Vušurović; head coach: Zoran Gajić

Italy–Lorenzo Bernardi, Vigor Bovolenta, Cristian Casoli, Mirko Corsano, Alessandro Fei, Leondino Giombini, Marco Meoni, Samuele Papi, Andrea Sartoretti, Luca Tencati, Valerio Vermiglio, Hristo Zlatanov; head coach: Andrea Anastasi

Russia–Pavel Abramov, Roman Arkhipov, Aleksandr Gerasimov, Aleksey Kazakov, Vadim Khamuttskikh, Aleksandr Kosarev, Aleksey Kuleshov, Evgeniy Mitkov, Ruslan Olikhver, Igor Shulepov, Sergey Tetyukhin, Roman Yakovlev; head coach: Gennadiy Shipulin

XXIII EUROPEAN CHAMPIONSHIP
5–14 September 2003, Berlin, Karlsruhe, and Leipzig (Germany)

Preliminary round

Group A

5 Sep.	Poland–Greece	3–0	(25–14, 25–22, 25–19)	Leipzig
5 Sep.	Russia–Bulgaria	3–0	(25–0, 25–0, 25–0)*	Leipzig
5 Sep.	Serbia and Montenegro–Netherlands	3–1	(30–28, 21–25, 25–22, 25–18)	Leipzig
6 Sep.	Russia–Poland	3–1	(25–19, 25–23, 23–25, 25–20)	Leipzig

(continued)

Group A (continued)

6 Sep.	Netherlands–Greece	3–2	(23–25, 25–21, 22–25, 25–14, 15–11)	Leipzig
6 Sep.	Serbia and Montenegro–Bulgaria	3–0	(25–22, 25–19, 25–18)	Leipzig
7 Sep.	Netherlands–Poland	3–2	(29–27, 21–25, 25–21, 24–26, 15–9)	Leipzig
7 Sep.	Serbia and Montenegro–Russia	3–1	(25–21, 21–25, 25–23, 25–15)	Leipzig
7 Sep.	Greece–Bulgaria	3–1	(25–20, 25–16, 20–25, 25–18)	Leipzig
10 Sep.	Netherlands–Russia	3–0	(25–21, 27–25, 25–21)	Karlsruhe
10 Sep.	Bulgaria–Poland	3–2	(25–22, 18–25, 22–25, 25–19, 15–11)	Karlsruhe
10 Sep.	Serbia and Montenegro–Greece	3–0	(25–15, 25–20, 25–15)	Karlsruhe
11 Sep.	Bulgaria–Netherlands	3–0	(26–24, 25–21, 26–24)	Karlsruhe
11 Sep.	Russia–Greece	3–2	(24–26, 27–25, 24–26, 25–20, 15–9)	Karlsruhe
11 Sep.	Poland–Serbia and Montenegro	3–2	(25–22, 22–25, 26–28, 25–19, 15–13)	Karlsruhe

	G	W/L	SW/SL	Pts.
1. Serbia and Montenegro	5	4/1	14/5	9
2. Russia	5	3/2	10/9	8
3. Netherlands	5	3/2	10/10	8
4. Poland	5	2/3	11/11	7
5. Bulgaria	5	2/3	7/11	7
6. Greece	5	1/4	7/13	6

*Russia won the match 3–1 (25–22, 23–25, 28–26, 25–20), but because Bulgarian player Matey Kaziyski was not eligible to play in the tournament (the Bulgarian Federation did not apply to list him on the collective license list), the results of the game were changed by the CEV Jury two days later.

Group B

5 Sep.	France–Spain	3–0	(25–17, 32–30, 25–19)	Karlsruhe
5 Sep.	Germany–Slovakia	3–1	(25–20, 25–16, 25–27, 25–16)	Karlsruhe
5 Sep.	Italy–Czech Republic	3–1	(25–19, 25–21, 22–25, 25–23)	Karlsruhe
6 Sep.	Italy–Spain	3–0	(25–16, 25–22, 25–16)	Karlsruhe
6 Sep.	Germany–Czech Republic	3–0	(25–19, 25–18, 25–20)	Karlsruhe
6 Sep.	France–Slovakia	3–0	(25–17, 25–19, 25–15)	Karlsruhe
7 Sep.	Czech Republic–Slovakia	3–1	(27–29, 25–23, 25–22, 25–22)	Karlsruhe

(continued)

Group B (continued)

7 Sep.	Italy–France	3–1	(25–21, 17–25, 26–24, 25–20)	Karlsruhe
7 Sep.	Germany–Spain	3–1	(26–24, 20–25, 25–20, 25–22)	Karlsruhe
10 Sep.	Spain–Czech Republic	3–1	(21–25, 25–16, 25–23, 26–24)	Leipzig
10 Sep.	France–Germany	3–1	(20–25, 26–24, 25–22, 25–19)	Leipzig
10 Sep.	Italy–Slovakia	3–0	(25–14, 25–12, 25–15)	Leipzig
11 Sep.	France–Czech Republic	3–0	(25–23, 25–20, 25–21)	Leipzig
11 Sep.	Spain–Slovakia	3–1	(25–21, 25–23, 20–25, 25–18)	Leipzig
11 Sep.	Italy–Germany	3–0	(25–17, 25–20, 25–19)	Leipzig

	G	W/L	SW/SL	Pts.
1. Italy	5	5/0	15/2	10
2. France	5	4/1	13/4	9
3. Germany	5	3/2	10/8	8
4. Spain	5	2/3	7/11	7
5. Czech Republic	5	1/4	5/13	6
6. Slovakia	5	0/5	3/15	5

Final round for 1–8 places (Berlin)

Semifinals (5–8 places)

13 Sep.	Netherlands–Spain	3–2	(21–25, 25–23, 22–25, 25–22, 18–16)
13 Sep.	Poland–Germany	3–1	(25–21, 23–25, 34–32, 25–22)

Game for 7th place

14 Sep.	Germany–Spain	3–1	(28–26, 21–25, 25–19, 28–26)

Game for 5th place

14 Sep.	Poland–Netherlands	3–0	(25–21, 25–20, 25–13)

Semifinals (1–4 places)

13 Sep.	Italy–Russia	3–0	(25–18, 25–18, 25–16)
13 Sep.	France–Serbia and Montenegro	3–2	(25–22, 19–25, 25–20, 22–25, 16–14)

Game for 3rd place

14 Sep.	Russia–Serbia and Montenegro	3–1	(25–11, 24–26, 25–19, 25–23)

Final

14 Sep.	Italy–France	3–2	(25–18, 40–42, 25–18, 27–29, 15–9)

Final standings

	G	W/L	SW/SL
1. Italy	7	7/0	21/4
2. France	7	5/2	18/9
3. Russia	7	4/3	13/13
4. Serbia and Montenegro	7	4/3	17/11
5. Poland	7	4/3	17/12
6. Netherlands	7	4/3	13/15
7. Germany	7	4/3	14/12
8. Spain	7	2/5	10/17
9. Bulgaria	5	2/3	7/11
9. Czech Republic	5	1/4	5/13
11. Greece	5	1/4	7/13
11. Slovakia	5	0/5	3/15

Total: 12 teams, 38 games

Rosters of the medalists

Italy–Francesco Biribanti, Matej Cernic, Paolo Cozzi, Alessandro Fei, Andrea Giani, Luigi Mastrangelo, Marco Meoni, Samuele Papi, Damiano Pippi, Andrea Sartoretti, Cristian Savani, Valerio Vermiglio; head coach: Gian Paolo Montali

France–Stéphane Antiga, Laurent Capet, Johan Cohen, Dominique Daquin, Loic De Kergret, Sébastien Frangolacci, Frantz Granvorka, Hubert Henno, Oliver Kieffer, Luc Marquet, Vincent Montméat, Mathias Patin; head coach: Philippe Blain

Russia–Pavel Abramov, Sergey Baranov, Andrey Egorchev, Aleksey Kazakov, Vadim Khamuttskikh, Aleksey Kuleshov, Evgeniy Mitkov, Semyon Poltavskiy, Igor Shulepov, Sergey Tetyukhin, Konstantin Ushakov, Roman Yakovlev; head coach: Gennadiy Shipulin

XXIV EUROPEAN CHAMPIONSHIP
2–11 September 2005, Rome (Italy), Belgrade (Serbia and Montenegro)

Preliminary round

Group A (Rome)

3 Sep.	Poland–Croatia	3–0	(25–22, 25–19, 25–21)
3 Sep.	Italy–Portugal	3–0	(25–19, 25–21, 25–20)
3 Sep.	Russia–Ukraine	3–0	(25–22, 25–23, 25–21)
4 Sep.	Croatia–Portugal	3–2	(25–23, 20–25, 21–25, 25–21, 15–7)
4 Sep.	Italy–Ukraine	3–0	(25–17, 25–23, 25–23)
4 Sep.	Russia–Poland	3–1	(25–27, 29–27, 29–27, 25–21)
5 Sep.	Portugal–Ukraine	3–2	(25–20, 20–25, 20–25, 25–21, 15–13)
5 Sep.	Italy–Poland	3–0	(26–24, 25–22, 25–19)

(continued)

Group A (Rome) (continued)

5 Sep.	Russia–Croatia	3–2	(21–25, 25–18, 25–20, 21–25, 15–11)
7 Sep.	Poland–Ukraine	3–1	(25–18, 21–25, 25–20, 25–21)
7 Sep.	Russia–Portugal	3–1	(23–25, 25–22, 25–21, 25–18)
7 Sep.	Italy–Croatia	3–1	(20–25, 26–24, 25–17, 25–19)
8 Sep.	Poland–Portugal	3–0	(25–23, 25–18, 25–16)
8 Sep.	Croatia–Ukraine	3–0	(25–21, 25–21, 25–21)
8 Sep.	Russia–Italy	3–1	(22–25, 25–22, 25–22, 25–22)

	G	W/L	SW/SL	Pts.
1. Russia	5	5/0	15/5	10
2. Italy	5	4/1	13/4	9
3. Poland	5	3/2	10/7	8
4. Croatia	5	2/3	9/11	7
5. Portugal	5	1/4	6/14	6
6. Ukraine	5	0/5	3/15	5

Group B (Belgrade)

2 Sep.	Greece–Netherlands	3–2	(25–20, 15–25, 23–25, 25–21, 15–11)
2 Sep.	France–Czech Republic	3–0	(25–23, 25–22, 25–20)
2 Sep.	Serbia and Montenegro–Spain	3–0	(25–22, 25–17, 25–15)
3 Sep.	France–Netherlands	3–1	(25–17, 25–22, 16–25, 25–20)
3 Sep.	Spain–Greece	3–1	(25–21, 24–26, 25–21, 25–20)
3 Sep.	Serbia and Montenegro–Czech Republic	3–1	(20–25, 25–23, 25–21, 25–22)
4 Sep.	Spain–France	3–2	(28–30, 16–25, 25–23, 33–31, 15–9)
4 Sep.	Czech Republic–Netherlands	3–0	(25–18, 25–22, 26–24)
4 Sep.	Serbia and Montenegro–Greece	3–0	(25–20, 25–15, 29–27)
6 Sep.	Czech Republic–Spain	3–2	(25–17, 22–25, 17–25, 25–14, 15–11)
6 Sep.	Serbia and Montenegro–Netherlands	3–0	(25–20, 25–18, 25–19)
6 Sep.	Greece–France	3–2	(25–22, 26–28, 20–25, 28–26, 15–12)
7 Sep.	Spain–Netherlands	3–1	(21–25, 25–20, 25–21, 25–18)
7 Sep.	Greece–Czech Republic	3–1	(30–32, 25–22, 25–19, 25–16)
7 Sep.	Serbia and Montenegro–France	3–2	(25–16, 20–25, 23–25, 25–19, 15–9)

	G	W/L	SW/SL	Pts.
1. Serbia and Montenegro	5	5/0	15/3	10
2. Spain	5	3/2	11/10	8
3. Greece	5	3/2	10/11	8
4. France	5	2/3	12/10	7
5. Czech Republic	5	2/3	8/11	7
6. Netherlands	5	0/5	4/15	5

Final round for 1–4 places (Rome)

Semifinals

10 Sep.	Russia–Spain	3–2	(15–25, 27–25, 25–12, 19–25, 15–13)
10 Sep.	Italy–Serbia and Montenegro	3–2	(25–15, 19–25, 25–19, 23–25, 15–8)

Game for 3rd place

11 Sep.	Serbia and Montenegro–Spain	3–0	(25–18, 25–21, 25–22)

Final

11 Sep.	Italy–Russia	3–2	(25–22, 14–25, 15–25, 25–19, 15–10)

Final standings

	G	W/L	SW/SL
1. Italy	7	6/1	19/8
2. Russia	7	6/1	20/10
3. Serbia and Montenegro	7	6/1	20/6
4. Spain	7	3/4	13/16
5. Poland	5	3/2	10/7
6. Greece	5	3/2	10/11
7. France	5	2/3	12/10
8. Croatia	5	2/3	9/11
9. Czech Republic	5	2/3	8/11
10. Portugal	5	1/4	6/14
11. Netherlands	5	0/5	4/15
12. Ukraine	5	0/5	3/15

Total: 12 teams, 34 games

Rosters of the medalists

Italy–Matej Cernic, Alberto Cisolla, Mirko Corsano, Paolo Cozzi, Alessandro Fei, Michal Lasko, Luigi Mastrangelo, Alessandro Paparoni, Cristian Savani, Giacomo Sintini, Luca Tencati, Valerio Vermiglio; head coach: Gian Paolo Montali

Russia–Pavel Abramov, Nikolay Apalikov, Sergey Baranov, Andrey Egorchev, Aleksey Kazakov, Taras Khtey, Sergey Makarov, Vladimir Melnik, Semyon Poltavskiy, Sergey Tetyukhin, Konstantin Ushakov, Aleksey Verbov; head coach: Zoran Gajić

Serbia and Montenegro–Novica Bjelica, Dejan Bojović, Slobodan Boškan, Andrija Gerić, Nikola Grbić, Ivan Ilić, Bojan Janić, Ivan Miljković, Aleksandar Mitrović, Marko Samardžić, Dragan Stanković, Goran Vujević; head coach: Ljuba Travica

XXV EUROPEAN CHAMPIONSHIP
6–16 September 2007, Moscow and Saint Petersburg (Russia)

Preliminary round

Group A (St. Petersburg)

6 Sep.	Serbia–Netherlands	3–0	(25–23, 25–21, 25–18)
7 Sep.	Greece–Netherlands	3–2	(25–20, 22–25, 19–25, 25–19, 15–13)
7 Sep.	Germany–Serbia	3–1	(22–25, 25–21, 25–20, 25–17)
8 Sep.	Germany–Greece	3–0	(25–17, 25–19, 25–15)
9 Sep.	Netherlands–Germany	3–0	(25–15, 26–14, 25–19)
9 Sep.	Serbia–Greece	3–1	(25–23, 25–23, 24–26, 25–22)

	G	W/L	SW/SL	Pts.
1. Serbia	3	2/1	7/4	5
2. Germany	3	2/1	6/4	5
3. Netherlands	3	1/2	5/6	4
4. Greece	3	1/2	4/8	4

Group B (Moscow)

6 Sep.	Russia–Belgium	3–0	(25–17, 25–20, 25–22)
7 Sep.	Belgium–Poland	3–1	(25–22, 23–25, 25–14, 26–24)
7 Sep.	Russia–Turkey	3–0	(25–20, 25–17, 25–18)
8 Sep.	Poland–Turkey	3–1	(20–25, 25–18, 25–20, 25–11)
9 Sep.	Belgium–Turkey	3–2	(25–27, 21–25, 31–29, 25–23, 15–10)
9 Sep.	Russia–Poland	3–0	(25–22, 25–23, 25–14)

	G	W/L	SW/SL	Pts.
1. Russia	3	3/0	9/0	6
2. Belgium	3	2/1	6/6	5
3. Poland	3	1/2	4/7	4
4. Turkey	3	0/3	3/9	3

Group C (St. Petersburg)

6 Sep.	Spain–Slovenia	3–1	(16–25, 25–20, 25–21, 25–18)
6 Sep.	France–Slovakia	3–1	(25–23, 25–23, 24–26, 25–15)
7 Sep.	Slovakia–Slovenia	3–1	(21–25, 25–21, 34–32, 27–25)
8 Sep.	Spain–Slovakia	3–0	(25–15, 25–16, 25–20)
8 Sep.	France–Slovenia	3–0	(25–17, 25–18, 25–13)
9 Sep.	Spain–France	3–0	(25–22, 25–23, 25–22)

	G	W/L	SW/SL	Pts.
1. Spain	3	3/0	9/1	6
2. France	3	2/1	6/4	5
3. Slovakia	3	1/2	4/7	4
4. Slovenia	3	0/3	2/9	3

Group D (Moscow)

6 Sep.	Bulgaria–Croatia	3–2	(24–26, 23–25, 25–12, 25–20, 15–10)
6 Sep.	Italy–Finland	3–2	(25–21, 25–18, 21–25, 22–25, 15–13)
7 Sep.	Finland–Croatia	3–1	(25–22, 28–26, 26–28, 25–14)
8 Sep.	Finland–Bulgaria	3–0	(25–22, 28–26, 25–23)
8 Sep.	Italy–Croatia	3–1	(26–24, 23–25, 25–23, 25–18)
9 Sep.	Bulgaria–Italy	3–0	(25–20, 25–18, 25–21)

	G	W/L	SW/SL	Pts.
1. Finland	3	2/1	8/4	5
2. Bulgaria	3	2/1	6/5	5
3. Italy	3	2/1	6/6	5
4. Croatia	3	0/3	4/9	3

Preliminary round II (head-to-head games were carried over from the preliminary round)

Group E (St. Petersburg)

11 Sep.	Spain–Netherlands	3–1	(25–23, 20–25, 25–22, 25–22)
11 Sep.	Serbia–France	3–2	(25–23, 22–25, 25–23, 33–35, 15–12)
11 Sep.	Germany–Slovakia	3–0	(25–23, 25–15, 25–16)
12 Sep.	Netherlands–France	3–2	(25–11, 25–23, 21–25, 20–25, 15–12)
12 Sep.	Spain–Germany	3–1	(25–19, 15–25, 26–24, 26–24)
12 Sep.	Serbia–Slovakia	3–0	(25–18, 25–23, 25–23)
13 Sep.	Germany–France	3–0	(25–14, 25–22, 25–21)
13 Sep.	Spain–Serbia	3–2	(26–24, 25–19, 24–26, 22–25, 15–10)
13 Sep.	Netherlands–Slovakia	3–1	(30–28, 22–25, 25–18, 25–17)

	G	W/L	SW/SL	Pts.
1. Spain	5	5/0	15/4	10
2. Serbia	5	3/2	12/8	8
3. Germany	5	3/2	10/7	8
4. Netherlands	5	3/2	10/9	8
5. France	5	1/4	7/13	6
6. Slovakia	5	0/5	2/15	5

Group F (Moscow)

11 Sep.	Finland–Poland	3–0	(25–20, 29–27, 25–21)
11 Sep.	Italy–Belgium	3–0	(25–22, 25–21, 25–23)
11 Sep.	Russia–Bulgaria	3–0	(25–22, 25–18, 25–21)
12 Sep.	Finland–Belgium	3–1	(21–25, 25–17, 25–23, 25–21)
12 Sep.	Bulgaria–Poland	3–2	(25–20, 16–25, 26–24, 21–25, 15–13)
12 Sep.	Russia–Italy	3–2	(25–21, 25–15, 20–25, 19–25, 15–10)
13 Sep.	Bulgaria–Belgium	3–1	(22–25, 25–23, 25–23, 25–17)
13 Sep.	Italy–Poland	3–2	(25–23, 25–23, 26–28, 20–25, 15–9)
13 Sep.	Russia–Finland	3–2	(22–25, 28–26, 22–25, 25–16, 15–8)

	G	W/L	SW/SL	Pts.
1. Russia	5	5/0	15/4	10
2. Finland	5	3/2	13/7	8
3. Italy	5	3/2	11/10	8
4. Bulgaria	5	3/2	9/9	8
5. Belgium	5	1/4	5/13	6
6. Poland	5	0/5	5/15	5

Final round for 1–4 places (Moscow)

Semifinals

15 Sep.	Spain–Finland	3–2	(25–23, 19–25, 22–25, 26–24, 15–10)
15 Sep.	Russia–Serbia	3–0	(27–25, 25–22, 25–15)

Game for 3rd place

16 Sep.	Serbia–Finland	3–1	(25–18, 23–25, 25–21, 25–16)

Final

16 Sep.	Spain–Russia	3–2	(25–18, 20–25, 24–26, 30–28, 16–14)

Final standings

	G	W/L	SW/SL
1. Spain	8	8/0	24/9
2. Russia	8	7/1	23/7
3. Serbia	8	5/3	18/13
4. Finland	8	4/4	19/14
5. Germany	6	4/2	13/7
6. Italy	6	4/2	14/11
7. Netherlands	6	3/3	12/12
8. Bulgaria	6	4/2	12/11
9. France	6	2/4	10/13

(continued)

	G	W/L	SW/SL
10. Belgium	6	2/4	8/15
11. Poland	6	1/5	8/16
12. Slovakia	6	1/5	5/16
13. Greece	3	1/2	4/8
14. Croatia	3	0/3	4/9
15. Turkey	3	0/3	3/9
16. Slovenia	3	0/3	2/9

Total: 16 teams, 46 games

Rosters of the medalists

Spain–Guillermo Falasca, Miguel Ángel Falasca, Enrique de la Fuente, Julián García-Torres, Guillermo Hernán, José Luis Lobato, José Luis Moltó, Rafael Pascual, Ibán Pérez, Israel Rodríguez, Manuel Sevillano, Javier Subiela; head coach: Andrea Anastasi

Russia–Pavel Abramov, Yuriy Berezhko, Sergey Grankin, Vadim Khamuttskikh, Aleksandr Kosarev, Pavel Kruglov, Aleksey Kuleshov, Aleksey Ostapenko, Semyon Poltavskiy, Sergey Tetyukhin, Aleksey Verbov, Aleksandr Volkov; head coach: Vladimir Alekno

Serbia–Slobodan Boškan, Andrija Gerić, Nikola Grbić, Bojan Janić, Nikola Kovačević, Ivan Miljković, Miloš Nikić, Vlado Petković, Marko Podraščanin, Marko Samardžić, Dragan Stanković, Saša Starović; head coach: Igor Kolaković

XXVI EUROPEAN CHAMPIONSHIP
3–13 September 2009, Istanbul and Izmir (Turkey)

Preliminary round

Group A (Izmir)

3 Sep.	Poland–France	3–1	(18–25, 25–17, 25–22, 25–18)
3 Sep.	Germany–Turkey	3–2	(26–24, 23–25, 25–22, 30–32, 15–13)
4 Sep.	Poland–Germany	3–1	(25–17, 25–23, 27–29, 25–14)
5 Sep.	France–Germany	3–1	(21–25, 25–14, 25–20, 25–23)
5 Sep.	Poland–Turkey	3–0	(25–23, 25–18, 25–17)
6 Sep.	France–Turkey	3–0	(25–16, 25–21, 25–23)

	G	W/L	SW/SL	Pts.
1. Poland	3	3/0	9/2	6
2. France	3	2/1	7/4	5
3. Germany	3	1/2	5/8	4
4. Turkey	3	0/3	2/9	3

Group B (Istanbul)

3 Sep.	Russia–Estonia	3–1	(20–25, 25–17, 25–18, 25–15)
3 Sep.	Netherlands–Finland	3–2	(25–21, 22–25, 28–30, 25–15, 18–16)
4 Sep.	Netherlands–Estonia	3–1	(27–29, 25–19, 25–18, 30–28)
5 Sep.	Russia–Netherlands	3–2	(25–23, 25–22, 21–25, 23–25, 15–10)
5 Sep.	Finland–Estonia	3–0	(25–18, 25–22, 25–21)
6 Sep.	Russia–Finland	3–0	(25–12, 25–14, 25–17)

	G	W/L	SW/SL	Pts.
1. Russia	3	3/0	9/3	6
2. Netherlands	3	2/1	8/6	5
3. Finland	3	1/2	5/6	4
4. Estonia	3	0/3	2/9	3

Group C (Izmir)

3 Sep.	Spain–Slovenia	3–0	(25–20, 25–19, 25–20)
4 Sep.	Greece–Spain	3–0	(25–23, 25–20, 25–21)
4 Sep.	Slovakia–Slovenia	3–0	(25–20, 25–21, 30–28)
5 Sep.	Greece–Slovakia	3–2	(19–25, 30–28, 25–23, 21–25, 15–12)
6 Sep.	Greece–Slovenia	3–1	(34–32, 26–24, 23–25, 25–21)
6 Sep.	Spain–Slovakia	3–2	(25–18, 21–25, 25–18, 19–25, 15–11)

	G	W/L	SW/SL	Pts.
1. Greece	3	3/0	9/3	6
2. Spain	3	2/1	6/5	5
3. Slovakia	3	1/2	7/6	4
4. Slovenia	3	0/3	1/9	3

Group D (Istanbul)

3 Sep.	Bulgaria–Serbia	3–2	(21–25, 25–17, 19–25, 25–22, 15–11)
4 Sep.	Bulgaria–Italy	3–0	(26–24, 25–22, 25–22)
4 Sep.	Serbia–Czech Republic	3–0	(25–22, 26–24, 25–14)
5 Sep.	Italy–Czech Republic	3–0	(25–12, 28–26, 25–20)
6 Sep.	Serbia–Italy	3–1	(25–23, 19–25, 25–12, 25–21)
6 Sep.	Bulgaria–Czech Republic	3–1	(25–19, 23–25, 25–20, 25–17)

	G	W/L	SW/SL	Pts.
1. Bulgaria	3	3/0	9/3	6
2. Serbia	3	2/1	8/4	5
3. Italy	3	1/2	4/6	4
4. Czech Republic	3	0/3	1/9	3

Preliminary round II (head-to-head games were carried over from the preliminary round)

Group E (Izmir)

8 Sep.	Germany–Greece	3–1	(25–13, 33–31, 21–25, 25–21)
8 Sep.	Poland–Spain	3–2	(18–25, 25–20, 25–18, 23–25, 17–15)
8 Sep.	France–Slovakia	3–1	(25–23, 24–26, 25–22, 25–21)
9 Sep.	Germany–Spain	3–1	(19–25, 27–25, 25–23, 25–20)
9 Sep.	Poland–Slovakia	3–2	(21–25, 25–15, 25–10, 14–25, 16–14)
9 Sep.	France–Greece	3–1	(25–18, 30–32, 25–18, 25–23)
10 Sep.	Germany–Slovakia	3–1	(25–22, 21–25, 25–16, 25–21)
10 Sep.	France–Spain	3–1	(25–21, 25–15, 25–27, 25–17)
10 Sep.	Poland–Greece	3–0	(25–22, 28–26, 25–20)

	G	W/L	SW/SL	Pts.
1. Poland	5	5/0	15/6	10
2. France	5	4/1	13/7	9
3. Germany	5	3/2	11/9	8
4. Greece	5	2/3	8/11	7
5. Spain	5	1/4	7/14	6
6. Slovakia	5	0/5	8/15	5

Group F (Istanbul)

8 Sep.	Russia–Serbia	3–1	(25–15, 17–25, 25–21, 25–19)
8 Sep.	Netherlands–Italy	3–1	(25–22, 23–25, 25–21, 27–25)
8 Sep.	Bulgaria–Finland	3–0	(25–22, 25–15, 25–20)
9 Sep.	Russia–Italy	3–0	(25–23, 25–21, 25–21)
9 Sep.	Bulgaria–Netherlands	3–1	(25–15, 26–24, 21–25, 28–26)
9 Sep.	Serbia–Finland	3–0	(25–20, 25–14, 25–22)
10 Sep.	Russia–Bulgaria	3–0	(25–21, 25–23, 25–22)
10 Sep.	Italy–Finland	3–0	(27–25, 25–19, 27–25)
10 Sep.	Serbia–Netherlands	3–1	(25–20, 25–23, 21–25, 25–23)

	G	W/L	SW/SL	Pts.
1. Russia	5	5/0	15/3	10
2. Bulgaria	5	4/1	12/6	9
3. Serbia	5	3/2	12/8	8
4. Netherlands	5	2/3	10/12	7
5. Italy	5	1/4	5/12	6
6. Finland	5	0/5	2/15	5

Final round for 1–4 places (Izmir)

Semifinals

12 Sep.	Poland–Bulgaria	3–0	(25–19, 30–28, 25–20)
12 Sep.	France–Russia	3–2	(25–18, 25–22, 25–27, 15–25, 17–15)

Game for 3rd place

13 Sep.	Bulgaria–Russia	3–0	(25–18, 26–24, 25–21)

Final

13 Sep.	Poland–France	3–1	(29–27, 25–21, 16–25, 26–24)

Final standings

	G	W/L	SW/SL
1. Poland	8	8/0	24/7
2. France	8	6/2	20/12
3. Bulgaria	8	6/2	18/10
4. Russia	8	6/2	20/10
5. Serbia	6	4/2	15/8
6. Germany	6	4/2	14/11
7. Netherlands	6	3/3	13/13
8. Greece	6	3/3	11/12
9. Spain	6	2/4	10/14
10. Italy	6	2/4	8/12
11. Slovakia	6	1/5	11/15
12. Finland	6	1/5	5/15
13. Turkey	3	0/3	2/9
14. Estonia	3	0/3	2/9
15. Slovenia	3	0/3	1/9
16. Czech Republic	3	0/3	1/9

Total: 16 teams, 46 games

Rosters of the medalists

Poland–Michał Bąkiewicz, Zbigniew Bartman, Piotr Gacek, Marcel Gromadowski, Piotr Gruszka, Krzysztof Ignaczak, Jakub Jarosz, Bartosz Kurek, Marcin Możdżonek, Piotr Nowakowski, Daniel Pliński, Michał Ruciak, Paweł Woicki, Paweł Zagumny; head coach: Daniel Castellani

France–Stéphane Antiga, Yannick Bazin, Jean-François Exiga, Baptiste Geiler, Hubert Henno, Oliver Kieffer, Antonin Rouzier, Édouard Rowlandson, Guillaume Samica, Jean-Philippe Sol, Toafa Takaniko, Jean-Stéphane Tolar, Samuel Tuia, Romain Vadeleux; head coach: Philippe Blain

Bulgaria–Todor Aleksiev, Metodi Ananiev, Georgi Bratoev, Valentin Bratoev, Krasimir Gaydarski, Vladislav Ivanov, Matey Kaziyski, Vladimir Nikolov, Teodor Salparov, Tsvetan Sokolov, Teodor Todorov, Khristo Tsvetanov, Viktor Yosifov, Andrey Zhekov; head coach: Silvano Prandi

XXVII EUROPEAN CHAMPIONSHIP
10–18 September 2011, Innsbruck and Vienna (Austria), Karlovy Vary, and Prague (Czech Republic)

Preliminary round

Group A (Vienna)

10 Sep.	Slovenia–Austria	3–0	(25–20, 25–21, 25–20)
10 Sep.	Serbia–Turkey	3–0	(25–16, 25–18, 25–20)
11 Sep.	Serbia–Slovenia	3–1	(25–9, 25–23, 23–25, 25–23)
11 Sep.	Turkey–Austria	3–0	(25–21, 25–22, 25–20)
12 Sep.	Slovenia–Turkey	3–2	(25–18, 25–23, 16–25, 19–25, 15–12)
12 Sep.	Serbia–Austria	3–0	(25–16, 25–19, 25–16)

	G	W/L	SW/SL	Pts.
1. Serbia	3	3/0	9/1	9
2. Slovenia	3	2/1	7/5	5
3. Turkey	3	1/2	5/6	4
4. Austria	3	0/3	0/9	0

Group B (Karlovy Vary)

10 Sep.	Russia–Estonia	3–0	(25–17, 25–19, 25–17)
10 Sep.	Czech Republic–Portugal	3–2	(25–20, 20–25, 21–25, 25–16, 15–13)
11 Sep.	Russia–Portugal	3–1	(25–15, 23–25, 25–22, 25–13)
11 Sep.	Czech Republic–Estonia	3–0	(25–20, 25–14, 25–20)
12 Sep.	Estonia–Portugal	3–0	(25–23, 25–17, 25–22)
12 Sep.	Russia–Czech Republic	3–0	(25–19, 25–14, 25–18)

	G	W/L	SW/SL	Pts.
1. Russia	3	3/0	9/1	9
2. Czech Republic	3	2/1	6/5	5
3. Estonia	3	1/2	3/6	3
4. Portugal	3	0/3	3/9	1

Group C (Innsbruck)

10 Sep.	France–Finland	3–1	(25–14, 17–25, 31–29, 28–26)
10 Sep.	Italy–Belgium	3–1	(22–25, 25–18, 29–27, 25–15)
11 Sep.	Belgium–France	3–1	(31–29, 34–36, 25–20, 26–24)
11 Sep.	Italy–Finland	3–0	(25–23, 27–25, 25–21)
12 Sep.	Finland–Belgium	3–0	(25–21, 25–22, 25–22)
12 Sep.	France–Italy	3–2	(26–28, 22–25, 25–17, 25–21, 15–11)

	G	W/L	SW/SL	Pts.
1. Italy	3	2/1	8/4	7
2. France	3	2/1	7/6	5
3. Finland	3	1/2	4/6	3
4. Belgium	3	1/2	4/7	3

Group D (Prague)

10 Sep.	Slovakia–Bulgaria	3–2	(26–24, 27–25, 24–26, 19–25, 17–15)
10 Sep.	Poland–Germany	3–1	(25–19, 25–20, 22–25, 25–22)
11 Sep.	Slovakia–Germany	3–1	(25–23, 24–26, 26–24, 27–25)
11 Sep.	Bulgaria–Poland	3–1	(19–25, 25–22, 25–22, 25–23)
12 Sep.	Bulgaria–Germany	3–1	(25–19, 25–27, 26–24, 25–23)
12 Sep.	Slovakia–Poland	3–1	(23–25, 25–21, 25–18, 25–23)

	G	W/L	SW/SL	Pts.
1. Slovakia	3	3/0	9/4	8
2. Bulgaria	3	2/1	8/5	7
3. Poland	3	1/2	5/7	3
4. Germany	3	0/3	3/9	0

Playoff round

Elimination games*

14 Sep.	France–Turkey	3–1	(25–19, 25–23, 19–25, 25–21)	Vienna
14 Sep.	Finland–Slovenia	3–2	(25–18, 21–25, 25–23, 18–25, 15–12)	Vienna
14 Sep.	Bulgaria–Estonia	3–0	(25–20, 25–23, 25–22)	Karlovy Vary
14 Sep.	Poland–Czech Republic	3–1	(25–23, 22–25, 31–29, 25–18)	Karlovy Vary

*These games were played only between teams that placed second or third in their groups in the preliminary round; the winners of elimination games advanced to the quarterfinals.

Quarterfinals

15 Sep.	Italy–Finland	3–1	(25–18, 25–20, 29–31, 25–21)	Vienna
15 Sep.	Serbia–France	3–1	(32–30, 25–20, 23–25, 26–24)	Vienna
15 Sep.	Poland–Slovakia	3–0	(25–23, 25–17, 25–19)	Karlovy Vary
15 Sep.	Russia–Bulgaria	3–1	(22–25, 25–19, 25–18, 25–19)	Karlovy Vary

Final round for 1–4 places (Vienna)

Semifinals (1–4 places)

17 Sep.	Italy–Poland	3–0	(25–22, 25–21, 25–21)
17 Sep.	Serbia–Russia	3–2	(25–23, 17–25, 22–25, 33–31, 15–13)

Game for 3rd place

18 Sep.	Poland–Russia	3–1	(25–23, 18–25, 25–21, 25–19)

Final

18 Sep.	Serbia–Italy	3–1	(17–25, 25–20, 25–23, 26–24)

Final standings

	G	W/L	SW/SL
1. Serbia	6	6/0	18/5
2. Italy	6	4/2	15/8
3. Poland	7	4/3	14/12
4. Russia	6	4/2	15/8
5. Slovakia	4	3/1	9/7
6. Bulgaria	5	3/2	12/8
7. France	5	3/2	11/10
8. Finland	5	2/3	8/11
9. Slovenia	4	2/2	9/8
10. Czech Republic	4	2/2	7/8
11. Turkey	4	1/3	6/9
12. Estonia	4	1/3	3/9
13. Belgium	3	1/2	4/7
14. Portugal	3	0/3	3/9
15. Germany	3	0/3	3/9
16. Austria	3	0/3	0/9

Total: 16 teams, 36 games

Rosters of the medalists

Serbia–Aleksandar Atanasijević, Nikola Kovačević, Uroš Kovačević, Ivan Miljković, Mihajlo Mitić, Miloš Nikić, Vlado Petković, Marko Podraščanin, Milan Rašić, Nikola Rosić, Dragan Stanković, Saša Starović, Miloš Terzić, Filip Vujić; head coach: Igor Kolaković

Italy–Andrea Bari, Rocco Barone, Emanuele Birarelli, Dante Boninfante, Simone Buti, Andrea Giovi, Michal Lasko, Gabriele Maruotti, Luigi Mastrangelo, Simone Parodi, Giulio Sabbi, Cristian Savani, Dragan Travica, Ivan Zaytsev; head coach: Mauro Berruto

Poland–Fabian Drzyzga, Piotr Gruszka, Krzysztof Ignaczak, Jakub Jarosz, Karol Kłos, Grzegorz Kosok, Michał Kubiak, Bartosz Kurek, Mateusz Mika, Marcin Możdżonek, Piotr Nowakowski, Michał Ruciak, Paweł Zatorski, Łukasz Żygadło; head coach: Andrea Anastasi

Women's European Championships

10–18 September 1949, Prague (Czechoslovakia)

Date	Winner–Loser	Final Score	(Partial Scores)
10 Sep.	Czechoslovakia–France	3–0	(15–3, 15–0, 15–9)
11 Sep.	Romania–Hungary	3–1	(15–10, 13–15, 15–6, 15–9)
11 Sep.	USSR–Poland	3–0	(15–13, 15–4, 15–3)
12 Sep.	Poland–Romania	3–0	(15–10, 15–3, 15–7)
12 Sep.	France–Hungary	3–1	(15–17, 15–12, 15–2, 15–11)
12 Sep.	Czechoslovakia–Netherlands	3–0	(15–8, 15–0, 15–1)
13 Sep.	Poland–France	3–0	(15–13, 15–7, 15–6)
13 Sep.	Hungary–Netherlands	3–0	(15–1, 15–4, 15–3)
14 Sep.	USSR–Romania	3–0	(15–5, 15–0, 15–6)
14 Sep.	Poland–Netherlands	3–0	(15–0, 15–6, 15–4)
14 Sep.	Czechoslovakia–Hungary	3–0	(15–2, 15–6, 15–1)
15 Sep.	USSR–France	3–0	(15–1, 15–4, 15–2)
15 Sep.	Romania–Netherlands	3–0	(15–5, 15–3, 15–1)
15 Sep.	Czechoslovakia–Poland	3–0	(15–13, 16–14, 15–13)
16 Sep.	Poland–Hungary	3–0	(15–4, 15–6, 15–9)
16 Sep.	USSR–Netherlands	3–0	(15–1, 15–4, 15–10)
16 Sep.	Romania–France	3–1	(4–15, 15–10, 15–1, 15–11)
17 Sep.	USSR–Czechoslovakia	3–0	(15–10, 16–14, 15–11)
17 Sep.	France–Netherlands	3–0	(15–0, 15–0, 15–7)
18 Sep.	USSR–Hungary	3–0	(15–0, 15–1, 15–0)
18 Sep.	Czechoslovakia–Romania	3–0	(15–1, 15–8, 15–3)

	G	W/L	SW/SL	Pts.
1. USSR	6	6/0	18/0	12
2. Czechoslovakia	6	5/1	15/3	11
3. Poland	6	4/2	12/6	10
4. Romania	6	3/3	9/11	9
5. France	6	2/4	7/13	8
6. Hungary	6	1/5	5/15	7
7. Netherlands	6	0/6	0/18	6

Final standings

	G	W/L	SW/SL
1. USSR	6	6/0	18/0
2. Czechoslovakia	6	5/1	15/3
3. Poland	6	4/2	12/6
4. Romania	6	3/3	9/11
5. France	6	2/4	7/13
6. Hungary	6	1/5	5/15
7. Netherlands	6	0/6	0/18

Total: 7 teams, 21 games

Rosters of the medalists

USSR–Anna Afanaseva, Taisiya Baryshnikova, Aleksandra Chudina, Militiya Kononova-Eremeeva, Serafima Kundirenko, Valentina Kvasheninnikova, Vera Missik, Valentina Oskolkova, Tamara Petrova, Anna Ponomaryova, Valentina Sviridova, Aleksandra Zharova; head coach: Aleksandr Anikin

Czechoslovakia–Jindra Batková, Mária Bernovská, Alena Čadilová, Božena Cígrová, Jitka Cvilinková, Bronislava Dostálová, Jarmila Hroudová, Milena Krimlová, Naďa Marynčáková, Jaroslava Mirovická, Božena Valášková, Zdeňka Zaplatílková; head coach: Miroslav Rovný

Poland–Jadwiga Brześniowska, Aleksandra English, Irena Felchnerowska, Urszula Figwer, Romualda Gruszczyńska, Elżbieta Kurtz, Halina Orzechowska, Krystyna Paprot, Maria Pogorzelska, Halina Tomaszewska, Zofia Wojewódzka, Mirosława Zakrzewska; head coach: Lothar Geyer

II EUROPEAN CHAMPIONSHIP
14–22 October 1950, Sofia (Bulgaria)

14 Oct.	Poland–Bulgaria	3–0	(15–12, 15–7, 15–7)
15 Oct.	Czechoslovakia–Hungary	3–0	(15–7, 15–11, 15–3)
15 Oct.	USSR–Romania	3–0	(15–3, 15–0, 15–3)
16 Oct.	USSR–Hungary	3–0	(15–6, 15–7, 15–4)

(continued)

16 Oct.	Poland–Czechoslovakia	3–1	(15–9, 15–3, 12–15, 17–15)
17 Oct.	Bulgaria–Romania	3–1	(9–15, 15–9, 15–8, 15–8)
18 Oct.	Czechoslovakia–Bulgaria	3–0	(15–7, 15–13, 15–3)
18 Oct.	Romania–Hungary	3–2	(15–8, 12–15, 12–15, 15–4, 15–9)
19 Oct.	USSR–Poland	3–0	(15–5, 15–2, 16–14)
20 Oct.	Poland–Romania	3–0	(15–10, 15–6, 15–8)
20 Oct.	Bulgaria–Hungary	3–1	(13–15, 18–16, 15–9, 15–7)
21 Oct.	USSR–Czechoslovakia	3–0	(15–11, 15–5, 15–8)
22 Oct.	Czechoslovakia–Romania	3–0	(15–6, 15–9, 15–11)
22 Oct.	USSR–Bulgaria	3–0	(15–1, 15–3, 15–2)
22 Oct.	Poland–Hungary	3–0	(15–6, 15–5, 15–5)

	G	W/L	SW/SL	Pts.
1. USSR	5	5/0	15/0	10
2. Poland	5	4/1	12/4	9
3. Czechoslovakia	5	3/2	10/6	8
4. Bulgaria	5	2/3	6/11	7
5. Romania	5	1/4	4/14	6
6. Hungary	5	0/5	3/15	5

Final standings

	G	W/L	SW/SL
1. USSR	5	5/0	15/0
2. Poland	5	4/1	12/4
3. Czechoslovakia	5	3/2	10/6
4. Bulgaria	5	2/3	6/11
5. Romania	5	1/4	4/14
6. Hungary	5	0/5	3/15

Total: 6 teams, 15 games

Rosters of the medalists

USSR–Aleksandra Chudina, Militiya Kononova-Eremeeva, Serafima Kundirenko, Zinaida Kuzkina, Valentina Kvasheninnikova, Vera Ozerova, Tamara Petrova, Iraida Sedova, Zlata Starovoytova, Valentina Sviridova, Mariya Toporkova, Aleksandra Zharova; head coach: Valentina Oskolkova

Poland–Jadwiga Brześniowska, Aleksandra English, Romualda Gruszczyńska, Aleksandra Kubiak, Halina Orzechowska, Maria Pogorzelska, Emilia Szczawińska, Halina Tomaszewska, Zofia Wojewódzka, Mirosława Zakrzewska; head coach: Kazimierz Strycharzewski

Czechoslovakia–Jindra Batková, Soňa Burianová, Zdena Černá, Božena Cígrová, Libuše Houdková, Milena Krimlová, Lenka Kučerová, Jaroslava Mirovická, Jarmila Vojnarová, Zdena Zaplatílková; head coach: Jan Fiedler

III EUROPEAN CHAMPIONSHIP
15–22 September 1951, Paris (France)

Preliminary round

Group A

15 Sep.	France–Netherlands	3–0	(15–5, 15–6, 15–11)
16 Sep.	USSR–Netherlands	3–0	(15–4, 15–3, 15–9)
17 Sep.	USSR–France	3–0	(15–5, 15–1, 15–3)

	G	W/L	SW/SL	Pts.
1. USSR	2	2/0	6/0	4
2. France	2	1/1	3/3	3
3. Netherlands	2	0/2	0/6	2

Group B

15 Sep.	Poland–Yugoslavia	3–1	(13–15, 15–12, 15–5, 15–10)
16 Sep.	Poland–Italy	3–0	(15–5, 15–1, 15–3)
17 Sep.	Yugoslavia–Italy	3–0	(15–0, 15–7, 15–11)

	G	W/L	SW/SL	Pts.
1. Poland	2	2/0	6/1	4
2. Yugoslavia	2	1/1	4/3	3
3. Italy	2	0/2	0/6	2

Final round

Game for 5th place

| 20 Sep. | Netherlands–Italy | 3–2 | (15–5, 1–15, 15–10, 12–15, 15–6) |

Final group for 1–4 places

18 Sep.	USSR–Yugoslavia	3–0	(15–1, 15–4, 15–0)
19 Sep.	Poland–Yugoslavia	3–0	(17–15, 15–9, 15–9)
20 Sep.	USSR–France	3–0	(15–2, 15–1, 15–3)
21 Sep.	Yugoslavia–France	3–0	(15–8, 15–8, 17–15)
21 Sep.	USSR–Poland	3–0	(15–8, 15–3, 15–11)
22 Sep.	Poland–France	3–0	(15–13, 15–12, 15–4)

	G	W/L	SW/SL	Pts.
1. USSR	3	3/0	9/0	6
2. Poland	3	2/1	6/3	5
3. Yugoslavia	3	1/2	3/6	4
4. France	3	0/3	0/9	3

Final standings

	G	W/L	SW/SL
1. USSR	5	5/0	15/0
2. Poland	5	4/1	12/4
3. Yugoslavia	5	2/3	7/9
4. France	5	1/4	3/12
5. Netherlands	3	1/2	3/8
6. Italy	3	0/3	2/9

Total: 6 teams, 13 games

Rosters of the medalists

USSR–Tatyana Bunina, Aleksandra Chudina, Albina Ippolitova, Militiya Kononova-Eremeeva, Serafima Kundirenko, Aleksandra Kuryatnikova, Valentina Kvasheninnikova, Vera Ozerova, Tamara Petrova, Anna Ponomaryova, Mariya Toporkova, Aleksandra Zharova; head coach: Valentina Oskolkova

Poland–Aleksandra English, Irena Felchnerowska, Krystyna Hajec, Aleksandra Kubiak, Elżbieta Kurtz, Maria Pogorzelska, Emilia Szczawińska, Halina Tomaszewska, Katarzyna Welsyng, Zofia Wojewódzka; head coach: Zygmunt Kraus

Yugoslavia–Anica Flis, Tilka Gajšek, Dana Glumac, Desa Končar, Nataša Luković, Ančka Magušar, Štefanija Milošev, Branka Popović, Gordana Tkačuk, Liza Valentan; head coach: Branislav Marković

IV EUROPEAN CHAMPIONSHIP
15–26 June 1955, Bucharest (Romania)

15 Jun.	Romania–Hungary	3–0	(15–7, 15–13, 15–13)
15 Jun.	USSR–Bulgaria	3–0	(15–10, 15–6, 15–11)
15 Jun.	Czechoslovakia–Poland	3–2	(15–13, 15–4, 14–16, 7–15, 15–11)
17 Jun.	Czechoslovakia–Hungary	3–0	(15–5, 15–12, 15–6)
17 Jun.	Poland–Bulgaria	3–2	(15–9, 8–15, 15–5, 11–15, 15–10)
17 Jun.	USSR–Romania	3–0	(15–4, 15–5, 15–13)
19 Jun.	Poland–Hungary	3–0	(15–6, 15–12, 15–11)
19 Jun.	Romania–Bulgaria	3–2	(15–13, 10–15, 10–15, 15–7, 15–11)
19 Jun.	Czechoslovakia–USSR	3–2	(15–9, 8–15, 15–7, 7–15, 15–13)
22 Jun.	Czechoslovakia–Bulgaria	3–2	(15–5, 7–15, 15–10, 15–17, 15–7)
22 Jun.	USSR–Hungary	3–0	(15–8, 15–11, 15–3)
22 Jun.	Poland–Romania	3–2	(9–15, 15–5, 15–13, 15–17, 15–11)
26 Jun.	Czechoslovakia–Romania	3–0	(15–13, 15–4, 15–13)
26 Jun.	Bulgaria–Hungary	3–1	(12–15, 15–12, 15–13, 16–14)
26 Jun.	USSR–Poland	3–1	(15–9, 15–5, 9–15, 15–6)

	G	W/L	SW/SL	Pts.
1. Czechoslovakia	5	5/0	15/6	10
2. USSR	5	4/1	14/4	9
3. Poland	5	3/2	12/10	8
4. Romania	5	2/3	8/11	7
5. Bulgaria	5	1/4	9/13	6
6. Hungary	5	0/5	1/15	5

Final standings

	G	W/L	SW/SL
1. Czechoslovakia	5	5/0	15/6
2. USSR	5	4/1	14/4
3. Poland	5	3/2	12/10
4. Romania	5	2/3	8/11
5. Bulgaria	5	1/4	9/13
6. Hungary	5	0/5	1/15

Total: 6 teams, 15 games

Rosters of the medalists

Czechoslovakia–Jindra Holá, Drahuše Křížová, Lenka Kučerová, Božena Lútočková, Regina Matalíková, Alena Nečasová, Libuše Neugebauerová, Jaroslava Šindelářová, Svatava Štaudová, Běla Štulcová, Alžběta Technovská, Bohumila Valášková; head coach: Metoděj Mácha

USSR–Aleksandra Chudina, Sofya Gorbunova, Aino Huimerind, Lirika Ivanskaya, Liliya Kalenik, Lyudmila Meshcheryakova-Buldakova, Antonina Moiseeva-Ryzhova, Vera Ozerova, Natalya Pshenichnikova, Minjona Sakse-Khekhta, Zinaida Smolyaninova, Lidiya Strelnikova; head coach: Aleksey Yakushev

Poland–Jadwiga Abisiak, Danuta Chwalińska, Barbara Czeczótko-Szpyt, Krystyna Hajec, Danuta Jośko-Żochowska, Teresa Krogulec-Konopka, Wanda Tumidajewicz, Mirosława Zakrzewska-Kotula, Wanda Zarzycka, Klementyna Zielniok, Barbara Ziemba-Kocan; head coach: Lucjan Tyszecki

V EUROPEAN CHAMPIONSHIP
30 August–11 September 1958, České Budějovice, Liberec, and Prague (Czechoslovakia)

Preliminary round

Group A (Prague)

30 Aug.	GDR–France	3–0	(15–3, 15–13, 16–14)
31 Aug.	Czechoslovakia–France	3–0	(15–7, 15–5, 16–14)
1 Sep.	Czechoslovakia–GDR	3–0	(15–7, 15–11, 15–10)

	G	W/L	SW/SL	Pts.
1. Czechoslovakia	2	2/0	6/0	4
2. GDR	2	1/1	3/3	3
3. France	2	0/2	0/6	2

Group B (České Budějovice)

30 Aug.	Yugoslavia–FRG	3–0	(15–6, 15–3, 15–1)
31 Aug.	USSR–Yugoslavia	3–0	(15–3, 15–8, 15–2)
1 Sep.	USSR–FRG	3–0	(15–7, 15–6, 15–1)

	G	W/L	SW/SL	Pts.
1. USSR	2	2/0	6/0	4
2. Yugoslavia	2	1/1	3/3	3
3. FRG	2	0/2	0/6	2

Group C (Prague)

30 Aug.	Hungary–Netherlands	3–0	(15–11, 15–10, 15–5)
31 Aug.	Poland–Hungary	3–1	(15–5, 13–15, 15–11, 15–10)
1 Sep.	Poland–Netherlands	3–0	(15–4, 15–12, 15–7)

	G	W/L	SW/SL	Pts.
1. Poland	2	2/0	6/1	4
2. Hungary	2	1/1	4/3	3
3. Netherlands	2	0/2	0/6	2

Group D (Liberec)

30 Aug.	Romania–Austria	3–0	(15–0, 15–3, 15–3)
31 Aug.	Romania–Bulgaria	3–2	(5–15, 13–15, 17–15, 15–11, 15–12)
1 Sep.	Bulgaria–Austria	3–0	(15–0, 15–3, 15–1)

	G	W/L	SW/SL	Pts.
1. Romania	2	2/0	6/2	4
2. Bulgaria	2	1/1	5/3	3
3. Austria	2	0/2	0/6	2

Final round (Prague)

Final group for 9–12 places

3 Sep.	FRG–Austria	3–2	(15–6, 14–16, 13–15, 15–10, 15–10)
3 Sep.	France–Netherlands	3–2	(15–10, 9–15, 15–11, 11–15, 15–8)

(continued)

Final group for 9–12 places (continued)

5 Sep.	France–Austria	3–0	(15–0, 15–0, 15–11)
6 Sep.	Netherlands–FRG	3–0	(15–2, 15–10, 15–5)
8 Sep.	France–FRG	3–1	(15–4, 15–9, 3–15, 15–6)
9 Sep.	Netherlands–Austria	3–0	(15–8, 15–1, 15–9)

	G	W/L	SW/SL	Pts.
1. France	3	3/0	9/3	6
2. Netherlands	3	2/1	8/3	5
3. FRG	3	1/2	4/8	4
4. Austria	3	0/3	2/9	3

Final group for 1–8 places

3 Sep.	Yugoslavia–Hungary	3–1	(15–2, 15–12, 10–15, 18–16)
3 Sep.	Romania–GDR	3–2	(11–15, 11–15, 15–5, 15–2, 15–11)
3 Sep.	Czechoslovakia–Poland	3–2	(15–7, 11–15, 12–15, 15–12, 15–11)
3 Sep.	USSR–Bulgaria	3–0	(15–7, 15–8, 15–13)
4 Sep.	USSR–Yugoslavia	3–1	(13–15, 15–3, 15–5, 15–2)
4 Sep.	Poland–Romania	3–1	(5–15, 15–7, 15–8, 15–8)
4 Sep.	Czechoslovakia–Bulgaria	3–0	(15–4, 15–13, 15–12)
4 Sep.	Hungary–GDR	3–0	(15–8, 15–8, 15–10)
6 Sep.	Czechoslovakia–Yugoslavia	3–0	(15–4, 15–8, 15–5)
6 Sep.	Poland–GDR	3–0	(15–5, 15–1, 15–5)
6 Jun.	USSR–Hungary	3–0	(15–8, 15–11, 15–7)
6 Sep.	Romania–Bulgaria	3–1	(14–16, 15–8, 15–12, 15–11)
7 Sep.	Romania–Yugoslavia	3–1	(15–6, 18–16, 13–15, 15–11)
7 Sep.	Czechoslovakia–Hungary	3–0	(15–3, 15–5, 15–12)
7 Sep.	USSR–GDR	3–0	(15–5, 15–6, 15–4)
7 Sep.	Poland–Bulgaria	3–1	(15–12, 14–16, 15–8, 16–14)
8 Sep.	Poland–Yugoslavia	3–0	(15–1, 15–11, 15–1)
8 Sep.	Bulgaria–GDR	3–0	(15–2, 15–5, 15–11)
8 Sep.	Romania–Hungary	3–2	(10–15, 15–13, 15–12, 13–15, 15–10)
8 Sep.	USSR–Czechoslovakia	3–2	(15–9, 8–15, 15–13, 13–15, 15–11)
9 Sep.	Bulgaria–Yugoslavia	3–2	(15–5, 10–15, 13–15, 15–10, 15–9)
9 Sep.	Czechoslovakia–GDR	3–0	(15–12, 17–15, 15–0)
9 Sep.	USSR–Romania	3–0	(15–4, 15–8, 15–10)
9 Sep.	Poland–Hungary	3–1	(15–10, 13–15, 15–6, 15–10)
10 Sep.	GDR–Yugoslavia	3–1	(15–12, 11–15, 15–13, 15–10)
10 Sep.	Czechoslovakia–Romania	3–1	(15–13, 15–13, 12–15, 15–9)
10 Sep.	Bulgaria–Hungary	3–1	(15–6, 9–15, 15–6, 15–9)
10 Sep.	USSR–Poland	3–2	(13–15, 6–15, 15–10, 16–14, 15–11)

	G	W/L	SW/SL	Pts.
1. USSR	7	7/0	21/5	14
2. Czechoslovakia	7	6/1	20/6	13
3. Poland	7	5/2	19/9	12
4. Romania	7	4/3	14/15	11
5. Bulgaria	7	3/4	11/15	10
6. Hungary	7	1/6	8/18	8
7. Yugoslavia	7	1/6	8/19	8
8. GDR	7	1/6	5/19	8

Final standings

	G	W/L	SW/SL
1. USSR	9	9/0	27/5
2. Czechoslovakia	9	8/1	26/6
3. Poland	9	7/2	25/10
4. Romania	9	6/3	20/17
5. Bulgaria	9	4/5	16/18
6. Hungary	9	2/7	12/21
7. Yugoslavia	9	2/7	11/22
8. GDR	9	2/7	8/22
9. France	5	3/2	9/9
10. Netherlands	5	2/3	8/9
11. FRG	5	1/4	4/14
12. Austria	5	0/5	2/15

Total: 12 teams, 46 games

Rosters of the medalists

USSR–Lidiya Boldyreva, Tamara Bubchikova, Aleksandra Chudina, Alisa Galakhova-Krasheninnikova, Militiya Kononova-Eremeeva, Lyudmila Meshcheryakova-Buldakova, Antonina Moiseeva-Ryzhova, Minjona Sakse-Khekhta, Lidiya Strelnikova, Valentīna Varkeviča, Anna Vilciņa, Antonina Yashina; head coach: Aleksey Yakushev

Czechoslovakia–Soňa Holubová, Drahuše Křížová, Libuše Kyselková, Regina Matalíková, Hana Moravcová, Běla Paclíková, Naďa Špelinová, Božena Šteflová, Libuše Svozilová, Anna Uhrinová, Taťána Ulmonová, Svatava Vráželová; head coach: Josef Češpiva

Poland–Krystyna Czajkowska, Barbara Czeczótko–Szpyt, Maria Golimowska, Danuta Kordaczuk, Jadwiga Kostkiewicz, Mirosława Kotula, Halina Lenkiewicz, Maria Panek, Wanda Poleszczuk, Alicja Szewczyk, Krystyna Wleciał, Wanda Zarzycka; head coach: Zbigniew Szpyt

VI EUROPEAN CHAMPIONSHIP
22 October–2 November 1963, Braşov, Bucharest, Constanţa, and Craiova (Romania)

Preliminary round

Group A (Bucharest)

22 Oct.	Bulgaria–Turkey	3–0	(15–4, 15–3, 15–0)
23 Oct.	USSR–Bulgaria	3–0	(15–8, 15–10, 15–9)
24 Oct.	USSR–Turkey	3–0	(15–1, 15–3, 15–0)

	G	W/L	SW/SL	Pts.
1. USSR	2	2/0	6/0	4
2. Bulgaria	2	1/1	3/3	3
3. Turkey	2	0/2	0/6	2

Group B (Craiova)

22 Oct.	Czechoslovakia–Denmark	3–0	(15–6, 15–4, 15–2)
22 Oct.	Hungary–Netherlands	3–0	(15–11, 15–11, 16–14)
23 Oct.	Netherlands–Denmark	3–0	(15–0, 15–2, 15–2)
23 Oct.	Czechoslovakia–Hungary	3–1	(15–3, 9–15, 15–10, 16–14)
24 Oct.	Hungary–Denmark	3–0	(15–0, 15–5, 15–2)
24 Oct.	Czechoslovakia–Netherlands	3–1	(15–13, 18–16, 12–15, 15–9)

	G	W/L	SW/SL	Pts.
1. Czechoslovakia	3	3/0	9/2	6
2. Hungary	3	2/1	7/3	5
3. Netherlands	3	1/2	4/6	4
4. Denmark	3	0/3	0/9	3

Group C (Constanţa)

22 Oct.	Poland–FRG	3–0	(15–1, 15–6, 15–5)
23 Oct.	Poland–Yugoslavia	3–0	(15–10, 15–7, 15–8)
24 Oct.	Yugoslavia–FRG	3–1	(16–14, 15–2, 13–15, 15–11)

	G	W/L	SW/SL	Pts.
1. Poland	2	2/0	6/0	4
2. Yugoslavia	2	1/1	3/4	3
3. FRG	2	0/2	1/6	2

Group D (Constanţa)

22 Oct.	Romania–Austria	3–0	(15–0, 15–0, 15–3)
23 Oct.	Romania–GDR	3–1	(15–12, 16–18, 15–12, 15–3)
24 Oct.	GDR–Austria	3–0	(15–1, 15–0, 15–0)

	G	W/L	SW/SL	Pts.
1. Romania	2	2/0	6/1	4
2. GDR	2	1/1	4/3	3
3. Austria	2	0/2	0/6	2

Final round (head-to-head games were carried over from the preliminary round)

Final group for 9–13 places (Braşov)

26 Oct.	Turkey–Denmark	3–0	(15–9, 15–5, 15–2)
26 Oct.	Netherlands–Austria	3–0	(15–1, 15–0, 15–0)
27 Oct.	Turkey–FRG	3–1	(19–17, 12–15, 15–7, 15–12)
28 Oct.	Austria–Denmark	3–2	(15–6, 14–16, 8–15, 15–12, 15–13)
28 Oct.	Netherlands–FRG	3–0	(15–8, 15–8, 15–3)
29 Oct.	FRG–Austria	3–0	(15–11, 15–9, 15–4)
29 Oct.	Netherlands–Turkey	3–0	(15–8, 15–8, 15–9)
30 Oct.	FRG–Denmark	3–0	(15–6, 15–4, 15–5)
30 Oct.	Turkey–Austria	3–0	(15–2, 15–3, 15–3)

	G	W/L	SW/SL	Pts.
1. Netherlands	4	4/0	12/0	8
2. Turkey	4	3/1	9/4	7
3. FRG	4	2/2	7/6	6
4. Austria	4	1/3	3/11	5
5. Denmark	4	0/4	2/12	4

Final group for 1–8 places (Constanţa)

26 Oct.	Hungary–Yugoslavia	3–2	(15–12, 13–15, 15–10, 14–16, 15–8)
26 Oct.	Poland–GDR	3–2	(15–12, 10–15, 13–15, 15–3, 15–9)
26 Oct.	USSR–Czechoslovakia	3–0	(15–6, 15–9, 15–11)
26 Oct.	Romania–Bulgaria	3–2	(13–15, 15–12, 3–15, 15–11, 15–11)
27 Oct.	USSR–Yugoslavia	3–0	(15–5, 15–5, 15–6)
27 Oct.	Bulgaria–Czechoslovakia	3–2	(11–15, 15–10, 15–8, 12–15, 15–7)
27 Oct.	GDR–Hungary	3–0	(15–7, 15–3, 15–13)
27 Oct.	Poland–Romania	3–0	(15–12, 15–11, 15–5)
28 Oct.	Bulgaria–Yugoslavia	3–1	(12–15, 15–0, 15–5, 15–11)
28 Oct.	USSR–Hungary	3–0	(15–11, 15–8, 15–2)
28 Oct.	Poland–Czechoslovakia	3–0	(15–2, 17–15, 15–10)

(continued)

Final group for 1–8 places (Constanța) (continued)

29 Oct.	Bulgaria–Hungary	3–1	(15–4, 13–15, 16–14, 15–11)
29 Oct.	USSR–GDR	3–0	(15–11, 15–4, 15–2)
29 Oct.	Romania–Czechoslovakia	3–1	(5–15, 15–11, 15–6, 16–14)
31 Oct.	Romania–Yugoslavia	3–0	(15–7, 15–12, 15–11)
31 Oct.	Poland–Hungary	3–1	(15–5, 15–6, 10–15, 15–12)
31 Oct.	GDR–Czechoslovakia	3–0	(15–7, 15–6, 15–7)
1 Nov.	Czechoslovakia–Yugoslavia	3–0	(15–2, 15–9, 15–7)
1 Nov.	GDR–Bulgaria	3–0	(15–7, 15–5, 15–4)
1 Nov.	USSR–Poland	3–2	(8–15, 15–8, 15–17, 15–4, 15–10)
1 Nov.	Romania–Hungary	3–0	(15–8, 15–11, 15–11)
2 Nov.	GDR–Yugoslavia	3–0	(15–11, 15–10, 18–16)
2 Nov.	USSR–Romania	3–0	(15–0, 15–8, 15–3)
2 Nov.	Poland–Bulgaria	3–2	(15–10, 15–3, 5–15, 14–16, 15–10)

	G	W/L	SW/SL	Pts.
1. USSR	7	7/0	21/2	14
2. Poland	7	6/1	20/8	13
3. Romania	7	5/2	15/10	12
4. GDR	7	4/3	15/9	11
5. Bulgaria	7	3/4	13/16	10
6. Czechoslovakia	7	2/5	9/16	9
7. Hungary	7	1/6	6/20	8
8. Yugoslavia	7	0/7	3/21	7

Final standings

	G	W/L	SW/SL
1. USSR	8	8/0	24/2
2. Poland	8	7/1	23/8
3. Romania	8	6/2	18/10
4. GDR	8	5/3	18/9
5. Bulgaria	8	4/4	16/16
6. Czechoslovakia	9	4/5	15/17
7. Hungary	9	3/6	12/20
8. Yugoslavia	8	1/7	6/22
9. Netherlands	6	4/2	13/6
10. Turkey	6	3/3	9/10
11. FRG	6	2/4	8/12
12. Austria	6	1/5	3/17
13. Denmark	6	0/6	2/18

Total: 13 teams, 48 games

Rosters of the medalists

USSR–Lidiya Aleksandrova, Marita Aven-Katusheva, Galina Chesnokova, Alisa Galakhova-Krasheninnikova, Valentina Kamenyok-Vinogradova, Ninel Lukanina, Lyudmila Mikhaylovskaya, Antonina Moiseeva-Ryzhova, Tatyana Roshchina-Rodionova, Inna Ryskal, Tamara Tikhonina, Valentina Voloshchuk-Mishak; head coach: Oleg Chekhov

Poland–Krystyna Czajkowska, Ewa Dołmatow-Kuźmińska, Jadwiga Domańska, Maria Golimowska, Danuta Kordaczuk-Wagner, Józefa Ledwig, Krystyna Malinowska-Krupa, Jadwiga Marko, Maria Śliwka, Zofia Szczęśniewska, Krystyna Tabaka-Jakubowska, Lidia Żmuda; head coach: Stanisław Poburka

Romania–Alexandrina Chezan, Sonia Colceriu, Ileana Enculescu-Dulău, Elisabeta Goloşie, Doina Ivănescu-Corbeanu, Viorica Mirion, Ana Mocanu, Doina Popescu, Cornelia Timoşanu-Moraru, Natalia Todorovschi, Lia Vanea, Elena Verdeş; head coach: Gheorghe Constantinescu

VII EUROPEAN CHAMPIONSHIP
22 October–7 November 1967, Adana, Ankara, Istanbul, and Izmir (Turkey)

Preliminary round

Group A (Ankara)

26 Oct.	GDR–Hungary	3–0	(15–12, 15–8, 15–5)
26 Oct.	Romania–Italy	3–0	(15–8, 15–7, 15–7)
27 Oct.	Hungary–Romania	3–0	(15–12, 15–10, 15–6)
27 Oct.	GDR–Italy	3–0	(15–13, 15–1, 15–3)
28 Oct.	Hungary–Italy	3–0	(15–9, 15–2, 15–7)
28 Oct.	Romania–GDR	3–0	(16–14, 15–13, 15–9)

	G	W/L	SW/SL	Pts.
1. GDR	3	2/1	6/3	5
2. Hungary	3	2/1	6/3	5
3. Romania	3	2/1	6/3	5
4. Italy	3	0/3	0/9	3

Group B (Istanbul)

26 Oct.	Turkey–Sweden	3–0	(15–7, 15–10, 15–9)
26 Oct.	Bulgaria–Israel	3–0	(15–0, 15–1, 15–6)
27 Oct.	Bulgaria–Turkey	3–0	(15–3, 15–5, 15–8)
27 Oct.	Israel–Sweden	3–0	(15–1, 15–8, 15–2)
28 Oct.	Israel–Turkey	3–1	(15–11, 15–12, 10–15, 15–8)
28 Oct.	Bulgaria–Sweden	3–0	(15–2, 15–3, 15–4)

	G	W/L	SW/SL	Pts.
1. Bulgaria	3	3/0	9/0	6
2. Israel	3	2/1	6/4	5
3. Turkey	3	1/2	4/6	4
4. Sweden	3	0/3	0/9	3

Group C (Adana)

26 Oct.	Czechoslovakia–Belgium	3–0	(15–1, 15–0, 15–3)
26 Oct.	Poland–FRG	3–0	(15–0, 15–3, 15–2)
27 Oct.	FRG–Belgium	3–0	(15–8, 15–9, 15–13)
27 Oct.	Poland–Czechoslovakia	3–2	(15–9, 15–10, 5–15, 10–15, 15–6)
28 Oct.	Czechoslovakia–FRG	3–0	(15–0, 15–4, 15–2)
28 Oct.	Poland–Belgium	3–0	(15–3, 15–0, 15–3)

	G	W/L	SW/SL	Pts.
1. Poland	3	3/0	9/2	6
2. Czechoslovakia	3	2/1	8/3	5
3. FRG	3	1/2	3/6	4
4. Belgium	3	0/3	0/9	3

Group D (Izmir)

26 Oct.	Netherlands–Switzerland	3–0	(15–1, 15–5, 15–2)
27 Oct.	USSR–Switzerland	3–0	(15–2, 15–3, 15–2)
28 Oct.	USSR–Netherlands	3–0	(15–10, 15–7, 15–4)

	G	W/L	SW/SL	Pts.
1. USSR	2	2/0	6/0	4
2. Netherlands	2	1/1	3/3	3
3. Switzerland	2	0/2	0/6	2

Final round (head-to-head games were carried over from the preliminary round)

Final group for 9–15 places (Ankara)

2 Nov.	Romania–Belgium	3–0	(15–0, 15–0, 15–3)
2 Nov.	Italy–Sweden	3–0	(15–3, 15–3, 15–0)
2 Nov.	FRG–Switzerland	3–0	(15–5, 15–6, 15–12)
3 Nov.	FRG–Italy	3–0	(16–14, 15–8, 15–8)
3 Nov.	Turkey–Switzerland	3–1	(15–8, 10–15, 15–12, 15–7)
3 Nov.	Belgium–Sweden	3–0	(15–6, 15–9, 15–6)
4 Nov.	Italy–Turkey	3–1	(15–10, 15–12, 13–15, 15–1)
4 Nov.	FRG–Sweden	3–0	(15–5, 15–8, 15–3)

(continued)

Final group for 9–15 places (Ankara) (continued)

4 Nov.	Romania–Switzerland	3–0	(15–1, 15–1, 15–3)
6 Nov.	FRG–Turkey	3–2	(15–8, 15–7, 9–15, 12–15, 15–12)
6 Nov.	Romania–Sweden	3–0	(15–3, 15–0, 15–4)
6 Nov.	Switzerland–Belgium	3–2	(15–8, 6–15, 5–15, 15–6, 15–7)
7 Nov.	Italy–Switzerland	3–1	(15–11, 15–6, 15–17, 15–3)
7 Nov.	Turkey–Belgium	3–0	(15–9, 15–9, 15–8)
7 Nov.	Romania–FRG	3–0	(15–1, 15–2, 15–4)
8 Nov.	Romania–Turkey	3–0	(15–1, 15–0, 15–2)
8 Nov.	Italy–Belgium	3–0	(15–7, 15–10, 15–8)
8 Nov.	Switzerland–Sweden	3–1	(15–11, 15–9, 11–15, 15–11)

	G	W/L	SW/SL	Pts.
1. Romania	6	6/0	18/0	12
2. FRG	6	5/1	15/5	11
3. Italy	6	4/2	12/8	10
4. Turkey	6	3/3	12/10	9
5. Switzerland	6	2/4	8/15	8
6. Belgium	6	1/5	5/15	7
7. Sweden	6	0/6	1/18	6

Final group for 1–8 places (Izmir)

1 Nov.	Hungary–Israel	3–0	(15–7, 15–5, 15–4)
1 Nov.	Czechoslovakia–Netherlands	3–0	(15–1, 15–6, 15–8)
1 Nov.	USSR–Bulgaria	3–0	(15–5, 15–3, 15–0)
1 Nov.	Poland–GDR	3–1	(15–11, 17–15, 13–15, 15–10)
2 Nov.	Netherlands–Israel	3–0	(15–10, 15–10, 15–6)
2 Nov.	Czechoslovakia–Bulgaria	3–0	(15–6, 15–9, 15–10)
2 Nov.	Poland–Hungary	3–1	(15–8, 3–15, 17–15, 15–10)
2 Nov.	USSR–GDR	3–0	(15–1, 15–3, 15–2)
3 Nov.	Czechoslovakia–Israel	3–0	(15–4, 15–1, 15–2)
3 Nov.	Poland–Netherlands	3–0	(15–3, 15–10, 15–3)
3 Nov.	GDR–Bulgaria	3–0	(15–10, 15–13, 15–11)
3 Nov.	USSR–Hungary	3–0	(15–2, 15–0, 15–0)
5 Nov.	Poland–Israel	3–0	(15–2, 15–2, 15–4)
5 Nov.	GDR–Netherlands	3–1	(15–5, 17–15, 8–15, 15–5)
5 Nov.	Hungary–Bulgaria	3–0	(15–12, 15–12, 15–11)
5 Nov.	USSR–Czechoslovakia	3–0	(15–4, 15–10, 15–4)
6 Nov.	USSR–Israel	3–0	(15–7, 15–1, 15–1)
6 Nov.	Hungary–Netherlands	3–1	(15–2, 15–4, 12–15, 15–5)
6 Nov.	Poland–Bulgaria	3–0	(15–6, 15–10, 15–9)
6 Nov.	Czechoslovakia–GDR	3–0	(15–9, 15–13, 15–7)

(continued)

Final group for 1–8 places (Izmir) (continued)

7 Nov.	USSR–Poland	3–0	(15–7, 15–10, 15–10)
7 Nov.	GDR–Israel	3–0	(15–2, 15–2, 15–2)
7 Nov.	Bulgaria–Netherlands	3–1	(15–8, 11–15, 15–4, 15–10)
7 Nov.	Czechoslovakia–Hungary	3–1	(15–11, 15–8, 9–15, 15–6)

	G	W/L	SW/SL	Pts.
1. USSR	7	7/0	21/0	14
2. Poland	7	6/1	18/7	13
3. Czechoslovakia	7	5/2	17/7	12
4. GDR	7	4/3	13/10	11
5. Hungary	7	3/4	11/13	10
6. Bulgaria	7	2/5	6/16	9
7. Netherlands	7	1/6	6/18	8
8. Israel	7	0/7	0/21	7

Final standings

	G	W/L	SW/SL
1. USSR	8	8/0	24/0
2. Poland	9	8/1	24/7
3. Czechoslovakia	9	7/2	23/7
4. GDR	9	5/4	16/13
5. Hungary	9	5/4	17/13
6. Bulgaria	9	4/5	12/16
7. Netherlands	8	2/6	9/18
8. Israel	9	2/7	6/22
9. Romania	8	7/1	21/3
10. FRG	8	5/3	15/11
11. Italy	8	4/4	12/14
12. Turkey	8	3/5	13/16
13. Switzerland	8	2/6	8/21
14. Belgium	8	1/7	5/21
15. Sweden	8	0/8	1/24

Total: 15 teams, 63 games

Rosters of the medalists

USSR–Nelli Abramova, Galina Elnitskaya-Leonteva, Lyubov Evtushenko, Valentina Kamenyok-Vinogradova, Vera Lantratova, Lyudmila Meshcheryakova-Buldakova, Tatyana Ponyaeva-Tretyakova, Tatyana Roshchina-Rodionova, Inna Ryskal, Roza Salikhova, Nina Smoleeva, Valentina Voloshchuk-Mishak; head coach: Givi Akhvlediani

Poland–Halina Aszkiełowicz, Krystyna Czajkowska, Barbara Hermel, Krystyna Jakubowska, Krystyna Krupa, Józefa Ledwig, Janina Pluta, Elżbieta Porzec, Hanna Sojczuk, Zofia Szczęśniewska, Wanda Wiecha, Lidia Żmuda; head coach: Benedykt Krysik

Czechoslovakia–Júlia Bendeová, Věra Hrabáková, Irena Hrádková, Hilda Mazurová, Elena Poláková, Naďa Pražanová, Stanislava Rehbergerová, Karla Šašková, Jitka Senecká, Eva Široká, Paulina Steffková, Věra Štruncová; head coach: Metoděj Mácha

VIII EUROPEAN CHAMPIONSHIP
23 September–1 October 1971, Bologna, Gorizia, Imola, Modena, and Reggio Emilia (Italy)

Preliminary round

Group A (Gorizia)

23 Sep.	USSR–Sweden	3–0	(15–1, 15–5, 15–1)
24 Sep.	USSR–Switzerland	3–0	(15–3, 15–4, 15–0)
25 Sep.	Switzerland–Sweden	3–1	(15–10, 10–15, 15–10, 15–12)

	G	W/L	SW/SL	Pts.
1. USSR	2	2/0	6/0	4
2. Switzerland	2	1/1	3/4	3
3. Sweden	2	0/2	1/6	2

Group B (Gorizia)

23 Sep.	Italy–Austria	3–0	(15–2, 15–2, 15–5)
24 Sep.	Poland–Italy	3–0	(15–4, 15–7, 15–10)
25 Sep.	Poland–Austria	3–0	(15–0, 15–1, 15–1)

	G	W/L	SW/SL	Pts.
1. Poland	2	2/0	6/0	4
2. Italy	2	1/1	3/3	3
3. Austria	2	0/2	0/6	2

Group C (Reggio Emilia)

23 Sep.	FRG–France	3–2	(10–15, 15–3, 14–16, 15–8, 15–0)
24 Sep.	Czechoslovakia–France	3–0	(15–4, 15–2, 15–6)
25 Sep.	Czechoslovakia–FRG	3–0	(15–0, 15–7, 15–1)

	G	W/L	SW/SL	Pts.
1. Czechoslovakia	2	2/0	6/0	4
2. FRG	2	1/1	3/5	3
3. France	2	0/2	2/6	2

Group D (Reggio Emilia)

23 Sep.	GDR–Yugoslavia	3–0	(15–6, 15–7, 15–1)
24 Sep.	Romania–Yugoslavia	3–0	(15–2, 15–7, 15–1)
25 Sep.	GDR–Romania	3–2	(15–7, 8–15, 16–14, 13–15, 15–12)

	G	W/L	SW/SL	Pts.
1. GDR	2	2/0	6/2	4
2. Romania	2	1/1	5/3	3
3. Yugoslavia	2	0/2	0/6	2

Group E (Imola)

23 Sep.	Hungary–Israel	3–0	(15–7, 15–7, 15–6)
24 Sep.	Hungary–England	3–0	(15–1, 15–1, 15–1)
25 Sep.	Israel–England	3–0	(15–2, 15–2, 15–8)

	G	W/L	SW/SL	Pts.
1. Hungary	2	2/0	6/0	4
2. Israel	2	1/1	3/3	3
3. England	2	0/2	0/6	2

Group F (Modena)

23 Sep.	Netherlands–Denmark	3–0	(15–8, 15–4, 15–5)
24 Sep.	Bulgaria–Denmark	3–0	(15–2, 15–3, 15–3)
25 Sep.	Bulgaria–Netherlands	3–1	(9–15, 15–5, 15–6, 15–3)

	G	W/L	SW/SL	Pts.
1. Bulgaria	2	2/0	6/1	4
2. Netherlands	2	1/1	4/3	3
3. Denmark	2	0/2	0/6	2

Final round

Final group for 13–18 places (Reggio Emilia)

| 27 Sep. | Yugoslavia–Austria | 3–0 | (15–6, 15–0, 15–8) |
| 27 Sep. | Denmark–England | 3–0 | (15–12, 15–10, 15–13) |

(continued)

Final group for 13–18 places (Reggio Emilia) (continued)

27 Sep.	France–Sweden	3–0	(15–2, 15–5, 15–7)
28 Sep.	France–Yugoslavia	3–2	(15–6, 11–15, 15–13, 7–15, 15–12)
28 Sep.	Sweden–England	3–0	(15–8, 15–7, 15–13)
28 Sep.	Denmark–Austria	3–0	(15–4, 16–14, 15–6)
29 Sep.	Yugoslavia–England	3–0	(15–1, 15–5, 15–1)
29 Sep.	Sweden–Denmark	3–1	(15–6, 12–15, 15–2, 15–13)
29 Sep.	France–Austria	3–0	(15–4, 15–2, 15–8)
30 Sep.	Austria–England	3–0	(15–6, 15–4, 15–8)
30 Sep.	Yugoslavia–Sweden	3–0	(15–9, 15–4, 15–3)
30 Sep.	France–Denmark	3–0	(15–6, 15–9, 15–3)
1 Oct.	France–England	3–0	(15–6, 15–1, 15–3)
1 Oct.	Yugoslavia–Denmark	3–0	(15–12, 15–2, 15–11)
1 Oct.	Sweden–Austria	3–1	(3–15, 15–8, 15–7, 15–9)

	G	W/L	SW/SL	Pts.
1. France	5	5/0	15/2	10
2. Yugoslavia	5	4/1	14/3	9
3. Sweden	5	3/2	9/8	8
4. Denmark	5	2/3	7/9	7
5. Austria	5	1/4	4/12	6
6. England	5	0/5	0/15	5

Final group for 7–12 places (Bologna)

27 Sep.	FRG–Israel	3–2	(12–15, 11–15, 15–5, 15–3, 15–13)
27 Sep.	Romania–Netherlands	3–0	(15–6, 15–3, 15–0)
27 Sep.	Italy–Switzerland	3–0	(15–12, 15–12, 15–10)
28 Sep.	Romania–FRG	3–0	(15–6, 15–7, 15–5)
28 Sep.	Italy–Israel	3–0	(15–2, 15–10, 15–5)
28 Sep.	Netherlands–Switzerland	3–0	(15–13, 15–3, 15–11)
29 Sep.	FRG–Switzerland	3–0	(15–11, 15–6, 15–8)
29 Sep.	Italy–Netherlands	3–0	(15–13, 15–11, 15–11)
29 Sep.	Romania–Israel	3–0	(15–5, 15–6, 15–2)
30 Sep.	Romania–Switzerland	3–0	(15–7, 15–2, 15–4)
30 Sep.	Netherlands–Israel	3–1	(15–10, 15–8, 8–15, 15–11)
30 Sep.	Italy–FRG	3–2	(15–10, 2–15, 11–15, 17–15, 15–5)
1 Oct.	Israel–Switzerland	3–0	(15–7, 15–3, 15–10)
1 Oct.	Netherlands–FRG	3–1	(14–16, 15–9, 15–11, 15–4)
1 Oct.	Romania–Italy	3–0	(15–3, 15–4, 15–10)

	G	W/L	SW/SL	Pts.
1. Romania	5	5/0	15/0	10
2. Italy	5	4/1	12/5	9
3. Netherlands	5	3/2	9/8	8
4. FRG	5	2/3	9/11	7
5. Israel	5	1/4	6/12	6
6. Switzerland	5	0/5	0/15	5

Final group for 1–6 places (Reggio Emilia)

27 Sep.	USSR–GDR	3–0	(15–4, 15–6, 15–7)
27 Sep.	Bulgaria–Hungary	3–2	(15–9, 15–9, 9–15, 10–15, 15–10)
27 Sep.	Czechoslovakia–Poland	3–0	(15–13, 15–4, 15–8)
28 Sep.	Poland–Hungary	3–0	(15–11, 15–12, 15–12)
28 Sep.	USSR–Czechoslovakia	3–0	(15–11, 15–6, 15–8)
28 Sep.	Bulgaria–GDR	3–2	(15–5, 11–15, 15–12, 7–15, 15–11)
29 Sep.	Poland–GDR	3–0	(15–11, 15–12, 15–10)
29 Sep.	USSR–Bulgaria	3–0	(15–1, 15–3, 15–8)
29 Sep.	Czechoslovakia–Hungary	3–1	(9–15, 15–5, 15–13, 15–11)
30 Sep.	Hungary–GDR	3–0	(15–10, 16–14, 15–2)
30 Sep.	USSR–Poland	3–0	(15–8, 15–6, 15–13)
30 Sep.	Czechoslovakia–Bulgaria	3–0	(15–9, 15–12, 15–7)
1 Oct.	Czechoslovakia–GDR	3–2	(15–10, 12–15, 15–12, 6–15, 15–6)
1 Oct.	Poland–Bulgaria	3–2	(15–2, 15–6, 10–15, 14–16, 15–7)
1 Oct.	USSR–Hungary	3–0	(15–2, 15–5, 15–4)

	G	W/L	SW/SL	Pts.
1. USSR	5	5/0	15/0	10
2. Czechoslovakia	5	4/1	12/6	9
3. Poland	5	3/2	9/8	8
4. Bulgaria	5	2/3	8/13	7
5. Hungary	5	1/4	6/12	6
6. GDR	5	0/5	4/15	5

Final standings

	G	W/L	SW/SL
1. USSR	7	7/0	21/0
2. Czechoslovakia	7	6/1	18/6
3. Poland	7	5/2	15/8
4. Bulgaria	7	4/3	14/14
5. Hungary	7	3/4	12/12
6. GDR	7	2/5	10/17
7. Romania	7	6/1	20/3

(continued)

	G	W/L	SW/SL
8. Italy	7	5/2	15/8
9. Netherlands	7	4/3	13/11
10. FRG	7	3/4	12/16
11. Israel	7	2/5	9/15
12. Switzerland	7	1/6	3/19
13. France	7	5/2	17/8
14. Yugoslavia	7	4/3	14/9
15. Sweden	7	3/4	10/14
16. Denmark	7	2/5	7/15
17. Austria	7	1/6	4/18
18. England	7	0/7	0/21

Total: 18 teams, 63 games

Rosters of the medalists

USSR–Marytė Batutytė, Larisa Bergen, Galina Elnitskaya-Leonteva, Lyudmila Meshcheryakova-Buldakova, Tatyana Ponyaeva-Tretyakova, Anna Rostova, Inna Ryskal, Roza Salikhova, Tatyana Sarycheva, Tatyana Semyonova, Lyudmila Shchetinina, Nina Smoleeva; head coach: Givi Akhvlediani

Czechoslovakia–Jaroslava Baniová, Jana Hálková, Dora Jelínková, Darina Kodajová, Zuzana Malá, Mária Mališová, Anna Mifková, Elena Moskalová, Jana Semecká, Irena Svobodová, Ludmila Vindušková, Hana Vlasáková; head coach: Stanislav Šneberger

Poland–Celina Aszkiełowicz, Halina Aszkiełowicz-Wojno, Małgorzata Denisow, Barbara Hermel-Niemczyk, Krystyna Karasińska, Elżbieta Leżoń, Teresa Małowidzka, Barbara Miazek, Krystyna Mioduszewska, Bożena Modnicka, Krystyna Ostromęcka, Maria Zaucha; head coach: Zygmunt Krzyżanowski

IX EUROPEAN CHAMPIONSHIP
18–25 October 1975, Banja Luka, Belgrade, Negotin, and Rijeka (Yugoslavia)

Preliminary round

Group A (Rijeka)

18 Oct.	Yugoslavia–FRG	3–1	(15–11, 10–15, 15–10, 15–7)
18 Oct.	Hungary–GDR	3–1	(15–7, 9–15, 15–8, 15–13)
19 Oct.	Hungary–FRG	3–0	(15–4, 15–0, 15–10)
19 Oct.	GDR–Yugoslavia	3–0	(15–10, 15–8, 15–7)
20 Oct.	Hungary–Yugoslavia	3–0	(15–13, 15–4, 15–2)
20 Oct.	GDR–FRG	3–0	(15–7, 15–2, 15–4)

	G	W/L	SW/SL	Pts.
1. Hungary	3	3/0	9/1	6
2. GDR	3	2/1	7/3	5
3. Yugoslavia	3	1/2	3/7	4
4. FRG	3	0/3	1/9	3

Group B (Banja Luka)

18 Oct.	Bulgaria–Netherlands	3–0	(15–6, 15–3, 15–7)
18 Oct.	USSR–Romania	3–1	(15–10, 15–9, 8–15, 15–5)
19 Oct.	USSR–Netherlands	3–0	(15–10, 15–1, 15–10)
19 Oct.	Bulgaria–Romania	3–1	(15–8, 15–12, 9–15, 15–13)
20 Oct.	Romania–Netherlands	3–0	(15–10, 15–13, 15–12)
20 Oct.	USSR–Bulgaria	3–1	(15–4, 7–15, 15–12, 15–2)

	G	W/L	SW/SL	Pts.
1. USSR	3	3/0	9/2	6
2. Bulgaria	3	2/1	7/4	5
3. Romania	3	1/2	5/6	4
4. Netherlands	3	0/3	0/9	3

Group C (Negotin)

18 Oct.	Czechoslovakia–Italy	3–1	(13–15, 15–6, 15–3, 15–4)
18 Oct.	Poland–Belgium	3–0	(15–10, 15–4, 15–4)
19 Oct.	Italy–Belgium	3–1	(15–5, 15–8, 8–15, 15–7)
19 Oct.	Czechoslovakia–Poland	3–2	(15–8, 11–15, 8–15, 15–7, 15–13)
20 Oct.	Czechoslovakia–Belgium	3–0	(15–0, 15–9, 15–1)
20 Oct.	Poland–Italy	3–1	(15–2, 15–4, 8–15, 15–10)

	G	W/L	SW/SL	Pts.
1. Czechoslovakia	3	3/0	9/3	6
2. Poland	3	2/1	8/4	5
3. Italy	3	1/2	5/7	4
4. Belgium	3	0/3	1/9	3

Final round (head-to-head games were carried over from the preliminary round)

Final group for 7–12 places (Belgrade)

22 Oct.	Romania–FRG	3–0	(15–4, 15–6, 15–11)
22 Oct.	Yugoslavia–Belgium	3–0	(15–13, 15–9, 15–10)
22 Oct.	Netherlands–Italy	3–1	(16–14, 4–15, 15–5, 15–10)

(continued)

Final group for 7–12 places (Belgrade) (continued)

23 Oct.	FRG–Netherlands	3–1	(15–10, 10–15, 15–7, 15–5)
23 Oct.	Romania–Belgium	3–0	(15–2, 15–4, 15–4)
23 Oct.	Yugoslavia–Italy	3–2	(15–7, 12–15, 7–15, 15–13, 15–9)
24 Oct.	FRG–Belgium	3–1	(15–12, 9–15, 18–16, 15–5)
24 Oct.	Romania–Italy	3–0	(15–4, 15–7, 15–7)
24 Oct.	Yugoslavia–Netherlands	3–0	(16–14, 15–10, 15–9)
25 Oct.	Netherlands–Belgium	3–2	(14–16, 9–15, 15–0, 15–10, 19–17)
25 Oct.	Italy–FRG	3–0	(15–12, 15–4, 15–6)
25 Oct.	Romania–Yugoslavia	3–0	(15–8, 15–9, 17–15)

	G	W/L	SW/SL	Pts.
1. Romania	5	5/0	15/0	10
2. Yugoslavia	5	4/1	12/6	9
3. Italy	5	2/3	9/10	7
4. Netherlands	5	2/3	7/12	7
5. FRG	5	2/3	7/11	7
6. Belgium	5	0/5	4/15	5

Final group for 1–6 places (Belgrade)

22 Oct.	Hungary–Czechoslovakia	3–1	(15–13, 15–10, 6–15, 15–5)
22 Oct.	Bulgaria–Poland	3–1	(15–9, 12–15, 15–9, 15–4)
22 Oct.	USSR–GDR	3–0	(15–8, 15–8, 15–5)
23 Oct.	USSR–Hungary	3–0	(15–2, 15–8, 15–8)
23 Oct.	Czechoslovakia–Bulgaria	3–0	(15–9, 15–11, 15–10)
23 Oct.	GDR–Poland	3–2	(15–6, 11–15, 15–2, 9–15, 15–12)
24 Oct.	Hungary–Poland	3–1	(15–10, 9–15, 17–15, 15–6)
24 Oct.	USSR–Czechoslovakia	3–1	(12–15, 15–4, 15–5, 15–3)
24 Oct.	Bulgaria–GDR	3–1	(15–12, 6–15, 15–12, 15–12)
25 Oct.	GDR–Czechoslovakia	3–0	(15–10, 15–9, 15–2)
25 Oct.	USSR–Poland	3–0	(15–9, 15–4, 15–7)
25 Oct.	Hungary–Bulgaria	3–1	(13–15, 15–7, 15–5, 15–13)

	G	W/L	SW/SL	Pts.
1. USSR	5	5/0	15/2	10
2. Hungary	5	4/1	12/7	9
3. GDR	5	2/3	8/11	7
4. Bulgaria	5	2/3	8/11	7
5. Czechoslovakia	5	2/3	8/11	7
6. Poland	5	0/5	6/15	5

Final standings

	G	W/L	SW/SL
1. USSR	7	7/0	21/3
2. Hungary	7	6/1	18/7
3. GDR	7	4/3	14/11
4. Bulgaria	7	4/3	14/12
5. Czechoslovakia	7	4/3	14/12
6. Poland	7	2/5	12/16
7. Romania	7	5/2	17/6
8. Yugoslavia	7	4/3	12/12
9. Italy	7	2/5	11/16
10. FRG	7	2/5	7/17
11. Netherlands	7	2/5	7/18
12. Belgium	7	0/7	4/21

Total: 12 teams, 42 games

Rosters of the medalists

USSR–Larisa Bergen, Lyudmila Chernyshyova, Olga Kozakova, Natalya Kushnir, Lidiya Loginova, Evgeniya Nazarenko, Liliya Osadchaya, Anna Rostova, Tatyana Sarycheva, Lyudmila Shchetinina, Nina Smoleeva, Nadezhda Zezyulya-Radzevich; head coach: Givi Akhvlediani

Hungary–Éva Biszku, Gabriella Csapó Feketéné, Katalin Eichler Schadekné, Ágnes Gajdos Hubainé, Ágnes Juhász Szilvásyné, Katalin Marcus Halászné, Lúcia Radó Bánhegyiné, Judit Schlégl, Éva Sebok Szalayné, Emerencia Siry Királyné, Ildikó Szonyi, Ágnes Torma; head coach: Gabriella Attiláné Kotsis

GDR–Jutta Balster, Marie Böhm, Barbara Czekalla, Karen Heller, Hannelore Meincke, Monika Meißner, Ingrid Mierzwiak, Helga Offen, Cornelia Rickert, Helga Schaller, Christine Walther, Anke Westendorf; head coach: Dieter Grund

X EUROPEAN CHAMPIONSHIP
25 September–2 October 1977, Kotka, Lahti, Tampere, and Turku (Finland)

Preliminary round

Group A (Kotka)

25 Sep.	Finland–FRG	3–2	(12–15, 15–11, 10–15, 15–12, 15–8)
25 Sep.	Poland–Bulgaria	3–0	(16–14, 15–11, 15–5)
25 Sep.	GDR–Italy	3–0	(15–4, 15–10, 15–1)
26 Sep.	Poland–Italy	3–0	(15–8, 15–10, 15–6)
26 Sep.	GDR–FRG	3–0	(15–9, 15–2, 15–10)
26 Sep.	Bulgaria–Finland	3–0	(15–5, 15–4, 15–10)

(continued)

Group A (Kotka) (continued)

27 Sep.	GDR–Poland	3–0	(15–13, 15–11, 15–5)
27 Sep.	Italy–Finland	3–0	(15–8, 15–7, 15–8)
27 Sep.	Bulgaria–FRG	3–0	(15–13, 15–5, 15–7)
28 Sep.	Bulgaria–Italy	3–0	(15–5, 16–14, 15–5)
28 Sep.	GDR–Finland	3–0	(15–4, 15–9, 15–9)
28 Sep.	Poland–FRG	3–1	(15–13, 12–15, 15–9, 15–3)
29 Sep.	Bulgaria–GDR	3–2	(15–12, 15–7, 1–15, 12–15, 15–11)
29 Sep.	FRG–Italy	3–1	(15–1, 11–15, 15–5, 15–5)
29 Sep.	Poland–Finland	3–0	(15–2, 15–1, 15–1)

	G	W/L	SW/SL	Pts.
1. GDR	5	4/1	14/3	9
2. Poland	5	4/1	12/4	9
3. Bulgaria	5	4/1	12/5	9
4. FRG	5	1/4	6/13	6
5. Italy	5	1/4	4/12	6
6. Finland	5	1/4	3/14	6

Group B (Turku)

25 Sep.	Romania–Yugoslavia	3–2	(15–17, 15–8, 15–1, 16–18, 15–9)
25 Sep.	USSR–Czechoslovakia	3–0	(15–5, 15–9, 15–6)
25 Sep.	Hungary–Netherlands	3–0	(15–8, 15–12, 15–3)
26 Sep.	Hungary–Yugoslavia	3–0	(15–9, 15–4, 15–6)
26 Sep.	Czechoslovakia–Romania	3–2	(15–8, 15–10, 9–15, 14–16, 15–13)
26 Sep.	USSR–Netherlands	3–0	(15–1, 15–3, 15–10)
27 Sep.	USSR–Yugoslavia	3–0	(15–0, 15–8, 15–2)
27 Sep.	Hungary–Romania	3–2	(15–7, 9–15, 13–15, 15–8, 15–7)
27 Sep.	Czechoslovakia–Netherlands	3–0	(15–9, 15–7, 15–2)
28 Sep.	Yugoslavia–Netherlands	3–2	(12–15, 15–8, 15–1, 6–15, 15–10)
28 Sep.	USSR–Romania	3–1	(15–3, 15–7, 13–15, 15–4)
28 Sep.	Hungary–Czechoslovakia	3–1	(15–13, 14–16, 16–14, 15–5)
29 Sep.	Czechoslovakia–Yugoslavia	3–0	(15–13, 15–4, 16–14)
29 Sep.	Romania–Netherlands	3–2	(15–11, 11–15, 15–4, 13–15, 15–8)
29 Sep.	USSR–Hungary	3–0	(15–10, 15–2, 15–6)

	G	W/L	SW/SL	Pts.
1. USSR	5	5/0	15/1	10
2. Hungary	5	4/1	12/6	9
3. Czechoslovakia	5	3/2	10/8	8
4. Romania	5	2/3	11/13	7
5. Yugoslavia	5	1/4	5/14	6
6. Netherlands	5	0/5	4/15	5

Final round

Semifinals (9–12 places)

1 Oct.	Netherlands–Italy	3–2	(15–6, 5–15, 15–5, 11–15, 15–11) Lahti
1 Oct.	Yugoslavia–Finland	3–2	(16–18, 15–11, 2–15, 15–11, 15–8) Lahti

Game for 11th place

2 Oct.	Italy–Finland	3–1	(15–11, 15–5, 8–15, 15–6)	Lahti

Game for 9th place

2 Oct.	Yugoslavia–Netherlands	3–0	(15–9, 15–13, 15–2)	Lahti

Semifinals (5–8 places)

1 Oct.	Romania–Bulgaria	3–0	(15–11, 15–2, 15–5)	Kotka
1 Oct.	Czechoslovakia–FRG	3–0	(15–6, 15–4, 15–2)	Kotka

Game for 7th place

2 Oct.	Bulgaria–FRG	3–0	(15–6, 15–10, 15–6)	Kotka

Game for 5th place

2 Oct.	Czechoslovakia–Romania	3–0	(15–3, 15–3, 15–10)	Kotka

Semifinals (1–4 places)

1 Oct.	GDR–Hungary	3–0	(18–16, 15–6, 18–16)	Tampere
1 Oct.	USSR–Poland	3–0	(15–3, 15–1, 15–7)	Tampere

Game for 3rd place

2 Oct.	Hungary–Poland	3–2	(16–14, 10–15, 15–9, 5–15, 15–9) Tampere

Final

2 Oct.	USSR–GDR	3–0	(15–1, 15–2, 15–13)	Tampere

Final standings

	G	W/L	SW/SL
1. USSR	7	7/0	21/1
2. GDR	7	5/2	17/6
3. Hungary	7	5/2	15/11
4. Poland	7	4/3	14/10
5. Czechoslovakia	7	5/2	16/8
6. Romania	7	3/4	14/16

(continued)

	G	W/L	SW/SL
7. Bulgaria	7	5/2	15/8
8. FRG	7	1/6	6/19
9. Yugoslavia	7	3/4	11/16
10. Netherlands	7	1/6	7/20
11. Italy	7	2/5	9/16
12. Finland	7	1/6	6/20

Total: 12 teams, 42 games

Rosters of the medalists

USSR–Olga Belova, Lyudmila Borozna-Zhigiliy, Lyudmila Chernyshyova, Nadezhda Gorlovskaya, Nina Muradyan, Galina Myachina, Elena Petrunina, Lyudmila Shchetinina, Nina Smoleeva, Tatyana Sorokina, Mudīte Stūrmane, Nadezhda Zezyulya-Radzevich; head coach: Viktor Tyurin

GDR–Katharina Bullin, Barbara Czekalla, Karin Hahn, Gabriela Langanki, Andrea Mattke, Monika Meißner, Christine Mummhardt, Helga Offen, Cornelia Rickert, Gudrun Schröter, Annette Schultz, Anke Westendorf; head coach: Dieter Grund

Hungary–Irma Anker, Gyöngyi Bardi, Gabriella Csapó Feketéné, Zsuzsa Gálhidi Fadorné, Ágnes Juhász, Bernadett Kászegi, Zita Kutas, Katalin Marcus Halászné, Lúcia Radó Bánhegyiné, Judit Schlégl, Ildikó Szányi, Ágnes Torma; head coach: Ernő Hennig

XI EUROPEAN CHAMPIONSHIP
5–13 October 1979, Cannes, Évreux, Lyon, and Orléans (France)

Preliminary round

Group A (Orléans)

5 Oct.	Poland–FRG	3–1	(15–6, 15–1, 13–15, 15–7)
5 Oct.	USSR–Romania	3–2	(15–5, 15–12, 11–15, 12–15, 15–8)
6 Oct.	Romania–FRG	3–1	(15–7, 12–15, 15–11, 15–12)
6 Oct.	Poland–USSR	3–2	(15–10, 6–15, 15–12, 12–15, 15–12)
7 Oct.	USSR–FRG	3–0	(15–6, 15–2, 15–11)
7 Oct.	Romania–Poland	3–0	(15–5, 15–6, 15–10)

	G	W/L	SW/SL	Pts.
1. Romania	3	2/1	8/4	5
2. USSR	3	2/1	8/5	5
3. Poland	3	2/1	6/6	5
4. FRG	3	0/3	2/9	3

Group B (Cannes)

5 Oct.	GDR–Belgium	3–0	(15–1, 15–5, 15–3)
5 Oct.	Bulgaria–Czechoslovakia	3–0	(15–5, 15–10, 15–11)
6 Oct.	Bulgaria–Belgium	3–0	(15–4, 15–4, 15–3)
6 Oct.	GDR–Czechoslovakia	3–1	(15–6, 15–13, 13–15, 15–9)
7 Oct.	GDR–Bulgaria	3–0	(15–3, 16–14, 15–8)
7 Oct.	Czechoslovakia–Belgium	3–0	(15–7, 15–10, 15–5)

	G	W/L	SW/SL	Pts.
1. GDR	3	3/0	9/1	6
2. Bulgaria	3	2/1	6/3	5
3. Czechoslovakia	3	1/2	4/6	4
4. Belgium	3	0/3	0/9	3

Group C (Évreux)

5 Oct.	Hungary–Yugoslavia	3–1	(8–15, 15–3, 15–3, 15–12)
5 Oct.	Netherlands–France	3–0	(15–11, 15–9, 15–13)
6 Oct.	Yugoslavia–France	3–1	(15–4, 15–5, 9–15, 15–6)
6 Oct.	Hungary–Netherlands	3–2	(16–18, 15–13, 15–9, 8–15, 15–7)
7 Oct.	Netherlands–Yugoslavia	3–1	(15–3, 8–15, 15–8, 15–8)
7 Oct.	Hungary–France	3–0	(15–7, 15–3, 15–6)

	G	W/L	SW/SL	Pts.
1. Hungary	3	3/0	9/3	6
2. Netherlands	3	2/1	8/4	5
3. Yugoslavia	3	1/2	5/7	4
4. France	3	0/3	1/9	3

Final round (head-to-head games were carried over from the preliminary round)

Final group for 7–12 places (Cannes)

10 Oct.	Czechoslovakia–Yugoslavia	3–0	(15–11, 16–14, 15–6)
10 Oct.	FRG–Belgium	3–1	(15–7, 9–15, 15–4, 15–1)
10 Oct.	Poland–France	3–1	(15–12, 15–7, 9–15, 15–4)
11 Oct.	Czechoslovakia–FRG	3–0	(15–7, 15–13, 15–3)
11 Oct.	Poland–Yugoslavia	3–0	(15–11, 15–10, 15–6)
11 Oct.	France–Belgium	3–2	(14–16, 15–9, 15–4, 12–15, 15–12)
12 Oct.	FRG–Yugoslavia	3–1	(15–11, 5–15, 15–11, 15–8)
12 Oct.	Czechoslovakia–France	3–0	(15–7, 15–0, 15–13)
12 Oct.	Poland–Belgium	3–0	(15–5, 15–4, 15–5)
13 Oct.	Czechoslovakia–Poland	3–0	(15–11, 15–13, 15–5)
13 Oct.	Yugoslavia–Belgium	3–0	(15–9, 15–7, 15–11)
13 Oct.	FRG–France	3–0	(15–5, 15–9, 15–11)

	G	W/L	SW/SL	Pts.
1. Czechoslovakia	5	5/0	15/0	10
2. Poland	5	4/1	12/5	9
3. FRG	5	3/2	10/8	8
4. Yugoslavia	5	2/3	7/10	7
5. France	5	1/4	5/14	6
6. Belgium	5	0/5	3/15	5

Final group for 1–6 places (Lyon)

10 Oct.	Hungary–Romania	3–0	(16–14, 15–11, 15–8)
10 Oct.	USSR–Bulgaria	3–2	(15–10, 15–7, 10–15, 9–15, 15–11)
10 Oct.	GDR–Netherlands	3–0	(15–7, 15–4, 15–6)
11 Oct.	USSR–Hungary	3–1	(18–16, 15–6, 9–15, 15–8)
11 Oct.	Bulgaria–Netherlands	3–0	(17–15, 15–6, 15–6)
11 Oct.	GDR–Romania	3–0	(15–3, 15–5, 15–3)
12 Oct.	USSR–Netherlands	3–0	(15–6, 15–1, 15–1)
12 Oct.	GDR–Hungary	3–1	(15–4, 15–6, 7–15, 15–13)
12 Oct.	Bulgaria–Romania	3–0	(15–4, 15–10, 15–6)
13 Oct.	Romania–Netherlands	3–2	(15–12, 12–15, 13–15, 15–5, 15–10)
13 Oct.	Bulgaria–Hungary	3–2	(9–15, 11–15, 15–3, 15–10, 15–10)
13 Oct.	USSR–GDR	3–0	(15–9, 15–5, 15–7)

	G	W/L	SW/SL	Pts.
1. USSR	5	5/0	15/5	10
2. GDR	5	4/1	12/4	9
3. Bulgaria	5	3/2	11/8	8
4. Hungary	5	2/3	10/11	7
5. Romania	5	1/4	5/14	6
6. Netherlands	5	0/5	4/15	5

Final standings

	G	W/L	SW/SL
1. USSR	7	6/1	20/8
2. GDR	7	6/1	18/5
3. Bulgaria	7	5/2	17/8
4. Hungary	7	4/3	16/12
5. Romania	7	3/4	11/15
6. Netherlands	7	2/5	10/16
7. Czechoslovakia	7	5/2	16/6

(continued)

	G	W/L	SW/SL
8. Poland	7	5/2	15/10
9. FRG	7	3/4	11/14
10. Yugoslavia	7	2/5	9/16
11. France	7	1/6	5/20
12. Belgium	7	0/7	3/21

Total: 12 teams, 42 games

Rosters of the medalists

USSR–Elena Akhaminova-Sokolovskaya, Elena Andreyuk, Tatyana Cherkasova, Lyudmila Chernyshyova, Tatyana Kunitskaya, Lidiya Loginova, Irina Makogonova, Svetlana Nikishina-Kunysheva, Natalya Razumova-Starshova, Olga Solovova, Lyubov Timofeeva, Nadezhda Zezyulya-Radzevich; head coach: Nikolay Karpol

GDR–Katharina Bullin, Monika Burmeister, Barbara Czekalla, Brigitte Fetzer, Karin Hahn, Barbara Intrau, Andrea Mattke, Christine Mummhardt, Karin Püschel, Karla Roffeis, Annette Schultz, Anke Westendorf; head coach: Dieter Grund

Bulgaria–Tsvetana Bozhurina, Tanya Dimitrova, Tanya Gogova, Rumyana Kaisheva, Mariana Khalacheva, Rositsa Mikhaylova, Neli Mileva, Tanya Mumdzhieva, Silva Petrunova, Maya Stoeva, Verka Stoyanova, Anka Uzunova; head coach: Vasil Simov

XII EUROPEAN CHAMPIONSHIP
19–27 September 1981, Pernik and Sofia (Bulgaria)

Preliminary round

Group A (Pernik)

19 Sep.	Romania–Yugoslavia	3–0	(15–6, 15–4, 15–13)
19 Sep.	USSR–Czechoslovakia	3–0	(15–3, 15–9, 15–7)
20 Sep.	USSR–Yugoslavia	3–0	(15–3, 15–4, 15–3)
20 Sep.	Czechoslovakia–Romania	3–1	(16–14, 15–10, 12–15, 15–5)
21 Sep.	Czechoslovakia–Yugoslavia	3–0	(17–15, 15–12, 15–9)
21 Sep.	USSR–Romania	3–0	(15–9, 15–13, 15–6)

	G	W/L	SW/SL	Pts.
1. USSR	3	3/0	9/0	6
2. Czechoslovakia	3	2/1	6/4	5
3. Romania	3	1/2	4/6	4
4. Yugoslavia	3	0/3	0/9	3

Group B (Sofia)

19 Sep.	Poland–Netherlands	3–1	(15–12, 15–3, 13–15, 15–2)
19 Sep.	GDR–Italy	3–2	(14–16, 15–13, 6–15, 15–9, 15–9)
20 Sep.	GDR–Netherlands	3–2	(10–15, 15–7, 6–15, 15–13, 15–11)
20 Sep.	Poland–Italy	3–0	(15–12, 15–5, 15–0)
21 Sep.	Italy–Netherlands	3–0	(15–9, 15–8, 15–4)
21 Sep.	GDR–Poland	3–0	(15–11, 15–13, 15–9)

	G	W/L	SW/SL	Pts.
1. GDR	3	3/0	9/4	6
2. Poland	3	2/1	6/4	5
3. Italy	3	1/2	5/6	4
4. Netherlands	3	0/3	3/9	3

Group C (Sofia)

19 Sep.	Hungary–Turkey	3–0	(15–2, 15–3, 15–4)
19 Sep.	Bulgaria–FRG	3–0	(15–4, 16–14, 15–8)
20 Sep.	Bulgaria–Turkey	3–0	(15–4, 15–9, 15–4)
20 Sep.	Hungary–FRG	3–0	(15–4, 15–10, 15–11)
21 Sep.	FRG–Turkey	3–0	(15–10, 15–9, 15–1)
21 Sep.	Bulgaria–Hungary	3–2	(15–13, 6–15, 13–15, 15–5, 15–10)

	G	W/L	SW/SL	Pts.
1. Bulgaria	3	3/0	9/2	6
2. Hungary	3	2/1	8/3	5
3. FRG	3	1/2	3/6	4
4. Turkey	3	0/3	0/9	3

Final round (head-to-head games were carried over from the preliminary round)

Final group for 7–12 places (Pernik)

24 Sep.	Yugoslavia–Turkey	3–0	(19–17, 15–10, 15–2)
24 Sep.	Netherlands–FRG	3–2	(10–15, 8–15, 15–10, 15–11, 15–10)
24 Sep.	Romania–Italy	3–0	(15–11, 15–6, 15–5)
25 Sep.	FRG–Yugoslavia	3–2	(14–16, 15–11, 13–15, 15–8, 15–7)
25 Sep.	Italy–Turkey	3–0	(15–3, 15–10, 15–5)
25 Sep.	Romania–Netherlands	3–0	(15–8, 15–3, 15–13)
26 Sep.	Romania–Turkey	3–0	(15–6, 15–13, 15–6)
26 Sep.	Netherlands–Yugoslavia	3–0	(15–9, 15–2, 15–7)
26 Sep.	Italy–FRG	3–0	(15–13, 15–12, 17–15)
27 Sep.	Netherlands–Turkey	3–1	(6–15, 15–12, 15–5, 15–11)
27 Sep.	Italy–Yugoslavia	3–1	(15–3, 13–15, 15–6, 15–6)
27 Sep.	Romania–FRG	3–0	(15–4, 15–9, 15–2)

	G	W/L	SW/SL	Pts.
1. Romania	5	5/0	15/0	10
2. Italy	5	4/1	12/4	9
3. Netherlands	5	3/2	9/9	8
4. FRG	5	2/3	8/11	7
5. Yugoslavia	5	1/4	6/12	6
6. Turkey	5	0/5	1/15	5

Final group for 1–6 places (Sofia)

24 Sep.	Hungary–Czechoslovakia	3–1	(15–3, 11–15, 15–7, 15–5)
24 Sep.	Bulgaria–Poland	3–0	(15–6, 15–10, 15–5)
24 Sep.	USSR–GDR	3–0	(15–7, 15–10, 15–7)
25 Sep.	USSR–Poland	3–0	(15–10, 15–7, 17–15)
25 Sep.	Hungary–GDR	3–0	(15–7, 15–10, 15–2)
25 Sep.	Bulgaria–Czechoslovakia	3–1	(10–15, 15–3, 15–2, 15–9)
26 Sep.	USSR–Hungary	3–2	(15–12, 8–15, 15–0, 7–15, 15–7)
26 Sep.	Bulgaria–GDR	3–1	(15–3, 15–0, 11–15, 15–4)
26 Sep.	Poland–Czechoslovakia	3–2	(15–8, 15–12, 11–15, 8–15, 15–10)
27 Sep.	GDR–Czechoslovakia	3–1	(13–15, 17–15, 15–12, 15–11)
27 Sep.	Hungary–Poland	3–1	(15–10, 10–15, 15–10, 15–7)
27 Sep.	Bulgaria–USSR	3–0	(15–6, 15–13, 15–12)

	G	W/L	SW/SL	Pts.
1. Bulgaria	5	5/0	15/4	10
2. USSR	5	4/1	12/5	9
3. Hungary	5	3/2	13/8	8
4. GDR	5	2/3	7/10	7
5. Poland	5	1/4	4/14	6
6. Czechoslovakia	5	0/5	5/15	5

Final standings

	G	W/L	SW/SL
1. Bulgaria	7	7/0	21/4
2. USSR	7	6/1	18/5
3. Hungary	7	5/2	19/8
4. GDR	7	4/3	13/14
5. Poland	7	3/4	10/15
6. Czechoslovakia	7	2/5	11/16
7. Romania	7	5/2	16/6

(continued)

	G	W/L	SW/SL
8. Italy	7	4/3	14/10
9. Netherlands	7	3/4	12/15
10. FRG	7	2/5	8/17
11. Yugoslavia	7	1/6	6/18
12. Turkey	7	0/7	1/21

Total: 12 teams, 42 games

Rosters of the medalists

Bulgaria–Tsvetana Bozhurina, Tanya Dimitrova, Tanya Gogova, Rumyana Kaisheva, Vanya Manova, Rositsa Mikhaylova, Mila Rangelova, Galina Stancheva, Maya Stoeva, Zlatka Stoichkova, Verka Stoyanova, Anka Uzunova; head coach: Vasil Simov

USSR–Elena Akhaminova-Sokolovskaya, Tatyana Cherkasova, Lyudmila Chernyshyova, Lyubov Ivanova, Lidiya Loginova, Irina Makovonova, Svetlana Nikishina-Kunysheva, Nadezhda Orlova, Nadezhda Radzevich, Natalya Razumova-Starshova, Olga Solovova, Elena Volkova; head coach: Nikolay Karpol

Hungary–Gyöngyi Bardi Gerevichné, Beáta Bernáth Pomikálszkyné, Gabriella Csapó Feketéné, Zsuzsa Gálhidi, Ágnes Juhász Balajczáné, Mária Kőrös, Bernadett Kőszegi, Lúcia Radó Bánhegyiné, Éva Sebok Szalayné, Zsuzsa Szabó, Éva Szűcs, Ágnes Torma; head coach: Gabriella Attiláné Kotsis

XIII EUROPEAN CHAMPIONSHIP
17–25 September 1983, Cottbus, Rostock, and Schwerin (GDR)

Preliminary round

Group A (Schwerin)

17 Sep.	FRG–Poland	3–1	(15–10, 17–15, 4–15, 15–5)
17 Sep.	Bulgaria–France	3–0	(15–13, 15–4, 15–7)
18 Sep.	Bulgaria–FRG	3–0	(15–8, 15–10, 15–11)
18 Sep.	Poland–France	3–1	(15–8, 15–13, 13–15, 15–2)
19 Sep.	FRG–France	3–0	(15–11, 15–5, 15–2)
19 Sep.	Poland–Bulgaria	3–2	(15–11, 13–15, 15–9, 9–15, 15–11)

	G	W/L	SW/SL	Pts.
1. Bulgaria	3	2/1	8/3	5
2. FRG	3	2/1	6/4	5
3. Poland	3	2/1	7/6	5
4. France	3	0/3	1/9	3

Group B (Cottbus)

17 Sep.	USSR–Romania	3–1	(15–3, 8–15, 15–5, 15–5)	
17 Sep.	Czechoslovakia–Netherlands	3–0	(15–1, 15–4, 15–6)	
18 Sep.	Romania–Czechoslovakia	3–0	(15–9, 15–12, 15–8)	
18 Sep.	USSR–Netherlands	3–0	(15–4, 15–8, 15–5)	
19 Sep.	Romania–Netherlands	3–1	(15–17, 16–14, 15–7, 16–14)	
19 Sep.	USSR–Czechoslovakia	3–0	(15–4, 16–14, 15–5)	

	G	W/L	SW/SL	Pts.
1. USSR	3	3/0	9/1	6
2. Romania	3	2/1	7/4	5
3. Czechoslovakia	3	1/2	3/6	4
4. Netherlands	3	0/3	1/9	3

Group C (Rostock)

17 Sep.	GDR–Italy	3–0	(15–7, 16–14, 15–5)
17 Sep.	Hungary–Sweden	3–0	(15–4, 15–0, 15–2)
18 Sep.	Hungary–Italy	3–0	(15–11, 15–6, 15–3)
18 Sep.	GDR–Sweden	3–0	(15–6, 15–3, 15–5)
19 Sep.	GDR–Hungary	3–0	(15–10, 15–10, 15–10)
19 Sep.	Italy–Sweden	3–0	(15–8, 15–6, 15–12)

	G	W/L	SW/SL	Pts.
1. GDR	3	3/0	9/0	6
2. Hungary	3	2/1	6/3	5
3. Italy	3	1/2	3/6	4
4. Sweden	3	0/3	0/9	3

Final round (head-to-head games were carried over from the preliminary round)

Final group for 7–12 places (Cottbus)

22 Sep.	Czechoslovakia–Sweden	3–1	(14–16, 15–6, 15–11, 16–14)
22 Sep.	Italy–France	3–1	(15–7, 15–10, 11–15, 15–12)
22 Sep.	Poland–Netherlands	3–0	(15–4, 15–9, 15–3)
23 Sep.	Czechoslovakia–Italy	3–0	(15–8, 15–5, 15–4)
23 Sep.	Poland–Sweden	3–0	(15–9, 15–6, 15–6)
23 Sep.	France–Netherlands	3–1	(15–11, 15–13, 13–15, 15–7)
24 Sep.	Italy–Poland	3–0	(15–7, 15–7, 15–13)
24 Sep.	Netherlands–Sweden	3–0	(15–5, 15–11, 15–3)
24 Sep.	Czechoslovakia–France	3–2	(15–17, 15–8, 15–4, 10–15, 15–4)
25 Sep.	Italy–Netherlands	3–0	(15–12, 15–10, 15–12)
25 Sep.	France–Sweden	3–1	(15–11, 11–15, 15–7, 15–2)
25 Sep.	Poland–Czechoslovakia	3–2	(15–13, 10–15, 7–15, 15–9, 17–15)

	G	W/L	SW/SL	Pts.
1. Italy	5	4/1	12/4	9
2. Czechoslovakia	5	4/1	14/6	9
3. Poland	5	4/1	12/6	9
4. France	5	2/3	10/11	7
5. Netherlands	5	1/4	4/12	6
6. Sweden	5	0/5	2/15	5

Final group for 1–6 places (Rostock)

22 Sep.	Hungary–Bulgaria	3–0	(15–1, 15–7, 15–9)
22 Sep.	GDR–Romania	3–0	(15–3, 15–5, 15–7)
22 Sep.	USSR–FRG	3–0	(15–7, 16–14, 15–4)
23 Sep.	Hungary–Romania	3–0	(16–14, 15–13, 15–4)
23 Sep.	USSR–Bulgaria	3–1	(13–15, 15–8, 15–5, 15–10)
23 Sep.	GDR–FRG	3–1	(15–10, 15–8, 14–16, 15–6)
24 Sep.	FRG–Romania	3–1	(15–1, 14–16, 15–13, 15–2)
24 Sep.	GDR–Bulgaria	3–2	(15–6, 12–15, 11–15, 15–9, 15–9)
24 Sep.	USSR–Hungary	3–2	(8–15, 3–15, 15–13, 15–8, 15–6)
25 Sep.	Bulgaria–Romania	3–0	(15–12, 15–13, 15–7)
25 Sep.	Hungary–FRG	3–0	(15–11, 15–7, 15–10)
25 Sep.	GDR–USSR	3–2	(6–15, 11–15, 15–8, 15–3, 16–14)

	G	W/L	SW/SL	Pts.
1. GDR	5	5/0	15/5	10
2. USSR	5	4/1	14/7	9
3. Hungary	5	3/2	11/6	8
4. Bulgaria	5	2/3	9/9	7
5. FRG	5	1/4	4/13	6
6. Romania	5	0/5	2/15	5

Final standings

	G	W/L	SW/SL
1. GDR	7	7/0	21/5
2. USSR	7	6/1	20/7
3. Hungary	7	5/2	17/6
4. Bulgaria	7	3/4	14/12
5. FRG	7	3/4	10/14
6. Romania	7	2/5	8/16
7. Italy	7	4/3	12/10
8. Czechoslovakia	7	4/3	14/12
9. Poland	7	5/2	16/11

(continued)

	G	W/L	SW/SL
10. France	7	2/5	10/17
11. Netherlands	7	1/6	5/18
12. Sweden	7	0/7	2/21

Total: 12 teams, 42 games

Rosters of the medalists

GDR–Maike Arlt, Monika Beu, Andrea Heim, Catrin Heydrich, Grit Jensen, Ramona Landgraf, Heike Lehmann, Karia Mügge, Ute Oldenburg, Ariane Radfan, Sabine Schott, Martina Schwarz; head coach: Dieter Grund

USSR–Vesma Aistere, Elena Akhaminova-Sokolovskaya, Svetlana Badulina-Safronova, Lyudmila Bazyuk, Elena Chebukina-Ovchinnikova, Irina Kirillova-Parkhomchuk, Lyudmila Makarkina, Tatyana Myshyakova, Valentina Ogienko, Olga Pozdnyakova-Shkurnova, Natalya Razumova-Starshova, Elena Volkova; head coach: Vladimir Patkin

Hungary–Gyöngyi Bardi Gerevichné, Beáta Bernáth Pomikálszkyné, Raquel Chumpitaz Gállné, Gabriella Csapó Feketéné, Zsuzsa Gálhidi, Veronika Kastner, Mária Kőrös, Bernadett Kőszegi Szijártóné, Erzsébet Pálinkás Vargáné, Jolán Perecsi, Éva Szűcs, Ágnes Torma; head coach: Gabriella Attiláné Kotsis

XIV EUROPEAN CHAMPIONSHIP
29 September–6 October 1985, Arnhem, Beverwijk, Enschede, Leeuwarden, and Sittard (Netherlands)

Preliminary round

Group A (Beverwijk)

29 Sep.	Czechoslovakia–Bulgaria	3–1	(15–13, 15–12, 8–15, 15–7)
29 Sep.	GDR–Greece	3–0	(15–4, 15–3, 15–3)
30 Sep.	Czechoslovakia–Greece	3–0	(15–4, 15–4, 15–2)
30 Sep.	GDR–Bulgaria	3–1	(15–3, 15–17, 15–4, 16–14)
1 Oct.	Bulgaria–Greece	3–0	(15–6, 15–10, 15–2)
1 Oct.	GDR–Czechoslovakia	3–1	(15–11, 15–8, 13–15, 15–11)

	G	W/L	SW/SL	Pts.
1. GDR	3	3/0	9/2	6
2. Czechoslovakia	3	2/1	7/4	5
3. Bulgaria	3	1/2	5/6	4
4. Greece	3	0/3	0/9	3

Group B (Enschede)

29 Sep.	USSR–Poland	3–1	(15–1, 15–6, 6–15, 15–9)
29 Sep.	FRG–France	3–1	(16–14, 15–8, 13–15, 15–11)
30 Sep.	USSR–FRG	3–0	(15–1, 15–6, 15–11)
30 Sep.	Poland–France	3–0	(15–12, 15–13, 15–11)
1 Oct.	FRG–Poland	3–1	(15–9, 15–9, 3–15, 15–9)
1 Oct.	USSR–France	3–0	(15–6, 15–10, 15–6)

	G	W/L	SW/SL	Pts.
1. USSR	3	3/0	9/1	6
2. FRG	3	2/1	6/5	5
3. Poland	3	1/2	5/6	4
4. France	3	0/3	1/9	3

Group C (Leeuwarden)

29 Sep.	Romania–Netherlands	3–0	(15–12, 15–10, 15–11)
29 Sep.	Italy–Hungary	3–2	(6–15, 15–12, 13–15, 16–14, 16–14)
30 Sep.	Netherlands–Italy	3–0	(15–11, 15–12, 15–8)
30 Sep.	Hungary–Romania	3–1	(15–13, 7–15, 15–8, 15–8)
1 Oct.	Italy–Romania	3–2	(15–11, 14–16, 11–15, 15–12, 15–11)
1 Oct.	Netherlands–Hungary	3–0	(15–12, 15–9, 15–6)

	G	W/L	SW/SL	Pts.
1. Netherlands	3	2/1	6/3	5
2. Italy	3	2/1	6/7	5
3. Romania	3	1/2	6/6	4
4. Hungary	3	1/2	5/7	4

Final round (head-to-head games were carried over from the preliminary round)

Final group for 7–12 places (Sittard)

3 Oct.	Poland–Greece	3–0	(15–5, 15–7, 15–7)
3 Oct.	Hungary–Bulgaria	3–2	(15–11, 12–15, 15–10, 10–15, 15–13)
3 Oct.	France–Romania	3–2	(15–11, 10–15, 15–2, 13–15, 15–7)
4 Oct.	Hungary–Greece	3–0	(15–8, 15–9, 15–3)
4 Oct.	France–Bulgaria	3–1	(17–15, 3–15, 15–8, 15–7)
4 Oct.	Poland–Romania	3–0	(15–4, 15–6, 15–3)
5 Oct.	France–Hungary	3–0	(15–7, 15–6, 15–6)
5 Oct.	Romania–Greece	3–0	(15–1, 15–6, 15–2)
5 Oct.	Poland–Bulgaria	3–0	(15–10, 15–12, 16–14)
6 Oct.	France–Greece	3–0	(15–8, 15–7, 15–0)
6 Oct.	Bulgaria–Romania	3–1	(15–8, 13–15, 15–5, 15–3)
6 Oct.	Hungary–Poland	3–0	(15–13, 15–8, 15–8)

	G	W/L	SW/SL	Pts.
1. Poland	5	4/1	12/3	9
2. France	5	4/1	12/6	9
3. Hungary	5	4/1	12/6	9
4. Bulgaria	5	2/3	9/10	7
5. Romania	5	1/4	7/12	6
6. Greece	5	0/5	0/15	5

Final group for 1–6 places (Arnhem)

3 Oct.	GDR–Italy	3–0	(16–14, 15–11, 15–3)
3 Oct.	Czechoslovakia–FRG	3–2	(11–15, 16–14, 15–10, 2–15, 15–10)
3 Oct.	USSR–Netherlands	3–2	(13–15, 9–15, 15–6, 15–9, 15–6)
4 Oct.	GDR–FRG	3–1	(15–4, 13–15, 15–3, 15–9)
4 Oct.	USSR–Italy	3–0	(15–9, 15–9, 15–6)
4 Oct.	Netherlands–Czechoslovakia	3–0	(15–11, 15–9, 15–11)
5 Oct.	Italy–FRG	3–1	(15–12, 6–15, 15–11, 15–10)
5 Oct.	USSR–Czechoslovakia	3–0	(15–9, 15–7, 15–8)
5 Oct.	GDR–Netherlands	3–0	(15–7, 15–4, 15–8)
6 Oct.	Czechoslovakia–Italy	3–1	(15–7, 15–9, 11–15, 15–8)
6 Oct.	Netherlands–FRG	3–1	(15–11, 13–15, 16–14, 15–13)
6 Oct.	USSR–GDR	3–0	(15–11, 15–10, 15–8)

	G	W/L	SW/SL	Pts.
1. USSR	5	5/0	15/2	10
2. GDR	5	4/1	12/5	9
3. Netherlands	5	3/2	11/7	8
4. Czechoslovakia	5	2/3	7/12	7
5. Italy	5	1/4	4/13	6
6. FRG	5	0/5	5/15	5

Final standings

	G	W/L	SW/SL
1. USSR	7	7/0	21/3
2. GDR	7	6/1	18/6
3. Netherlands	7	4/3	14/10
4. Czechoslovakia	7	4/3	13/13
5. Italy	7	3/4	10/17
6. FRG	7	2/5	11/17
7. Poland	7	4/3	14/9

(continued)

	G	W/L	SW/SL
8. France	7	4/3	13/12
9. Hungary	7	4/3	14/12
10. Bulgaria	7	2/5	11/16
11. Romania	7	2/5	12/15
12. Greece	7	0/7	0/21

Total: 12 teams, 42 games

Rosters of the medalists

USSR–Svetlana Badulina-Safronova, Elena Chebukina-Ovchinnikova, Irina Gorbatyuk, Diana Kachalova, Olga Krivosheeva, Marina Kumysh, Elena Kundaleva, Valentina Ogienko, Yuliya Saltsevich, Svetlana Shakhova, Tatyana Sidorenko, Elena Volkova; head coach: Vladimir Patkin

GDR–Maike Arlt, Monika Beu, Kathleen Bonath, Grit Jensen, Heike Jensen, Ramona Landgraf, Heike Lehmann, Ute Oldenburg, Ariane Radfan, Monika Schwarz, Dörte Stüdemann, Petra Zendel; head coach: Siegfried Köhler

Netherlands–Jantien Berg, Agnes Brunninkhuis, Martje de Vries, Marian Hagen, Bianca Hooymans, Carolien Keulen, Irene Klunder, Ingrid Piersma, Els Tuynman, Petra van der Linde, Ellen van Eijk, Helena van Eijkeren; head coach: Peter Murphy

XV EUROPEAN CHAMPIONSHIP
25 September–3 October 1987, Auderghem, Eupen, and Gent (Belgium)

Preliminary round

Group A (Eupen)

25 Sep.	USSR–Czechoslovakia	3–1	(15–13, 11–15, 15–1, 15–2)
25 Sep.	Netherlands–Poland	3–1	(14–16, 15–11, 15–11, 15–7)
25 Sep.	Italy–FRG	3–2	(15–7, 12–15, 9–15, 15–7, 15–12)
26 Sep.	USSR–FRG	3–0	(15–7, 15–3, 15–6)
26 Sep.	Czechoslovakia–Netherlands	3–1	(15–11, 12–15, 15–10, 15–1)
26 Sep.	Poland–Italy	3–1	(7–15, 15–13, 15–9, 15–7)
27 Sep.	Czechoslovakia–FRG	3–1	(15–11, 14–16, 15–10, 15–9)
27 Sep.	Netherlands–Italy	3–1	(15–4, 15–12, 13–15, 15–9)
27 Sep.	USSR–Poland	3–0	(15–3, 15–2, 15–6)
29 Sep.	USSR–Italy	3–0	(15–9, 15–4, 15–1)
29 Sep.	Czechoslovakia–Poland	3–0	(15–3, 15–13, 15–5)
29 Sep.	Netherlands–FRG	3–2	(8–15, 7–15, 15–13, 15–5, 15–11)
30 Sep.	Italy–Czechoslovakia	3–0	(15–11, 15–8, 15–4)
30 Sep.	FRG–Poland	3–0	(15–13, 15–13, 15–9)
30 Sep.	USSR–Netherlands	3–1	(15–10, 15–4, 13–15, 15–2)

	G	W/L	SW/SL	Pts.
1. USSR	5	5/0	15/2	10
2. Czechoslovakia	5	3/2	10/8	8
3. Netherlands	5	3/2	11/10	8
4. Italy	5	2/3	8/11	7
5. FRG	5	1/4	8/12	6
6. Poland	5	1/4	4/13	6

Group B (Gent)

25 Sep.	GDR–Bulgaria	3–0	(15–11, 16–14, 15–9)
25 Sep.	Romania–Belgium	3–0	(15–9, 15–3, 15–9)
25 Sep.	France–Hungary	3–2	(15–12, 15–10, 15–17, 11–15, 15–12)
26 Sep.	Bulgaria–Romania	3–0	(15–7, 15–11, 15–7)
26 Sep.	Hungary–Belgium	3–0	(15–7, 15–13, 15–3)
26 Sep.	GDR–France	3–0	(15–1, 15–8, 15–8)
27 Sep.	Bulgaria–Belgium	3–0	(15–11, 15–2, 15–7)
27 Sep.	France–Romania	3–0	(15–12, 15–6, 15–8)
27 Sep.	GDR–Hungary	3–0	(15–8, 15–6, 15–6)
29 Sep.	Bulgaria–Hungary	3–0	(15–7, 15–9, 15–13)
29 Sep.	GDR–Romania	3–0	(15–2, 15–9, 15–10)
29 Sep.	France–Belgium	3–0	(15–2, 15–6, 15–6)
30 Sep.	GDR–Belgium	3–0	(15–4, 15–6, 15–6)
30 Sep.	Romania–Hungary	3–1	(15–10, 15–10, 8–15, 15–5)
30 Sep.	Bulgaria–France	3–0	(15–9, 15–3, 15–10)

	G	W/L	SW/SL	Pts.
1. GDR	5	5/0	15/0	10
2. Bulgaria	5	4/1	12/3	9
3. France	5	3/2	9/8	8
4. Romania	5	2/3	6/10	7
5. Hungary	5	1/4	6/12	6
6. Belgium	5	0/5	0/15	5

Final round

Semifinals (9–12 places)

2 Oct.	Hungary–Poland	3–0	(15–10, 15–6, 15–10)	Auderghem
2 Oct.	FRG–Belgium	3–0	(15–9, 15–5, 15–8)	Auderghem

Game for 11th place

3 Oct.	Poland–Belgium	3–0	(15–6, 15–9, 15–11)	Auderghem

Game for 9th place

3 Oct.	FRG–Hungary	3–1	(15–4, 15–9, 13–15, 15–10)	Auderghem

Semifinals (5–8 places)

2 Oct.	Italy–France	3–0	(15–10, 15–13, 15–6)	Auderghem
2 Oct.	Netherlands–Romania	3–2	(15–5, 10–15, 11–15, 15–13, 15–9)	Auderghem

Game for 7th place

3 Oct.	France–Romania	3–2	(15–12, 15–17, 15–10, 11–15, 15–12)	Auderghem

Game for 5th place

3 Oct.	Netherlands–Italy	3–1	(15–5, 15–12, 12–15, 15–13)	Auderghem

Semifinals (1–4 places)

2 Oct.	USSR–Bulgaria	3–0	(15–9, 15–6, 15–10)	Gent
2 Oct.	GDR–Czechoslovakia	3–0	(15–9, 15–13, 15–2)	Gent

Game for 3rd place

3 Oct.	Czechoslovakia–Bulgaria	3–0	(15–10, 15–10, 15–12)	Gent

Final

3 Oct.	GDR–USSR	3–2	(8–15, 15–9, 18–20, 15–9, 15–11)	Gent

Final standings

	G	W/L	SW/SL
1. GDR	7	7/0	21/2
2. USSR	7	6/1	20/5
3. Czechoslovakia	7	4/3	13/11
4. Bulgaria	7	4/3	12/9
5. Netherlands	7	5/2	17/13
6. Italy	7	3/4	12/14
7. France	7	4/3	12/13
8. Romania	7	2/5	10/16
9. FRG	7	3/4	14/13
10. Hungary	7	2/5	10/15
11. Poland	7	2/5	7/16
12. Belgium	7	0/7	0/21

Total: 12 teams, 42 games

Rosters of the medalists

GDR–Maike Arlt, Monika Beu, Kathleen Bonath, Grit Jensen, Heike Jensen, Susanne Lahme, Kathrin Langschwager, Anke Lindemann, Ute Oldenburg, Ariane Radfan, Steffi Schmidt, Dörte Stüdemann; head coach: Siegfried Köhler

USSR–Svetlana Badulina-Safronova, Elena Chebukina-Ovchinnikova, Irina Gorbatyuk, Diana Kachalova, Irina Kirillova-Parkhomchuk, Marina Kiryakova, Olga Krivosheeva, Marina Kumysh, Marina Nikulina-Pankova, Valentina Ogienko, Irina Smirnova-Ilchenko, Elena Volkova; head coach: Vladimir Patkin

Czechoslovakia–Daniela Cuníková, Eva Dostálová, Leona Goldemundová, Vladěna Holubová, Stanislava Králová, Táňa Krempaská, Romana Kumpochová, Simona Mandelová, Ivana Matějíčková, Pavlína Šenoldová, Eva Trnková, Lucie Václavíková; head coach: Josef Stolařík

XVI EUROPEAN CHAMPIONSHIP
2–10 September 1989, Hamburg, Karlsruhe, Sindelfingen, and Stuttgart (FRG)

Preliminary round

Group A (Hamburg)

2 Sep.	USSR–Turkey	3–0	(15–5, 15–9, 15–8)
2 Sep.	Romania–Yugoslavia	3–0	(15–4, 15–4, 16–14)
2 Sep.	FRG–Finland	3–0	(15–6, 15–11, 15–8)
3 Sep.	USSR–Romania	3–0	(15–7, 16–14, 16–14)
3 Sep.	FRG–Yugoslavia	3–0	(15–3, 15–5, 15–3)
3 Sep.	Turkey–Finland	3–1	(5–15, 15–9, 16–14, 15–8)
4 Sep.	USSR–Yugoslavia	3–0	(15–12, 17–16, 15–8)
4 Sep.	Romania–Finland	3–0	(15–9, 15–10, 15–6)
4 Sep.	FRG–Turkey	3–0	(15–7, 15–10, 15–8)
6 Sep.	USSR–Finland	3–0	(15–3, 15–1, 15–7)
6 Sep.	Romania–FRG	3–2	(15–13, 8–15, 15–13, 13–15, 16–14)
6 Sep.	Yugoslavia–Turkey	3–0	(15–0, 15–0, 15–0)*
7 Sep.	Yugoslavia–Finland	3–0	(15–10, 15–7, 15–3)
7 Sep.	Romania–Turkey	3–1	(15–12, 9–15, 15–7, 15–12)
7 Sep.	USSR–FRG	3–0	(15–9, 15–7, 15–4)

*The original result of the game—Yugoslavia won 3–0 (15–5, 16–14, 15–12)—was changed because Turkish player Gamze Adanır tested positive for doping after the game.

	G	W/L	SW/SL	Pts.
1. USSR	5	5/0	15/0	10
2. Romania	5	4/1	12/6	9
3. FRG	5	3/2	11/6	8
4. Yugoslavia	5	2/3	6/9	7
5. Turkey	5	1/4	4/13	6
6. Finland	5	0/5	1/15	5

Group B (Karlsruhe)

2 Sep.	Bulgaria–France	3–1	(15–5, 15–10, 13–15, 15–2)
2 Sep.	Italy–Czechoslovakia	3–0	(15–9, 15–11, 15–13)
2 Sep.	GDR–Poland	3–0	(15–6, 15–7, 15–9)
3 Sep.	Italy–France	3–1	(15–10, 14–16, 15–2, 15–8)
3 Sep.	Czechoslovakia–Poland	3–1	(15–12, 15–12, 12–15, 15–10)
3 Sep.	GDR–Bulgaria	3–0	(15–11, 15–12, 15–9)
4 Sep.	Italy–Poland	3–0	(15–9, 15–5, 15–10)
4 Sep.	Czechoslovakia–Bulgaria	3–1	(15–3, 15–8, 12–15, 15–10)
4 Sep.	GDR–France	3–1	(15–6, 15–4, 14–16, 15–3)
6 Sep.	Bulgaria–Poland	3–1	(15–3, 14–16, 15–13, 15–10)
6 Sep.	GDR–Italy	3–0	(15–11, 15–13, 15–4)
6 Sep.	Czechoslovakia–France	3–1	(15–9, 13–15, 15–4, 15–10)
7 Sep.	Bulgaria–Italy	3–1	(15–12, 16–14, 12–15, 15–8)
7 Sep.	GDR–Czechoslovakia	3–2	(15–6, 15–4, 10–15, 8–15, 15–12)
7 Sep.	Poland–France	3–1	(15–9, 15–11, 11–15, 15–12)

	G	W/L	SW/SL	Pts.
1. GDR	5	5/0	15/3	10
2. Italy	5	3/2	10/7	8
3. Czechoslovakia	5	3/2	11/9	8
4. Bulgaria	5	3/2	10/9	8
5. Poland	5	1/4	5/13	6
6. France	5	0/5	5/15	5

Final round

Semifinals (9–12 places)

9 Sep.	France–Turkey	3–1	(15–5, 15–8, 14–16, 15–11)	Sindelfingen
9 Sep.	Poland–Finland	3–0	(15–7, 15–2, 15–3)	Sindelfingen

Game for 11th place

10 Sep.	Turkey–Finland	3–1	(15–6, 15–8, 12–15, 16–14)	Sindelfingen

Game for 9th place

10 Sep.	Poland–France	3–2	(15–12, 12–15, 17–15, 7–15, 15–13)	Sindelfingen

Semifinals (5–8 places)

9 Sep.	Czechoslovakia–Yugoslavia	3–1	(15–4, 15–12, 16–17, 15–9)	Stuttgart
9 Sep.	FRG–Bulgaria	3–1	(12–15, 15–9, 16–14, 15–6)	Stuttgart

Game for 7th place

10 Sep.	Bulgaria–Yugoslavia	3–0	(15–11, 15–9, 15–3)	Stuttgart

Game for 5th place

10 Sep.	Czechoslovakia–FRG	3–0	(15–4, 16–14, 15–7)	Stuttgart

Semifinals (1–4 places)

9 Sep.	USSR–Italy	3–0	(15–10, 15–7, 15–8)	Stuttgart
9 Sep.	GDR–Romania	3–0	(17–15, 15–6, 15–4)	Stuttgart

Game for 3rd place

10 Sep.	Italy–Romania	3–0	(15–5, 15–6, 15–3)	Stuttgart

Final

10 Sep.	USSR–GDR	3–1	(8–15, 16–14, 15–13, 15–13)	Stuttgart

Final standings

	G	W/L	SW/SL
1. USSR	7	7/0	21/1
2. GDR	7	6/1	19/6
3. Italy	7	4/3	13/10
4. Romania	7	4/3	12/12
5. Czechoslovakia	7	5/2	17/10
6. FRG	7	4/3	14/10
7. Bulgaria	7	4/3	14/12
8. Yugoslavia	7	2/5	7/15
9. Poland	7	3/4	11/15
10. France	7	1/6	10/19
11. Turkey	7	2/5	8/17
12. Finland	7	0/7	2/21

Total: 12 teams, 42 games

Rosters of the medalists

USSR–Elena Batukhtina-Tyurina, Elena Chebukina-Ovchinnikova, Inna Dashuk, Irina Kirillova-Parkhomchuk, Svetlana Korytova, Galina Lebedeva, Valentina Ogienko, Irina Shcherbakova, Tatyana Sidorenko, Irina Smirnova-Ilchenko, Olga Tolmachyova, Marina Vyalitsyna; head coach: Nikolay Karpol

GDR–Annette Heymann, Grit Jensen-Naumann, Anne Krüger, Susanne Lahme, Ute Oldenburg-Steppin, Ines Pianka, Manuela Pietsch, Constanze Radfan, Christina Schultz, Dörte Stüdemann-Techel, Katja Weimann, Brit Wiedemann; head coach: Siegfried Köhler

Italy–Manuela Benelli, Liliana Bernardi, Sabrina Bertini, Helga Chiostrini, Cinzia Flamigni, Barbara Fontanesi, Mirna Marabissi, Fabiana Mele, Patrizia Prati, Fanny Pudioli, Sabina Turrini, Alessandra Zambelli; head coach: Sergio Guerra

XVII EUROPEAN CHAMPIONSHIP
28 September–6 October 1991, Bari, Ravenna, and Rome (Italy)

Preliminary round

Group A (Ravenna)

28 Sep.	Greece–France	3–2	(15–9, 8–15, 10–15, 15–5, 15–13)
28 Sep.	USSR–Bulgaria	3–0	(15–7, 15–2, 15–11)
28 Sep.	Italy–Albania	3–0	(15–3, 15–12, 15–1)
29 Sep.	USSR–France	3–0	(15–6, 15–11, 15–13)
29 Sep.	Italy–Bulgaria	3–0	(15–7, 15–9, 15–9)
29 Sep.	Greece–Albania	3–1	(15–7, 6–15, 15–8, 16–14)
30 Sep.	Bulgaria–France	3–1	(12–15, 16–14, 15–9, 15–9)
30 Sep.	USSR–Albania	3–0	(15–2, 15–7, 15–6)
30 Sep.	Italy–Greece	3–0	(15–1, 15–6, 15–7)
2 Oct.	Italy–France	3–0	(15–6, 15–6, 15–12)
2 Oct.	USSR–Greece	3–0	(15–7, 15–2, 15–3)
2 Oct.	Bulgaria–Albania	3–1	(15–7, 6–15, 15–11, 15–3)
3 Oct.	Bulgaria–Greece	3–1	(13–15, 15–5, 15–7, 15–3)
3 Oct.	France–Albania	3–0	(15–4, 15–1, 15–9)
3 Oct.	USSR–Italy	3–0	(15–6, 15–6, 15–9)

	G	W/L	SW/SL	Pts.
1. USSR	5	5/0	15/0	10
2. Italy	5	4/1	12/3	9
3. Bulgaria	5	3/2	9/9	8
4. Greece	5	2/3	7/12	7
5. France	5	1/4	6/12	6
6. Albania	5	0/5	2/15	5

Group B (Bari)

28 Sep.	Poland–Yugoslavia	3–2	(13–15, 11–15, 15–4, 15–7, 15–5)
28 Sep.	Netherlands–Czechoslovakia	3–0	(17–15, 17–15, 15–13)
28 Sep.	Germany–Romania	3–1	(15–4, 15–6, 12–15, 15–12)
29 Sep.	Netherlands–Poland	3–0	(15–7, 15–8, 15–4)
29 Sep.	Czechoslovakia–Germany	3–1	(15–11, 3–15, 15–10, 15–3)
29 Sep.	Romania–Yugoslavia	3–0	(15–9, 15–7, 15–2)
30 Sep.	Czechoslovakia–Poland	3–2	(15–8, 3–15, 15–9, 9–15, 15–6)
30 Sep.	Netherlands–Romania	3–0	(15–10, 15–7, 15–11)
30 Sep.	Germany–Yugoslavia	3–0	(15–6, 15–2, 15–1)
2 Oct.	Romania–Czechoslovakia	3–1	(15–11, 15–10, 6–15, 15–2)
2 Oct.	Netherlands–Yugoslavia	3–0	(15–4, 15–4, 15–1)
2 Oct.	Germany–Poland	3–0	(15–12, 15–8, 15–10)
3 Oct.	Germany–Netherlands	3–2	(12–15, 16–14, 15–4, 14–16, 15–13)
3 Oct.	Czechoslovakia–Yugoslavia	3–0	(15–3, 15–6, 15–2)
3 Oct.	Romania–Poland	3–1	(15–13, 16–17, 15–4, 15–11)

	G	W/L	SW/SL	Pts.
1. Netherlands	5	4/1	14/3	9
2. Germany	5	4/1	13/6	9
3. Romania	5	3/2	10/8	8
4. Czechoslovakia	5	3/2	10/9	8
5. Poland	5	1/4	6/14	6
6. Yugoslavia	5	0/5	2/15	5

Final round for 1–8 places (Rome)

Semifinals (5–8 places)

5 Oct.	Romania–Greece	3–1	(15–9, 15–8, 5–15, 15–10)
5 Oct.	Czechoslovakia–Bulgaria	3–1	(15–5, 15–7, 14–16, 15–12)

Game for 7th place

6 Oct.	Bulgaria–Greece	3–2	(15–12, 15–11, 12–15, 11–15, 15–13)

Game for 5th place

6 Oct.	Czechoslovakia–Romania	3–1	(15–10, 5–15, 16–14, 15–10)

Semifinals (1–4 places)

5 Oct.	Netherlands–Italy	3–1	(12–15, 15–6, 15–7, 16–14)
5 Oct.	USSR–Germany	3–0	(15–6, 15–3, 15–11)

Game for 3rd place

| 6 Oct. | Germany–Italy | 3–1 | (9–15, 15–8, 15–7, 15–10) |

Final

| 6 Oct. | USSR–Netherlands | 3–0 | (15–4, 15–2, 15–3) |

Final standings

	G	W/L	SW/SL
1. USSR	7	7/0	21/0
2. Netherlands	7	5/2	17/7
3. Germany	7	5/2	16/10
4. Italy	7	4/3	14/9
5. Czechoslovakia	7	5/2	16/11
6. Romania	7	4/3	14/12
7. Bulgaria	7	4/3	13/14
8. Greece	7	2/5	10/18
9. France	5	1/4	6/12
9. Poland	5	1/4	6/14
11. Albania	5	0/5	2/15
11. Yugoslavia	5	0/5	2/15

Total: 12 teams, 38 games

Rosters of the medalists

USSR–Elena Batukhtina-Tyurina, Elena Chebukina-Ovchinnikova, Inna Dashuk, Inessa Emelyanova-Sargsyan, Svetlana Korytova, Galina Lebedeva, Natalya Morozova, Marina Nikulina-Pankova, Valentina Ogienko, Tatyana Sidorenko, Irina Smirnova-Ilchenko, Svetlana Vasilevskaya; head coach: Nikolay Karpol

Netherlands–Cintha Boersma, Erna Brinkman, Heleen Crielaard, Marjolein de Jong, Kirsten Gleis, Aafke Hament, Femke Hoekstra, Vera Koenen, Irena Machovcak, Madelon Maurice, Ingrid Piersma, Henriëtte Weersing; head coach: Peter Murphy

Germany–Maike Arlt, Silka Jäger, Susanne Lahme, Michaela Luckner, Ute Oldenburg-Steppin, Ines Pianka, Ariane Radfan, Constanze Radfan, Renate Riek, Christina Schultz, Karin Steyaert, Brit Wiedemann; head coach: Siegfried Köhler

XVIII EUROPEAN CHAMPIONSHIP
24 September–2 October 1993, Brno and Zlín (Czech Republic)

Preliminary round

Group A (Brno)

24 Sep.	Italy–Netherlands	3–2	(15–13, 8–15, 15–1, 15–17, 15–8)
24 Sep.	Czechoslovakia–Bulgaria	3–1	(15–8, 8–15, 17–16, 15–10)
24 Sep.	Croatia–Latvia	3–1	(15–13, 11–15, 16–14, 15–12)
25 Sep.	Bulgaria–Netherlands	3–1	(15–11, 12–15, 15–10, 15–9)
25 Sep.	Czechoslovakia–Latvia	3–0	(15–11, 15–13, 15–11)
25 Sep.	Italy–Croatia	3–0	(15–5, 15–8, 15–7)
26 Sep.	Latvia–Bulgaria	3–2	(8–15, 15–8, 15–2, 15–17, 15–7)
26 Sep.	Czechoslovakia–Italy	3–1	(11–15, 15–13, 15–7, 15–7)
26 Sep.	Netherlands–Croatia	3–1	(15–11, 15–8, 13–15, 15–1)
28 Sep.	Bulgaria–Italy	3–2	(15–5, 10–15, 15–9, 7–15, 15–6)
28 Sep.	Croatia–Czechoslovakia	3–1	(4–15, 15–2, 15–13, 15–13)
28 Sep.	Netherlands–Latvia	3–2	(13–15, 15–4, 8–15, 15–8, 15–8)
29 Sep.	Croatia–Bulgaria	3–0	(15–7, 15–11, 16–14)
29 Sep.	Italy–Latvia	3–0	(16–14, 15–13, 16–14)
29 Sep.	Netherlands–Czechoslovakia	3–2	(15–6, 13–15, 12–15, 15–10, 15–9)

	G	W/L	SW/SL	Pts.
1. Italy	5	3/2	12/8	8
2. Czechoslovakia	5	3/2	12/8	8
3. Croatia	5	3/2	10/8	8
4. Netherlands	5	3/2	12/11	8
5. Bulgaria	5	2/3	9/12	7
6. Latvia	5	1/4	6/14	6

Group B (Zlín)

24 Sep.	Germany–Greece	3–0	(15–4, 15–5, 15–7)
24 Sep.	Ukraine–Russia	3–0	(15–10, 15–13, 15–7)
24 Sep.	Belarus–Romania	3–1	(15–8, 15–8, 14–16, 17–16)
25 Sep.	Ukraine–Germany	3–0	(15–9, 15–8, 15–5)
25 Sep.	Russia–Belarus	3–0	(15–5, 15–3, 15–6)
25 Sep.	Romania–Greece	3–2	(13–15, 16–14, 15–17, 15–2, 15–9)
26 Sep.	Ukraine–Belarus	3–1	(15–7, 15–13, 9–15, 15–6)
26 Sep.	Russia–Greece	3–1	(15–5, 10–15, 15–7, 15–3)
26 Sep.	Germany–Romania	3–0	(15–4, 15–10, 15–8)
28 Sep.	Ukraine–Greece	3–1	(15–5, 15–2, 12–15, 15–6)
28 Sep.	Russia–Romania	3–0	(15–4, 15–7, 15–5)
28 Sep.	Germany–Belarus	3–2	(12–15, 15–3, 12–15, 15–9, 15–10)

(continued)

Group B (Zlín) (continued)

29 Sep.	Ukraine–Romania	3–1	(15–7, 15–12, 10–15, 15–12)
29 Sep.	Russia–Germany	3–0	(15–3, 15–7, 15–9)
29 Sep.	Belarus–Greece	3–1	(15–5, 15–4, 10–15, 15–5)

	G	W/L	SW/SL	Pts.
1. Ukraine	5	5/0	15/3	10
2. Russia	5	4/1	12/4	9
3. Germany	5	3/2	9/8	8
4. Belarus	5	2/3	9/11	7
5. Romania	5	1/4	5/14	6
6. Greece	5	0/5	5/15	5

Final round for 1–8 places (Brno)

Semifinals (5–8 places)

1 Oct.	Croatia–Belarus	3–0	(15–12, 16–14, 15–4)
1 Oct.	Germany–Netherlands	3–2	(15–12, 13–15, 15–4, 15–17, 15–11)

Game for 7th place

2 Oct.	Netherlands–Belarus	3–0	(15–10, 15–3, 15–12)

Game for 5th place

2 Oct.	Germany–Croatia	3–2	(15–9, 13–15, 13–15, 15–9, 15–9)

Semifinals (1–4 places)

1 Oct.	Czechoslovakia–Ukraine	3–2	(14–16, 15–5, 15–11, 6–15, 22–20)
1 Oct.	Russia–Italy	3–1	(15–9, 12–15, 16–14, 15–2)

Game for 3rd place

2 Oct.	Ukraine–Italy	3–1	(15–17, 15–8, 15–6, 17–15)

Final

2 Oct.	Russia–Czechoslovakia	3–0	(17–15, 15–3, 15–6)

Final standings

	G	W/L	SW/SL
1. Russia	7	6/1	18/5
2. Czechoslovakia	7	4/3	15/13
3. Ukraine	7	6/1	20/7

(continued)

	G	W/L	SW/SL
4. Italy	7	3/4	14/14
5. Germany	7	5/2	15/12
6. Croatia	7	4/3	15/11
7. Netherlands	7	4/3	17/14
8. Belarus	7	2/5	9/17
9. Bulgaria	5	2/3	9/12
9. Romania	5	1/4	5/14
11. Latvia	5	1/4	6/14
11. Greece	5	0/5	5/15

Total: 12 teams, 38 games

Rosters of the medalists

Russia–Evgeniya Artamonova, Elena Batukhtina-Tyurina, Elena Chebukina-Ovchinnikova, Tatyana Grachyova, Mariya Likhtenshteyn, Tatyana Menshova, Natalya Morozova, Marina Nikulina-Pankova, Valentina Ogienko, Irina Smirnova-Ilchenko, Yuliya Timonova, Elizaveta Tishchenko; head coach: Nikolay Karpol

Czechoslovakia–Jaroslava Bajerová, Jana Jurášová, Stanislava Králová, Jana Pechová, Marcela Ritschelová, Eva Šilhanová, Eva Štěpančíková, Lucie Václavíková, Michaela Večerková, Ester Volicerová, Eva Vostřejšová, Zdena Zimmermannová; head coach: Milan Kafka

Ukraine–Maryna Dubinina, Tetyana Ilyina, Hanna Kalashnykova, Olha Kolomiyets, Alla Kravets, Vita Mateshchuk, Mariya Polyakova, Iryna Pukhalska, Svitlana Sulym, Lyudmyla Trotsyuk, Yuliya Volivach, Olena Voronkina; head coach: Volodymyr Buzayev

XIX EUROPEAN CHAMPIONSHIP
23 September–1 October 1995, Arnhem and Groningen (Netherlands)

Preliminary round

Group A (Groningen)

23 Sep.	Germany–Ukraine	3–1	(15–6, 14–16, 15–8, 15–10)
23 Sep.	Belarus–Poland	3–1	(15–6, 15–8, 12–15, 15–12)
23 Sep.	Russia–Latvia	3–0	(15–5, 15–4, 15–1)
24 Sep.	Germany–Belarus	3–1	(12–15, 15–11, 15–6, 15–4)
24 Sep.	Ukraine–Latvia	3–1	(15–9, 15–3, 14–16, 15–5)
24 Sep.	Russia–Poland	3–0	(15–12, 15–7, 15–10)
25 Sep.	Ukraine–Belarus	3–1	(15–8, 6–15, 15–9, 15–6)
25 Sep.	Russia–Germany	3–0	(15–5, 15–4, 15–5)

(continued)

Group A (Groningen) (continued)

25 Sep.	Poland–Latvia	3–1	(15–2, 15–9, 4–15, 16–14)
27 Sep.	Russia–Belarus	3–0	(15–12, 15–7, 15–12)
27 Sep.	Germany–Latvia	3–0	(15–9, 15–1, 15–2)
27 Sep.	Ukraine–Poland	3–2	(15–10, 11–15, 12–15, 15–12, 15–8)
28 Sep.	Belarus–Latvia	3–0	(15–5, 15–13, 15–6)
28 Sep.	Germany–Poland	3–1	(15–13, 15–7, 8–15, 15–12)
28 Sep.	Russia–Ukraine	3–0	(17–15, 15–12, 15–10)

	G	W/L	SW/SL	Pts.
1. Russia	5	5/0	15/0	10
2. Germany	5	4/1	12/6	9
3. Ukraine	5	3/2	10/10	8
4. Belarus	5	2/3	8/10	7
5. Poland	5	1/4	7/13	6
6. Latvia	5	0/5	2/15	5

Group B (Arnhem)

23 Sep.	Netherlands–Bulgaria	3–1	(15–9, 15–9, 8–15, 15–10)
23 Sep.	Italy–Czech Republic	3–1	(9–15, 15–8, 17–15, 15–6)
23 Sep.	Croatia–Turkey	3–0	(15–10, 15–6, 15–10)
24 Sep.	Netherlands–Italy	3–0	(15–10, 15–3, 15–5)
24 Sep.	Croatia–Bulgaria	3–1	(15–9, 15–8, 12–15, 15–11)
24 Sep.	Czech Republic–Turkey	3–2	(15–7, 9–15, 11–15, 15–2, 21–19)
25 Sep.	Bulgaria–Italy	3–1	(15–6, 15–4, 11–15, 15–2)
25 Sep.	Croatia–Czech Republic	3–0	(15–11, 15–5, 15–10)
25 Sep.	Netherlands–Turkey	3–0	(15–11, 15–7, 15–12)
27 Sep.	Bulgaria–Czech Republic	3–0	(15–13, 15–3, 15–4)
27 Sep.	Italy–Turkey	3–0	(15–10, 15–12, 15–7)
27 Sep.	Croatia–Netherlands	3–2	(12–15, 15–11, 15–11, 12–15, 15–11)
28 Sep.	Bulgaria–Turkey	3–0	(15–13, 15–10, 15–3)
28 Sep.	Croatia–Italy	3–1	(15–6, 12–15, 15–8, 15–7)
28 Sep.	Netherlands–Czech Republic	3–0	(15–7, 15–4, 15–13)

	G	W/L	SW/SL	Pts.
1. Croatia	5	5/0	15/4	10
2. Netherlands	5	4/1	14/4	9
3. Bulgaria	5	3/2	11/7	8
4. Italy	5	2/3	8/10	7
5. Czech Republic	5	1/4	4/14	6
6. Turkey	5	0/5	2/15	5

Final round for 1–8 places (Arnhem)

Semifinals (5–8 places)

30 Sep.	Italy–Ukraine	3–1	(15–9, 8–15, 15–8, 15–13)
30 Sep.	Bulgaria–Belarus	3–0	(15–11, 15–7, 15–13)

Game for 7th place

1 Oct.	Ukraine–Belarus	3–0	(16–14, 15–10, 15–8)

Game for 5th place

1 Oct.	Bulgaria–Italy	3–2	(10–15, 15–9, 15–5, 4–15, 15–8)

Semifinals (1–4 places)

30 Sep.	Netherlands–Russia	3–1	(15–7, 15–7, 12–15, 15–7)
30 Sep.	Croatia–Germany	3–0	(15–7, 15–3, 15–2)

Game for 3rd place

1 Oct.	Russia–Germany	3–0	(15–6, 15–2, 15–10)

Final

1 Oct.	Netherlands–Croatia	3–0	(15–7, 15–13, 15–2)

Final standings

	G	W/L	SW/SL
1. Netherlands	7	6/1	20/5
2. Croatia	7	6/1	18/7
3. Russia	7	6/1	19/3
4. Germany	7	4/3	12/12
5. Bulgaria	7	5/2	17/9
6. Italy	7	3/4	13/14
7. Ukraine	7	4/3	14/13
8. Belarus	7	2/5	8/16
9. Poland	5	1/4	7/13
9. Czech Republic	5	1/4	4/14
11. Latvia	5	0/5	2/15
11. Turkey	5	0/5	2/15

Total: 12 teams, 38 games

Rosters of the medalists

Netherlands–Cintha Boersma, Erna Brinkman, Marjolein de Jong, Jolanda Elshof, Riëtte Fledderus, Jerine Fleurke, Petra Groenland, Marrit Leenstra, Elles Leferink, Irena Machovcak, Ingrid Visser, Henriëtte Weersing; head coach: Bert Goedkoop

Croatia–Tatjana Andrić, Elena Chebukina, Barbara Jelić, Željka Jovičić, Gordana Jurcan, Dušica Kalaba, Irina Kirillova, Slavica Kuzmanić, Snježana Mijić, Nataša Osmokrović, Marijana Ribičić, Vanesa Sršen-Kumar; head coach: Ivica Jelić

Russia–Evgeniya Artamonova, Elena Batukhtina-Tyurina, Inessa Emelyanova-Sargsyan, Elena Godina, Tatyana Grachyova, Mariya Likhtenshteyn, Tatyana Menshova, Natalya Morozova, Valentina Ogienko, Aleksandra Sorokina-Korukovets, Yuliya Timonova, Elizaveta Tishchenko; head coach: Nikolay Karpol

XX EUROPEAN CHAMPIONSHIP
27 September–5 October 1997, Brno and Zlín (Czech Republic)

Preliminary round

Group A (Zlín)

27 Sep.	Bulgaria–Netherlands	3–0	(15–5, 15–9, 15–10)
27 Sep.	Poland–Latvia	3–0	(15–7, 15–9, 15–10)
27 Sep.	Russia–Belarus	3–1	(15–11, 15–3, 9–15, 15–4)
28 Sep.	Bulgaria–Poland	3–0	(15–7, 15–8, 15–5)
28 Sep.	Latvia–Belarus	3–0	(15–12, 16–14, 15–8)
28 Sep.	Russia–Netherlands	3–0	(15–11, 15–5, 15–5)
29 Sep.	Belarus–Bulgaria	3–2	(15–13, 3–15, 15–13, 9–15, 15–11)
29 Sep.	Russia–Latvia	3–0	(15–2, 15–5, 15–8)
29 Sep.	Poland–Netherlands	3–1	(15–10, 4–15, 15–13, 15–4)
1 Oct.	Russia–Bulgaria	3–0	(15–3, 15–10, 15–12)
1 Oct.	Poland–Belarus	3–0	(15–5, 15–7, 15–12)
1 Oct.	Latvia–Netherlands	3–2	(12–15, 13–15, 15–7, 15–10, 15–13)
2 Oct.	Russia–Poland	3–1	(15–6, 15–13, 3–15, 15–7)
2 Oct.	Netherlands–Belarus	3–0	(15–4, 15–12, 15–10)
2 Oct.	Bulgaria–Latvia	3–0	(15–2, 15–9, 15–6)

	G	W/L	SW/SL	Pts.
1. Russia	5	5/0	15/2	10
2. Bulgaria	5	3/2	11/6	8
3. Poland	5	3/2	10/7	8
4. Latvia	5	2/3	6/11	7
5. Netherlands	5	1/4	6/12	6
6. Belarus	5	1/4	4/14	6

Group B (Brno)

27 Sep.	Italy–Ukraine	3–0	(15–12, 15–9, 15–11)
27 Sep.	Czech Republic–Romania	3–0	(15–11, 15–7, 15–8)
27 Sep.	Croatia–Germany	3–0	(15–7, 15–2, 15–9)
28 Sep.	Ukraine–Romania	3–0	(15–11, 15–10, 15–13)
28 Sep.	Croatia–Czech Republic	3–0	(15–4, 15–9, 15–8)
28 Sep.	Italy–Germany	3–1	(15–10, 14–16, 16–14, 15–10)
29 Sep.	Croatia–Romania	3–0	(15–7, 15–6, 15–13)
29 Sep.	Czech Republic–Italy	3–0	(15–9, 15–5, 15–7)
29 Sep.	Germany–Ukraine	3–0	(15–7, 15–9, 15–13)
1 Oct.	Italy–Romania	3–0	(15–5, 15–10, 15–7)
1 Oct.	Czech Republic–Germany	3–0	(15–10, 15–12, 15–3)
1 Oct.	Croatia–Ukraine	3–0	(15–7, 15–11, 15–6)
2 Oct.	Romania–Germany	3–0	(17–15, 16–14, 15–7)
2 Oct.	Croatia–Italy	3–1	(16–14, 14–16, 15–13, 15–7)
2 Oct.	Ukraine–Czech Republic	3–1	(11–15, 16–14, 15–11, 15–12)

	G	W/L	SW/SL	Pts.
1. Croatia	5	5/0	15/1	10
2. Czech Republic	5	3/2	10/6	8
3. Italy	5	3/2	10/7	8
4. Ukraine	5	2/3	6/10	7
5. Germany	5	1/4	4/12	6
6. Romania	5	1/4	3/12	6

Final round for 1–8 places (Brno)

Semifinals (5–8 places)

4 Oct.	Poland–Ukraine	3–0	(15–8, 15–10, 15–13)
4 Oct.	Italy–Latvia	3–0	(15–9, 15–4, 15–12)

Game for 7th place

5 Oct.	Ukraine–Latvia	3–1	(13–15, 15–5, 15–9, 15–7)

Game for 5th place

5 Oct.	Italy–Poland	3–0	(15–13, 15–9, 15–10)

Semifinals (1–4 places)

4 Oct.	Russia–Czech Republic	3–0	(15–4, 15–2, 15–1)
4 Oct.	Croatia–Bulgaria	3–1	(15–2, 10–15, 15–12, 15–12)

Game for 3rd place

5 Oct.   Czech Republic–Bulgaria   3–0   (15–13, 15–10, 15–7)

Final

5 Oct.   Russia–Croatia   3–0   (15–7, 15–12, 15–9)

Final standings

	G	W/L	SW/SL
1. Russia	7	7/0	21/2
2. Croatia	7	6/1	18/5
3. Czech Republic	7	4/3	13/9
4. Bulgaria	7	3/4	12/12
5. Poland	7	4/3	13/10
6. Italy	7	5/2	16/7
7. Ukraine	7	3/4	9/14
8. Latvia	7	2/5	7/17
9. Netherlands	5	1/4	6/12
9. Germany	5	1/4	4/12
11. Belarus	5	1/4	4/14
11. Romania	5	1/4	3/12

Total: 12 teams, 38 games

Rosters of the medalists

Russia–Evgeniya Artamonova, Elena Batukhtina-Tyurina, Anastasiya Belikova, Olga Chukanova, Elena Godina, Tatyana Grachyova, Tatyana Menshova, Natalya Morozova, Natalya Safronova, Irina Tebenikhina, Elizaveta Tishchenko, Elena Vasilevskaya; head coach: Nikolay Karpol

Croatia–Marija Anzulović, Elena Chebukina, Biljana Gligorović, Barbara Jelić, Ana Kaštelan, Irina Kirillova, Slavica Kuzmanić, Snježana Mijić, Sonja Percan, Marijana Ribičić, Tatyana Sidorenko, Vanesa Sršen-Kumar; head coach: Ivica Jelić

Czech Republic–Jaroslava Bajerová, Kateřina Bucková, Jana Drštková, Světlana Janáčková, Kateřina Jenčková, Zdeňka Mocová, Marcela Ritschelová, Martina Schwobová, Eva Štěpančíková, Jana Vávrová, Michaela Večerková, Ester Volicerová; head coach: Pavel Řeřábek

XXI EUROPEAN CHAMPIONSHIP
20–25 September 1999, Perugia and Rome (Italy)

Preliminary round

Group A (Rome)

20 Sep.	Italy–Romania	3–1	(21–25, 25–20, 25–17, 25–17)
20 Sep.	Russia–Netherlands	3–0	(26–24, 25–11, 25–20)
21 Sep.	Italy–Netherlands	3–1	(25–17, 22–25, 25–19, 25–17)
21 Sep.	Russia–Romania	3–0	(25–17, 25–18, 25–20)
22 Sep.	Russia–Italy	3–1	(22–25, 25–21, 27–25, 25–19)
22 Sep.	Netherlands–Romania	3–2	(17–25, 23–25, 25–21, 25–21, 15–9)

	G	W/L	SW/SL	Pts.
1. Russia	3	3/0	9/1	6
2. Italy	3	2/1	7/5	5
3. Netherlands	3	1/2	4/8	4
4. Romania	3	0/3	3/9	3

Group B (Perugia)

20 Sep.	Croatia–Bulgaria	3–0	(25–21, 25–19, 25–17)
20 Sep.	Germany–Poland	3–2	(21–25, 25–14, 25–19, 16–25, 15–13)
21 Sep.	Bulgaria–Germany	3–1	(25–22, 25–21, 21–25, 25–21)
21 Sep.	Croatia–Poland	3–0	(26–24, 26–24, 25–23)
22 Sep.	Poland–Bulgaria	3–2	(25–23, 15–25, 32–30, 22–25, 15–11)
22 Sep.	Germany–Croatia	3–0	(25–19, 25–23, 25–13)

	G	W/L	SW/SL	Pts.
1. Croatia	3	2/1	6/3	5
2. Germany	3	2/1	7/5	5
3. Bulgaria	3	1/2	5/7	4
4. Poland	3	1/2	5/8	4

Final round (Rome)

Semifinals (5–8 places)

24 Sep.	Romania–Bulgaria	3–1	(25–22, 25–21, 21–25, 25–22)
24 Sep.	Netherlands–Poland	3–1	(29–27, 22–25, 25–23, 25–23)

Game for 7th place

25 Sep.	Bulgaria–Poland	3–1	(25–19, 25–22, 20–25, 25–20)

Game for 5th place

| 25 Sep. | Netherlands–Romania | 3–0 | (25–19, 25–22, 25–16) |

Semifinals (1–4 places)

| 24 Sep. | Croatia–Italy | 3–2 | (25–22, 16–25, 22–25, 25–23, 15–13) |
| 24 Sep. | Russia–Germany | 3–0 | (25–14, 25–9, 25–16) |

Game for 3rd place

| 25 Sep. | Italy–Germany | 3–0 | (25–20, 25–20, 25–19) |

Final

| 25 Sep. | Russia–Croatia | 3–0 | (25–18, 25–19, 25–12) |

Final standings

	G	W/L	SW/SL
1. Russia	5	5/0	15/1
2. Croatia	5	3/2	9/8
3. Italy	5	3/2	12/8
4. Germany	5	2/3	7/11
5. Netherlands	5	3/2	10/9
6. Romania	5	1/4	6/13
7. Bulgaria	5	2/3	9/11
8. Poland	5	1/4	7/14

Total: 8 teams, 20 games

Rosters of the medalists

Russia–Evgeniya Artamonova, Anastasiya Belikova, Ekaterina Gamova, Elena Godina, Natalya Morozova, Elena Plotnikova, Natalya Safronova, Elena Sennikova, Lyubov Shashkova-Sokolova, Irina Tebenikhina, Elizaveta Tishchenko, Elena Vasilevskaya; head coach: Nikolay Karpol

Croatia–Barbara Jelić, Mia Jerkov, Ana Kaštelan, Slavica Kuzmanić, Nataša Leto, Mariya Likhtenshteyn, Maja Poljak, Marijana Ribičić, Beti Rimac, Ingrid Šišković, Tihana Stipanović, Ivana Troha; head coach: Ivica Jelić

Italy–Vania Beccaria, Sabrina Bertini, Antonella Bragaglia, Maurizia Cacciatori, Elisa Galastri, Simona Gioli, Manuela Leggeri, Eleonora Lo Bianco, Paola Paggi, Francesca Piccinini, Simona Rinieri, Elisa Togut; head coach: Angiolino Frigoni

XXII EUROPEAN CHAMPIONSHIP
22–30 September 2001, Sofia and Varna (Bulgaria)

Preliminary round

Group A (Varna)

22 Sep.	Russia–France	3–0	(25–23, 25–22, 25–16)
22 Sep.	Romania–Czech Republic	3–1	(25–21, 24–26, 25–21, 25–22)
22 Sep.	Bulgaria–Greece	3–1	(21–25, 25–15, 25–22, 25–16)
23 Sep.	France–Czech Republic	3–1	(25–19, 25–19, 24–26, 25–19)
23 Sep.	Russia–Greece	3–0	(25–13, 25–20, 25–19)
23 Sep.	Bulgaria–Romania	3–1	(25–20, 16–25, 25–20, 25–17)
24 Sep.	Russia–Czech Republic	3–0	(25–12, 25–15, 25–13)
24 Sep.	Romania–Greece	3–0	(26–24, 25–15, 29–27)
24 Sep.	Bulgaria–France	3–2	(25–16, 19–25, 20–25, 25–20, 15–13)
26 Sep.	Russia–Romania	3–0	(25–17, 25–13, 25–10)
26 Sep.	France–Greece	3–2	(16–25, 25–23, 24–26, 25–20, 15–11)
26 Sep.	Bulgaria–Czech Republic	3–0	(25–19, 25–21, 25–23)
27 Sep.	Romania–France	3–0	(25–21, 25–15, 25–12)
27 Sep.	Czech Republic–Greece	3–1	(25–18, 23–25, 25–20, 25–13)
27 Sep.	Russia–Bulgaria	3–0	(25–22, 25–16, 25–12)

	G	W/L	SW/SL	Pts.
1. Russia	5	5/0	15/0	10
2. Bulgaria	5	4/1	12/7	9
3. Romania	5	3/2	10/7	8
4. France	5	2/3	8/12	7
5. Czech Republic	5	1/4	5/13	6
6. Greece	5	0/5	4/15	5

Group B (Sofia)

22 Sep.	Germany–Netherlands	3–1	(24–26, 25–22, 25–15, 25–18)
22 Sep.	Italy–Poland	3–1	(25–17, 25–15, 20–25, 25–21)
22 Sep.	Ukraine–Croatia	3–0	(27–25, 25–16, 25–16)
23 Sep.	Poland–Germany	3–1	(19–25, 25–19, 26–24, 25–16)
23 Sep.	Italy–Ukraine	3–0	(27–25, 25–21, 25–15)
23 Sep.	Croatia–Netherlands	3–1	(29–27, 22–25, 25–20, 25–18)
24 Sep.	Ukraine–Poland	3–2	(25–14, 19–25, 23–25, 25–16, 15–11)
24 Sep.	Italy–Netherlands	3–2	(20–25, 17–25, 26–24, 25–16, 15–11)
24 Sep.	Croatia–Germany	3–2	(28–30, 25–20, 25–11, 20–25, 15–12)
26 Sep.	Netherlands–Ukraine	3–2	(20–25, 25–20, 31–29, 22–25, 16–14)
26 Sep.	Italy–Germany	3–0	(25–19, 25–19, 25–17)
26 Sep.	Poland–Croatia	3–0	(25–15, 30–28, 25–18)

(continued)

Group B (Sofia) (continued)

27 Sep.	Ukraine–Germany	3–1	(25–23, 22–25, 25–19, 25–21)
27 Sep.	Italy–Croatia	3–1	(25–22, 20–25, 25–17, 25–14)
27 Sep.	Netherlands–Poland	3–0	(25–18, 26–24, 25–19)

	G	W/L	SW/SL	Pts.
1. Italy	5	5/0	15/4	10
2. Ukraine	5	3/2	11/9	8
3. Netherlands	5	2/3	10/11	7
4. Poland	5	2/3	9/10	7
5. Croatia	5	2/3	7/12	7
6. Germany	5	1/4	7/13	6

Final round for 1–8 places (Varna)

Semifinals (5–8 places)

| 29 Sep. | Poland–Romania | 3–0 | (25–20, 25–22, 25–21) |
| 29 Sep. | Netherlands–France | 3–2 | (24–26, 25–23, 27–25, 21–25, 15–11) |

Game for 7th place

| 30 Sep. | Romania–France | 3–1 | (25–18, 22–25, 25–19, 25–23) |

Game for 5th place

| 30 Sep. | Netherlands–Poland | 3–2 | (25–22, 22–25, 25–19, 21–25, 15–9) |

Semifinals (1–4 places)

| 29 Sep. | Russia–Ukraine | 3–0 | (25–18, 25–19, 25–17) |
| 29 Sep. | Italy–Bulgaria | 3–0 | (25–18, 25–12, 25–21) |

Game for 3rd place

| 30 Sep. | Bulgaria–Ukraine | 3–1 | (25–23, 22–25, 25–21, 25–21) |

Final

| 30 Sep. | Russia–Italy | 3–2 | (21–25, 25–23, 25–23, 18–25, 15–6) |

Final standings

	G	W/L	SW/SL
1. Russia	7	7/0	21/2
2. Italy	7	6/1	20/7
3. Bulgaria	7	5/2	15/11
4. Ukraine	7	3/4	12/15

(continued)

	G	W/L	SW/SL
5. Netherlands	7	4/3	16/15
6. Poland	7	3/4	14/13
7. Romania	7	4/3	13/11
8. France	7	2/5	11/18
9. Croatia	5	2/3	7/12
9. Czech Republic	5	1/4	5/13
11. Germany	5	1/4	7/13
11. Greece	5	0/5	4/15

Total: 12 teams, 38 games

Rosters of the medalists

Russia–Evgeniya Artamonova, Elena Batukhtina-Tyurina, Inessa Emelyanova-Sargsyan, Ekaterina Gamova, Elena Godina, Tatyana Grachyova, Natalya Morozova, Elena Plotnikova, Olga Potashova, Lyubov Shashkova-Sokolova, Elizaveta Tishchenko, Elena Vasilevskaya; head coach: Nikolay Karpol

Italy–Vania Beccaria, Maurizia Cacciatori, Paola Cardullo, Silvia Croatto, Manuela Leggeri, Eleonora Lo Bianco, Anna Vania Mello, Darina Mifkova, Paola Paggi, Francesca Piccinini, Simona Rinieri, Elisa Togut; head coach: Marco Bonitta

Bulgaria–Aneta Germanova, Iliana Gocheva, Anna Ivanova, Elena Kunova, Marina Marik, Neli Marinova-Neshich, Iliyana Petkova, Radostina Rangelova, Emiliya Serafimova, Vanya Sokolova, Desislava Velichkova, Antonina Zetova; head coach: Emil Trenev

XXIII EUROPEAN CHAMPIONSHIP
20–28 September 2003, Ankara and Antalya (Turkey)

Preliminary round

Group A (Ankara)

20 Sep.	Germany–Slovakia	3–0	(25–14, 25–15, 25–16)
20 Sep.	Russia–Serbia and Montenegro	3–1	(25–13, 18–25, 25–17, 25–18)
20 Sep.	Turkey–Romania	3–0	(25–22, 25–20, 25–17)
21 Sep.	Russia–Slovakia	3–0	(27–25, 25–17, 25–19)
21 Sep.	Germany–Romania	3–0	(25–22, 25–22, 25–22)
21 Sep.	Turkey–Serbia and Montenegro	3–0	(25–23, 25–20, 25–20)
22 Sep.	Romania–Slovakia	3–2	(25–14, 25–10, 22–25, 28–30, 15–8)
22 Sep.	Germany–Serbia and Montenegro	3–0	(25–15, 25–22, 25–22)
22 Sep.	Turkey–Russia	3–0	(25–21, 25–22, 26–24)
24 Sep.	Romania–Serbia and Montenegro	3–1	(25–11, 25–21, 23–25, 25–22)

(continued)

Group A (Ankara) (continued)

24 Sep.	Germany–Russia	3–0	(25–22, 27–25, 25–19)
24 Sep.	Turkey–Slovakia	3–0	(25–20, 25–20, 25–14)
25 Sep.	Russia–Romania	3–0	(25–16, 25–17, 25–22)
25 Sep.	Serbia and Montenegro–Slovakia	3–0	(28–26, 25–12, 27–25)
25 Sep.	Germany–Turkey	3–2	(25–16, 25–16, 22–25, 12–25, 15–10)

		G	W/L	SW/SL	Pts.
1.	Germany	5	5/0	15/2	10
2.	Turkey	5	4/1	14/3	9
3.	Russia	5	3/2	9/7	8
4.	Romania	5	2/3	6/12	7
5.	Serbia and Montenegro	5	1/4	5/12	6
6.	Slovakia	5	0/5	2/15	5

Group B (Antalya)

20 Sep.	Poland–Netherlands	3–2	(25–22, 25–19, 32–34, 23–25, 15–5)
20 Sep.	Ukraine–Bulgaria	3–1	(25–23, 25–19, 23–25, 25–19)
20 Sep.	Italy–Czech Republic	3–0	(25–18, 25–16, 25–22)
21 Sep.	Poland–Ukraine	3–1	(25–19, 23–25, 25–19, 25–23)
21 Sep.	Bulgaria–Czech Republic	3–0	(25–13, 25–17, 25–16)
21 Sep.	Netherlands–Italy	3–0	(25–20, 25–19, 25–18)
22 Sep.	Poland–Bulgaria	3–2	(25–17, 25–22, 22–25, 20–25, 15–12)
22 Sep.	Netherlands–Czech Republic	3–2	(25–14, 18–25, 25–17, 20–25, 15–10)
22 Sep.	Italy–Ukraine	3–0	(25–23, 25–22, 25–14)
24 Sep.	Netherlands–Bulgaria	3–1	(22–25, 25–23, 25–18, 26–24)
24 Sep.	Ukraine–Czech Republic	3–2	(25–21, 25–14, 22–25, 22–25, 15–7)
24 Sep.	Italy–Poland	3–1	(20–25, 25–22, 25–20, 25–22)
25 Sep.	Netherlands–Ukraine	3–0	(25–15, 25–18, 25–20)
25 Sep.	Bulgaria–Italy	3–2	(25–19, 20–25, 25–21, 15–25, 19–17)
25 Sep.	Poland–Czech Republic	3–1	(25–19, 23–25, 25–22, 25–16)

		G	W/L	SW/SL	Pts.
1.	Netherlands	5	4/1	14/6	9
2.	Poland	5	4/1	13/9	9
3.	Italy	5	3/2	11/7	8
4.	Bulgaria	5	2/3	10/11	7
5.	Ukraine	5	2/3	7/12	7
6.	Czech Republic	5	0/5	5/15	5

Final round for 1–8 places (Ankara)

Semifinals (5–8 places)

27 Sep.	Russia–Bulgaria	3–2	(25–21, 28–30, 25–15, 26–28, 15–11)
27 Sep.	Italy–Romania	3–1	(21–25, 25–15, 28–26, 25–21)

Game for 7th place

28 Sep.	Bulgaria–Romania	3–1	(25–21, 20–25, 25–20, 25–22)

Game for 5th place

28 Sep.	Russia–Italy	3–0	(25–16, 25–14, 25–20)

Semifinals (1–4 places)

27 Sep.	Poland–Germany	3–2	(25–23, 20–25, 22–25, 25–22, 15–9)
27 Sep.	Turkey–Netherlands	3–0	(25–17, 25–22, 25–22)

Game for 3rd place

28 Sep.	Germany–Netherlands	3–2	(25–20, 25–15, 24–26, 23–25, 18–16)

Final

28 Sep.	Poland–Turkey	3–0	(25–17, 25–14, 25–17)

Final standings

	G	W/L	SW/SL
1. Poland	7	6/1	19/11
2. Turkey	7	5/2	17/6
3. Germany	7	6/1	20/7
4. Netherlands	7	4/3	16/12
5. Russia	7	5/2	15/9
6. Italy	7	4/3	14/11
7. Bulgaria	7	3/4	15/15
8. Romania	7	2/5	8/18
9. Ukraine	5	2/3	7/12
9. Serbia and Montenegro	5	1/4	5/12
11. Czech Republic	5	0/5	5/15
11. Slovakia	5	0/5	2/15

Total: 12 teams, 38 games

Rosters of the medalists

Poland–Izabela Bełcik, Małgorzata Glinka, Dominika Leśniewicz, Maria Liktoras, Joanna Mirek, Agata Mróz, Małgorzata Niemczyk-Wolska, Anna Podolec, Aleksandra Przybysz, Katarzyna Skowrońska, Magdalena Śliwa, Dorota Świeniewicz; head coach: Andrzej Niemczyk

Turkey–Sinem Akap, Pelin Çelik, Neslihan Demir, Esra Gümüş, Natalia Hanikoğlu, Gülden Kayalar, Mesude Atilgan Kuyan, Aysun Özbek, Özlem Özçelik, Çiğdem Can Rasna, Seda Tokatlıoğlu, Bahar Urcu; head coach: Reşat Yazıcıoğulları

Germany–Christina Benecke, Atika Bouagaa, Cornelia Dumler, Christiane Fürst, Angelina Grün, Tanja Hart, Olessya Kulakova, Kathy Radzuweit, Julia Schlecht, Anika Schulz, Judith Sylvester, Kerstin Tzscherlich; head coach: Lee Hee-wan

XXIV EUROPEAN CHAMPIONSHIP
17–25 September 2005, Pula and Zagreb (Croatia)

Preliminary round

Group A (Zagreb)

17 Sep.	Romania–Croatia	3–1	(26–24, 25–18, 20–25, 27–25)
17 Sep.	Poland–Azerbaijan	3–0	(26–24, 25–20, 25–23)
17 Sep.	Serbia and Montenegro–Germany	3–1	(25–22, 17–25, 25–13, 25–16)
18 Sep.	Azerbaijan–Romania	3–1	(26–24, 23–25, 25–17, 25–19)
18 Sep.	Croatia–Serbia and Montenegro	3–1	(16–25, 25–19, 25–23, 25–16)
18 Sep.	Poland–Germany	3–2	(25–22, 23–25, 19–25, 28–26, 15–13)
19 Sep.	Serbia and Montenegro–Romania	3–2	(25–15, 19–25, 25–14, 24–26, 15–13)
19 Sep.	Azerbaijan–Germany	3–0	(26–24, 25–14, 25–21)
19 Sep.	Poland–Croatia	3–1	(25–16, 25–21, 22–25, 25–20)
21 Sep.	Azerbaijan–Serbia and Montenegro	3–1	(18–25, 25–19, 25–20, 28–26)
21 Sep.	Poland–Romania	3–0	(25–13, 25–19, 25–16)
21 Sep.	Croatia–Germany	3–0	(25–21, 25–22, 25–23)
22 Sep.	Poland–Serbia and Montenegro	3–1	(25–14, 25–23, 23–25, 25–21)
22 Sep.	Germany–Romania	3–1	(20–25, 25–18, 25–21, 25–17)
22 Sep.	Azerbaijan–Croatia	3–0	(25–23, 25–16, 25–22)

	G	W/L	SW/SL	Pts.
1. Poland	5	5/0	15/4	10
2. Azerbaijan	5	4/1	12/5	9
3. Croatia	5	2/3	8/10	7
4. Serbia and Montenegro	5	2/3	9/12	7
5. Romania	5	1/4	7/13	6
6. Germany	5	1/4	6/13	6

Group B (Pula)

17 Sep.	Bulgaria–Netherlands	3–2	(17–25, 25–18, 25–22, 17–25, 16–14)
17 Sep.	Italy–Spain	3–0	(25–21, 29–27, 25–21)
17 Sep.	Russia–Turkey	3–0	(25–23, 26–24, 25–20)
18 Sep.	Italy–Bulgaria	3–0	(25–23, 25–14, 25–20)
18 Sep.	Russia–Spain	3–1	(25–11, 25–23, 22–25, 25–18)
18 Sep.	Netherlands–Turkey	3–1	(25–22, 28–30, 25–21, 25–23)
19 Sep.	Bulgaria–Spain	3–0	(25–22, 25–12, 25–23)
19 Sep.	Italy–Turkey	3–0	(25–21, 25–21, 25–20)
19 Sep.	Russia–Netherlands	3–2	(18–25, 21–25, 25–20, 28–26, 15–9)
21 Sep.	Turkey–Spain	3–0	(25–22, 25–13, 25–21)
21 Sep.	Italy–Netherlands	3–1	(25–23, 25–19, 24–26, 25–18)
21 Sep.	Russia–Bulgaria	3–0	(25–23, 25–17, 25–21)
22 Sep.	Netherlands–Spain	3–0	(25–23, 25–20, 25–22)
22 Sep.	Italy–Russia	3–2	(22–25, 25–14, 25–16, 14–25, 15–12)
22 Sep.	Turkey–Bulgaria	3–1	(20–25, 25–14, 25–19, 25–23)

	G	W/L	SW/SL	Pts.
1. Italy	5	5/0	15/3	10
2. Russia	5	4/1	14/6	9
3. Netherlands	5	2/3	11/10	7
4. Turkey	5	2/3	7/10	7
5. Bulgaria	5	2/3	7/11	7
6. Spain	5	0/5	1/15	5

Final round for 1–8 places (Zagreb)

Semifinals (5–8 places)

24 Sep.	Turkey–Croatia	3–1	(18–25, 25–22, 25–23, 25–22)
24 Sep.	Netherlands–Serbia and Montenegro	3–0	(25–15, 25–11, 25–21)

Game for 7th place

25 Sep.	Serbia and Montenegro–Croatia	3–0	(25–22, 25–21, 25–14)

Game for 5th place

25 Sep.	Netherlands–Turkey	3–1	(25–18, 12–25, 25–21, 25–20)

Semifinals (1–4 places)

24 Sep.	Poland–Russia	3–2	(26–24, 25–22, 26–28, 20–25, 22–20)
24 Sep.	Italy–Azerbaijan	3–0	(25–19, 25–19, 25–22)

Game for 3rd place

25 Sep.	Russia–Azerbaijan	3–0	(25–20, 25–10, 25–21)

Final

25 Sep.	Poland–Italy	3–1	(25–23, 27–25, 21–25, 25–18)

Final standings

	G	W/L	SW/SL
1. Poland	7	7/0	21/7
2. Italy	7	6/1	19/6
3. Russia	7	5/2	19/9
4. Azerbaijan	7	4/3	12/11
5. Netherlands	7	4/3	17/11
6. Turkey	7	3/4	11/14
7. Serbia and Montenegro	7	3/4	12/15
8. Croatia	7	2/5	9/16
9. Bulgaria	5	2/3	7/11
9. Romania	5	1/4	7/13
11. Germany	5	1/4	6/13
11. Spain	5	0/5	1/15

Total: 12 teams, 38 games

Rosters of the medalists

Poland–Natalia Bamber, Izabela Bełcik, Małgorzata Glinka, Joanna Mirek, Agata Mróz, Aleksandra Przybysz, Sylwia Pycia, Milena Rosner, Katarzyna Skowrońska, Magdalena Śliwa, Dorota Świeniewicz, Mariola Zenik; head coach: Andrzej Niemczyk

Italy–Sara Anzanello, Jenny Barazza, Paola Cardullo, Elisa Cella, Nadia Centoni, Antonella Del Core, Simona Gioli, Eleonora Lo Bianco, Katja Luraschi, Serena Ortolani, Simona Rinieri, Elisa Togut; head coach: Marco Bonitta

Russia–Natalya Alimova, Mariya Borodakova, Olga Fadeeva, Ekaterina Gamova, Elena Godina, Ekaterina Kabeshova, Natalya Kurnosova, Yuliya Merkulova, Natalya Safronova, Olga Sazhina, Marina Sheshenina, Mariya Zhadan; head coach: Giovanni Caprara

XXV EUROPEAN CHAMPIONSHIP
20–30 September 2007, Charleroi and Hasselt (Belgium), Luxembourg City (Luxembourg)

Preliminary round

Group A (Charleroi)

20 Sep.	Azerbaijan–Belarus	3–0	(25–15, 25–23, 25–13)
20 Sep.	Italy–Germany	3–0	(25–22, 25–14, 29–27)
21 Sep.	Germany–Azerbaijan	3–0	(25–13, 25–22, 25–16)
22 Sep.	Germany–Belarus	3–1	(25–10, 25–18, 25–27, 25–17)
22 Sep.	Italy–Azerbaijan	3–0	(25–23, 25–14, 25–16)
23 Sep.	Italy–Belarus	3–1	(25–16, 25–22, 20–25, 25–16)

	G	W/L	SW/SL	Pts.
1. Italy	3	3/0	9/1	6
2. Germany	3	2/1	6/4	5
3. Azerbaijan	3	1/2	3/6	4
4. Belarus	3	0/3	2/9	3

Group B (Hasselt)

20 Sep.	Bulgaria–Spain	3–2	(26–28, 15–25, 33–31, 25–14, 15–13)
21 Sep.	Czech Republic–Bulgaria	3–2	(25–10, 22–25, 25–22, 23–25, 20–18)
21 Sep.	Poland–Spain	3–0	(25–21, 25–22, 25–20)
22 Sep.	Poland–Czech Republic	3–1	(25–17, 27–25, 18–25, 25–22)
23 Sep.	Czech Republic–Spain	3–0	(25–19, 25–23, 25–21)
23 Sep.	Poland–Bulgaria	3–2	(20–25, 27–25, 29–31, 25–13, 15–13)

	G	W/L	SW/SL	Pts.
1. Poland	3	3/0	9/3	6
2. Czech Republic	3	2/1	7/5	5
3. Bulgaria	3	1/2	7/8	4
4. Spain	3	0/3	2/9	3

Group C (Charleroi)

20 Sep.	Russia–Croatia	3–0	(25–23, 25–23, 25–14)
21 Sep.	France–Croatia	3–1	(25–21, 28–26, 22–25, 25–18)
21 Sep.	Russia–Turkey	3–0	(25–22, 28–26, 25–22)
22 Sep.	France–Turkey	3–0	(25–19, 25–16, 25–23)
23 Sep.	Russia–France	3–0	(25–19, 25–17, 25–20)
23 Sep.	Turkey–Croatia	3–2	(22–25, 22–25, 25–22, 25–20, 15–6)

	G	W/L	SW/SL	Pts.
1. Russia	3	3/0	9/0	6
2. France	3	2/1	6/4	5
3. Turkey	3	1/2	3/8	4
4. Croatia	3	0/3	3/9	3

Group D (Hasselt)

20 Sep.	Slovakia–Serbia	3–2	(14–25, 25–21, 25–20, 21–25, 15–11)
20 Sep.	Netherlands–Belgium	3–1	(25–19, 19–25, 25–23, 25–12)
21 Sep.	Netherlands–Slovakia	3–0	(25–16, 25–12, 25–16)
22 Sep.	Serbia–Netherlands	3–2	(25–18, 17–25, 25–14, 30–32, 15–13)
22 Sep.	Belgium–Slovakia	3–0	(25–14, 25–14, 26–24)
23 Sep.	Serbia–Belgium	3–2	(22–25, 25–20, 27–29, 25–17, 15–5)

	G	W/L	SW/SL	Pts.
1. Netherlands	3	2/1	8/4	5
2. Serbia	3	2/1	8/7	5
3. Belgium	3	1/2	6/6	4
4. Slovakia	3	1/2	3/8	4

Preliminary round II (head-to-head games were carried over from the preliminary round)

Group E (Charleroi)

25 Sep.	Italy–France	3–1	(24–26, 25–17, 25–10, 25–19)
25 Sep.	Germany–Turkey	3–0	(25–21, 25–21, 32–30)
25 Sep.	Russia–Azerbaijan	3–0	(25–23, 25–14, 25–17)
26 Sep.	Italy–Turkey	3–0	(25–23, 25–14, 25–22)
26 Sep.	Russia–Germany	3–0	(25–12, 25–23, 25–23)
26 Sep.	France–Azerbaijan	3–1	(25–14, 23–25, 25–17, 25–21)
27 Sep.	Italy–Russia	3–0	(25–15, 25–22, 25–19)
27 Sep.	Germany–France	3–0	(25–22, 25–13, 25–15)
27 Sep.	Turkey–Azerbaijan	3–0	(25–18, 25–19, 25–22)

	G	W/L	SW/SL	Pts.
1. Italy	5	5/0	15/1	10
2. Russia	5	4/1	12/3	9
3. Germany	5	3/2	9/6	8
4. France	5	2/3	7/10	7
5. Turkey	5	1/4	3/12	6
6. Azerbaijan	5	0/5	1/15	5

Group F (Hasselt)

25 Sep.	Netherlands–Bulgaria	3–0	(25–20, 25–23, 25–19)
25 Sep.	Poland–Serbia	3–0	(25–18, 25–20, 25–14)
25 Sep.	Belgium–Czech Republic	3–1	(25–16, 18–25, 25–17, 25–21)
26 Sep.	Serbia–Bulgaria	3–1	(20–25, 25–16, 25–19, 30–28)
26 Sep.	Netherlands–Czech Republic	3–0	(25–18, 25–17, 25–22)
26 Sep.	Poland–Belgium	3–0	(25–18, 25–20, 25–19)
27 Sep.	Serbia–Czech Republic	3–0	(25–18, 25–21, 25–17)
27 Sep.	Poland–Netherlands	3–1	(25–22, 25–18, 22–25, 25–21)
27 Sep.	Belgium–Bulgaria	3–1	(25–16, 25–19, 30–32, 25–22)

		G	W/L	SW/SL	Pts.
1.	Poland	5	5/0	15/4	10
2.	Serbia	5	4/1	12/8	9
3.	Netherlands	5	3/2	12/7	8
4.	Belgium	5	2/3	9/11	7
5.	Czech Republic	5	1/4	5/14	6
6.	Bulgaria	5	0/5	6/15	5

Final round for 1–4 places (Luxembourg City)

Semifinals

29 Sep.	Italy–Russia	3–0	(25–21, 25–22, 25–13)
29 Sep.	Serbia–Poland	3–0	(27–25, 25–21, 25–21)

Game for 3rd place

30 Sep.	Russia–Poland	3–1	(21–25, 25–22, 25–14, 25–20)

Final

30 Sep.	Italy–Serbia	3–0	(26–24, 25–18, 25–21)

Final standings

		G	W/L	SW/SL
1.	Italy	8	8/0	24/2
2.	Serbia	8	5/3	17/14
3.	Russia	8	6/2	18/7
4.	Poland	8	6/2	19/10
5.	Netherlands	6	4/2	15/7
6.	Germany	6	4/2	12/7
7.	Belgium	6	3/3	12/11
8.	France	6	3/3	10/11
9.	Czech Republic	6	2/4	8/14

(continued)

	G	W/L	SW/SL
10. Turkey	6	2/4	6/14
11. Bulgaria	6	1/5	9/17
12. Azerbaijan	6	1/5	4/15
13. Slovakia	3	1/2	3/8
14. Croatia	3	0/3	3/9
15. Spain	3	0/3	2/9
16. Belarus	3	0/3	2/9

Total: 16 teams, 46 games

Rosters of the medalists

Italy–Taismaris Aguero, Jenny Barazza, Paola Cardullo, Paola Croce, Antonella Del Core, Francesca Ferretti, Valentina Fiorin, Simona Gioli, Martina Guiggi, Eleonora Lo Bianco, Serena Ortolani, Manuela Secolo; head coach: Massimo Barbolini

Serbia–Jovana Brakočević, Vesna Čitaković-Đurišić, Suzana Ćebić, Ivana Isailović, Nataša Krsmanović, Jasna Majstorović, Brižitka Molnar, Jelena Nikolić, Maja Ognjenović, Maja Simanić, Anja Spasojević, Jovana Vesović; head coach: Zoran Terzić

Russia–Marina Akulova, Svetlana Akulova, Natalya Alimova, Olga Fateeva, Ekaterina Gamova, Elena Godina, Ekaterina Kabeshova, Tatyana Kosheleva, Yuliya Merkulova, Natalya Safronova, Yuliya Sedova, Lyubov Shashkova-Sokolova; head coach: Giovanni Caprara

XXVI EUROPEAN CHAMPIONSHIP
25 September–4 October 2009, Bydgoszcz, Katowice, Łódź, and Wrocław (Poland)

Preliminary round

Group A (Łódź)

25 Sep.	Netherlands–Croatia	3–0	(25–11, 25–18, 25–12)
25 Sep.	Poland–Spain	3–2	(25–15, 25–20, 19–25, 23–25, 15–11)
26 Sep.	Poland–Croatia	3–0	(25–18, 25–13, 25–16)
26 Sep.	Netherlands–Spain	3–0	(25–17, 25–13, 25–15)
27 Sep.	Netherlands–Poland	3–0	(25–18, 25–13, 25–23)
27 Sep.	Spain–Croatia	3–2	(15–25, 25–22, 25–15, 22–25, 15–13)

	G	W/L	SW/SL	Pts.
1. Netherlands	3	3/0	9/0	6
2. Poland	3	2/1	6/5	5
3. Spain	3	1/2	5/8	4
4. Croatia	3	0/3	2/9	3

Group B (Wrocław)

25 Sep.	Turkey–France	3–0	(25–22, 25–9, 25–15)
25 Sep.	Italy–Germany	3–0	(25–15, 25–22, 25–22)
26 Sep.	Italy–Turkey	3–0	(25–20, 25–16, 25–14)
26 Sep.	Germany–France	3–1	(25–19, 25–17, 19–25, 28–26)
27 Sep.	Italy–France	3–1	(25–22, 25–22, 23–25, 25–15)
27 Sep.	Germany–Turkey	3–2	(23–25, 23–25, 18–25, 25–21, 15–9)

	G	W/L	SW/SL	Pts.
1. Italy	3	3/0	9/1	6
2. Germany	3	2/1	6/6	5
3. Turkey	3	1/2	5/6	4
4. France	3	0/3	2/9	3

Group C (Bydgoszcz)

25 Sep.	Belgium–Belarus	3–1	(26–28, 25–20, 27–25, 25–22)
25 Sep.	Russia–Bulgaria	3–0	(25–19, 25–9, 25–14)
26 Sep.	Bulgaria–Belgium	3–2	(24–26, 25–22, 17–25, 25–21, 15–6)
26 Sep.	Russia–Belarus	3–0	(25–19, 25–12, 25–15)
27 Sep.	Bulgaria–Belarus	3–1	(17–25, 25–20, 25–11, 25–20)
27 Sep.	Russia–Belgium	3–2	(25–13, 18–25, 20–25, 25–18, 15–9)

	G	W/L	SW/SL	Pts.
1. Russia	3	3/0	9/2	6
2. Bulgaria	3	2/1	6/6	5
3. Belgium	3	1/2	7/7	4
4. Belarus	3	0/3	2/9	3

Group D (Katowice)

25 Sep.	Serbia–Azerbaijan	3–0	(25–12, 25–21, 25–19)
25 Sep.	Slovakia–Czech Republic	3–2	(25–21, 17–25, 19–25, 25–23, 15–13)
26 Sep.	Azerbaijan–Slovakia	3–2	(25–13, 19–25, 25–18, 22–25, 15–12)
26 Sep.	Serbia–Czech Republic	3–0	(25–19, 25–21, 25–18)
27 Sep.	Serbia–Slovakia	3–0	(25–15, 25–19, 25–16)
27 Sep.	Czech Republic–Azerbaijan	3–2	(25–21, 25–18, 23–25, 20–25, 15–13)

	G	W/L	SW/SL	Pts.
1. Serbia	3	3/0	9/0	6
2. Azerbaijan	3	1/2	5/8	4
3. Czech Republic	3	1/2	5/8	4
4. Slovakia	3	1/2	5/8	4

Preliminary round II (head-to-head games were carried over from the preliminary round)

Group E (Łódź)

29 Sep.	Russia–Spain	3–1	(25–21, 26–24, 19–25, 25–20)
29 Sep.	Netherlands–Bulgaria	3–0	(25–19, 25–20, 25–18)
29 Sep.	Poland–Belgium	3–1	(25–16, 21–25, 25–19, 25–12)
30 Sep.	Bulgaria–Spain	3–1	(25–20, 25–16, 21–25, 25–18)
30 Sep.	Poland–Russia	3–1	(24–26, 25–22, 25–22, 25–22)
30 Sep.	Netherlands–Belgium	3–0	(25–17, 25–19, 25–20)
1 Oct.	Spain–Belgium	3–2	(23–25, 25–19, 21–25, 25–23, 15–13)
1 Oct.	Netherlands–Russia	3–2	(25–19, 19–25, 23–25, 25–19, 15–12)
1 Oct.	Poland–Bulgaria	3–1	(18–25, 25–20, 25–21, 25–23)

	G	W/L	SW/SL	Pts.
1. Netherlands	5	5/0	15/2	10
2. Poland	5	4/1	12/8	9
3. Russia	5	3/2	12/9	8
4. Bulgaria	5	2/3	7/12	7
5. Spain	5	1/4	7/14	6
6. Belgium	5	0/5	7/15	5

Group F (Katowice)

29 Sep.	Italy–Azerbaijan	3–0	(29–27, 25–23, 25–13)
29 Sep.	Germany–Czech Republic	3–0	(28–26, 25–12, 25–15)
29 Sep.	Turkey–Serbia	3–1	(24–26, 25–16, 25–23, 25–19)
30 Sep.	Italy–Czech Republic	3–0	(25–16, 25–20, 25–23)
30 Sep.	Germany–Serbia	3–2	(25–9, 23–25, 25–27, 25–17, 15–8)
30 Sep.	Turkey–Azerbaijan	3–1	(25–23, 25–19, 17–25, 25–17)
1 Oct.	Italy–Serbia	3–0	(25–19, 25–18, 25–22)
1 Oct.	Germany–Azerbaijan	3–0	(25–17, 25–13, 25–12)
1 Oct.	Turkey–Czech Republic	3–0	(25–16, 25–20, 25–23)

	G	W/L	SW/SL	Pts.
1. Italy	5	5/0	15/0	10
2. Germany	5	4/1	12/7	9

(continued)

	G	W/L	SW/SL	Pts.
3. Turkey	5	3/2	11/8	8
4. Serbia	5	2/3	9/9	7
5. Czech Republic	5	1/4	3/14	6
6. Azerbaijan	5	0/5	3/15	5

Final round for 1–4 places (Łódź)

Semifinals

3 Oct.	Netherlands–Poland	3–1	(25–11, 25–15, 20–25, 25–20)
3 Oct.	Italy–Germany	3–1	(25–10, 22–25, 25–12, 25–22)

Game for 3rd place

4 Oct.	Poland–Germany	3–0	(25–16, 25–19, 25–23)

Final

4 Oct.	Italy–Netherlands	3–0	(25–16, 25–19, 25–20)

Final standings

	G	W/L	SW/SL
1. Italy	8	8/0	24/2
2. Netherlands	8	7/1	21/6
3. Poland	8	6/2	19/11
4. Germany	8	5/3	16/14
5. Turkey	6	4/2	14/8
6. Russia	6	4/2	15/9
7. Serbia	6	3/3	12/9
8. Bulgaria	6	3/3	10/13
9. Spain	6	2/4	10/16
10. Czech Republic	6	1/5	5/17
11. Belgium	6	1/5	10/16
12. Azerbaijan	6	1/5	6/17
13. Slovakia	3	1/2	5/8
14. Belarus	3	0/3	2/9
14. France	3	0/3	2/9
16. Croatia	3	0/3	2/9

Total: 16 teams, 46 games

Rosters of the medalists

Italy–Taismaris Aguero, Valentina Arrighetti, Jenny Barazza, Lucia Bosetti, Paola Cardullo, Lucia Crisanti, Antonella Del Core, Simona Gioli, Eleonora Lo Bianco,

Enrica Merlo, Serena Ortolani, Francesca Piccinini, Giulia Rondon, Manuela Secolo; head coach: Massimo Barbolini

Netherlands–Alice Blom, Robin de Kruijf, Manon Flier, Maret Grothues, Francien Huurman, Myrthe Schoot, Deborah Sgroot, Chaïne Staelens, Kim Staelens, Debby Stam, Janneke van Tienen, Ingrid Visser, Caroline Wensink, Sharon Zuidema; head coach: Avital Selinger

Poland–Natalia Bamber, Anna Barańska, Agnieszka Bednarek-Kasza, Izabela Bełcik, Eleonora Dziękiewicz, Katarzyna Gajgał, Aleksandra Jagieło, Joanna Kaczor, Klaudia Kaczorowska, Paulina Maj, Dorota Pykosz, Milena Sadurek, Anna Woźniakowska, Mariola Zenik; head coach: Jerzy Matlak*

---

*After three games, Jerzy Matlak left the Polish team to be with his wife in the hospital. After that the team was coached to the end of the tournament by his assistat, Piotr Makowski.

XXVII EUROPEAN CHAMPIONSHIP
23 September–2 October 2011, Busto Arsizio and Monza (Italy), Belgrade and Zrenjanin (Serbia)

Preliminary round

Group A (Belgrade)

24 Sep.	Germany–Ukraine	3–0	(25–17, 25–15, 25–17)
24 Sep.	Serbia–France	3–1	(20–25, 25–15, 25–11, 25–19)
25 Sep.	Germany–France	3–0	(25–18, 25–23, 25–18)
25 Sep.	Serbia–Ukraine	3–0	(25–18, 25–18, 25–14)
26 Sep.	France–Ukraine	3–0	(26–24, 25–14, 25–15)
26 Sep.	Germany–Serbia	3–1	(25–22, 25–15, 18–25, 25–17)

	G	W/L	SW/SL	Pts.
1. Germany	3	3/0	9/1	9
2. Serbia	3	2/1	7/4	6
3. France	3	1/2	4/6	3
4. Ukraine	3	0/3	0/9	0

Group B (Monza)

23 Sep.	Turkey–Azerbaijan	3–1	(23–25, 25–17, 25–19, 25–21)
23 Sep.	Italy–Croatia	3–0	(25–19, 25–20, 25–19)
24 Sep.	Croatia–Turkey	3–0	(25–21, 25–23, 25–22)
24 Sep.	Italy–Azerbaijan	3–1	(25–22, 25–22, 21–25, 25–16)
25 Sep.	Azerbaijan–Croatia	3–1	(27–25, 18–25, 25–21, 25–18)
25 Sep.	Turkey–Italy	3–2	(21–25, 28–26, 25–16, 22–25, 15–9)

	G	W/L	SW/SL	Pts.
1. Italy	3	2/1	8/4	7
2. Turkey	3	2/1	6/6	5
3. Azerbaijan	3	1/2	5/7	3
4. Croatia	3	1/2	4/6	3

Group C (Zrenjanin)

24 Sep.	Poland–Israel	3–0	(25–23, 25–7, 25–15)
24 Sep.	Czech Republic–Romania	3–0	(29–27, 25–19, 25–16)
25 Sep.	Romania–Israel	3–0	(25–17, 25–23, 25–14)
25 Sep.	Poland–Czech Republic	3–0	(25–20, 28–26, 25–20)
26 Sep.	Czech Republic–Israel	3–0	(25–11, 25–18, 25–16)
26 Sep.	Poland–Romania	3–0	(27–25, 25–18, 25–22)

	G	W/L	SW/SL	Pts.
1. Poland	3	3/0	9/0	9
2. Czech Republic	3	2/1	6/3	6
3. Romania	3	1/2	3/6	3
4. Israel	3	0/3	0/9	0

Group D (Busto Arsizio)

23 Sep.	Netherlands–Spain	3–0	(25–15, 25–14, 25–17)
23 Sep.	Russia–Bulgaria	3–0	(25–13, 26–24, 25–21)
24 Sep.	Netherlands–Bulgaria	3–0	(25–23, 25–17, 25–23)
24 Sep.	Russia–Spain	3–1	(32–30, 19–25, 25–20, 25–22)
25 Sep.	Russia–Netherlands	3–1	(26–24, 24–26, 25–15, 25–22)
25 Sep.	Spain–Bulgaria	3–0	(25–17, 25–18, 25–21)

	G	W/L	SW/SL	Pts.
1. Russia	3	3/0	9/2	9
2. Netherlands	3	2/1	7/3	6
3. Spain	3	1/2	4/6	3
4. Bulgaria	3	0/3	0/9	0

Playoff round

Elimination games*

27 Sep.	Turkey–Spain	3–0	(25–19, 25–17, 25–21)	Monza
27 Sep.	Netherlands–Azerbaijan	3–1	(23–25, 27–25, 25–16, 25–17)	Monza
28 Sep.	Serbia–Romania	3–0	(25–19, 25–15, 25–20)	Belgrade
28 Sep.	Czech Republic–France	3–1	(25–21, 23–25, 25–14, 25–14)	Belgrade

*These games were played only between teams which placed second or third in their groups in the preliminary round; the winners of elimination games advanced to the quarterfinals.

Quarterfinals

28 Sep.	Turkey–Russia	3–0	(27–25, 25–21, 25–19)	Monza
28 Sep.	Italy–Netherlands	3–1	(25–21, 25–20, 21–25, 25–18)	Monza
29 Sep.	Germany–Czech Republic	3–0	(25–18, 25–20, 25–17)	Belgrade
29 Sep.	Serbia–Poland	3–0	(25–14, 25–20, 26–24)	Belgrade

Final round for 1–4 places (Belgrade)

Semifinals

1 Oct.	Germany–Italy	3–0	(25–22, 25–22, 25–17)
1 Oct.	Serbia–Turkey	3–2	(25–10, 25–22, 23–25, 23–25, 15–12)

Game for 3rd place

2 Oct.	Turkey–Italy	3–2	(25–21, 15–25, 25–27, 25–19, 15–10)

Final

2 Oct.	Serbia–Germany	3–2	(16–25, 25–20, 19–25, 25–20, 15–9)

Final standings

	G	W/L	SW/SL
1. Serbia	7	6/1	19/8
2. Germany	6	5/1	17/4
3. Turkey	7	5/2	17/11
4. Italy	6	3/3	13/11
5. Poland	4	3/1	9/3
6. Russia	4	3/1	9/5
7. Netherlands	5	3/2	11/7
8. Czech Republic	5	3/2	9/7
9. Azerbaijan	4	1/3	6/10

(continued)

	G	W/L	SW/SL
10. France	4	1/3	5/9
11. Spain	4	1/3	4/9
12. Romania	4	1/3	3/9
13. Croatia	3	1/2	4/6
14. Bulgaria	3	0/3	0/9
15. Ukraine	3	0/3	0/9
16. Israel	3	0/3	0/9

Total: 16 teams, 36 games

Rosters of the medalists

Serbia–Ana Antonijević, Jovana Brakočević, Suzana Ćebić, Nataša Krsmanović, Ana Lazarević, Sanja Malagurski, Tijana Malešević, Brižitka Molnar, Jelena Nikolić, Nađa Ninković, Maja Ognjenović, Silvija Popović, Milena Rašić, Jovana Vesović; head coach: Zoran Terzić

Germany–Mareen Apitz, Maren Brinker, Regina Burchardt, Lenka Dürr, Christiane Fürst, Angelina Grün, Saskia Hippe, Berit Kauffeldt, Margareta Kozuch, Anne Matthes, Corina Ssuschke-Voigt, Lisa Thomsen, Kerstin Tzscherlich, Kathleen Weiss; head coach: Giovanni Guidetti

Turkey–Ergül Avcı, Büşra Cansu, Neslihan Demir, Eda Erdem, Esra Gümüş, Gizem Güreşen, Asuman Karakoyun, Özge Kırdar Çemberci, Gözde Kırdar Sonsirma, Gülden Kuzubaşıoğlu, Güldeniz Önal, Neriman Özsoy, Bahar Toksoy, Polen Uslupehlivan; head coach: Marco Aurélio Motta

Records

MEN'S EUROPEAN CHAMPIONSHIPS

Most consecutive games won, all editions
46 (USSR, 26 September 1977–30 September 1989)

Most consecutive games won by 3–0 result, all editions
16 (USSR, 14 October 1950–20 June 1955)

Most consecutive games lost, all editions
24 (Spain, 26 September 1981–10 September 2003)

Most consecutive games lost by 0–3 result, all editions
20 (Denmark, 30 August 1958–27 September 1971)

Most editions by player
8 (Andrija Gerić, Yugoslavia/Serbia, 1995–2009)
8 (Nikola Grbić, Yugoslavia/Serbia, 1995–2009)

Most medals by a player, all editions
6 (Aleksandr Savin, USSR, all gold, 1975–1985)
6 (Vyacheslav Zaytsev, USSR, all gold, 1975–1985)
6 (Andrea Gardini, Italy, 4 gold, 1 silver, and 1 bronze, 1989–1999)
6 (Andrea Giani, Italy, 4 gold, 1 silver, and 1 bronze, 1991–1999, 2003)
6 (Slobodan Boškan, Yugoslavia/Serbia, 1 gold, 1 silver, and 4 bronze, 1995–2001, 2005–2007)
6 (Andrija Gerić, Yugoslavia/Serbia, 1 gold, 1 silver, and 4 bronze, 1995–2001, 2005–2007)
6 (Nikola Grbić, Yugoslavia/Serbia, 1 gold, 1 silver, and 4 bronze, 1995–2001, 2005–2007)

Most medals by a head coach, all editions
  6 (Vyacheslav Platonov, USSR, all gold, 1977–1985, 1991)

Most gold medals by a player, all editions
  6 (Aleksandr Savin, USSR, 1975–1985)
  6 (Vyacheslav Zaytsev, USSR, 1975–1985)

Most gold medals by a head coach, all editions
  6 (Vyacheslav Platonov, USSR, 1977–1985, 1991)

Most points in a one set, one team, until 1997, without tie-break
  24 (Finland against Romania, first set, 25 September 1971)

Fewest points in a one set, one team, until 1997
  0 (28 times)

Most points in a one set, one team, since 1999 (rally point system)
  42 (France against Italy, second set, 14 September 2003)

Fewest points in a one set, one team, since 1999 (rally point system)
  9 (Czech Republic against Italy, third set, 15 September 2001)
  9 (Slovenia against Serbia, first set, 11 September 2011)

Most points in a tie-break (since 1989), one team
  19 (France against Ukraine, 11 September 1997)
  19 (France against Italy, 13 September 2001)

Fewest points in a tie-break (since 1989), one team
  6 (Romania against Yugoslavia, 23 September 1989)
  6 (Poland against Germany, 4 September 1993)

Largest difference in points, winning team, three sets game, until 1997
  43 (Czechoslovakia–FRG, 3–0 [15–1, 15–1, 15–0], 2 September 1958)
  43 (GDR–Denmark, 3–0 [15–0, 15–1, 15–1], 28 October 1963)

Largest difference in points, winning team, three sets game, since 1999
  34 (Italy–Slovakia, 3–0 [25–14, 25–12, 25–15], 10 September 2003)

Largest difference in points, winning team, four sets game, until 1997
  33 (Poland–Finland, 3–1 [12–15, 15–2, 15–1, 15–6], 30 August 1958)

Largest difference in points, winning team, four sets game, since 1999
  27 (Yugoslavia–France, 3–1 [25–12, 25–17, 25–27, 25–17], 8 September 1999)
  27 (Czech Republic–Slovenia, 3–1 [25–15, 21–25, 25–17, 25–12],
    8 September 2001)
  27 (Italy–Germany, 3–1 [25–14, 25–16, 23–25, 25–16], 9 September 2001)

Largest difference in points, winning team, five sets game, until 1997
  23 (Italy–Netherlands, 3–2 [16–18, 15–12, 9–15, 15–1, 15–1], 1 September 1958)

Largest difference in points, winning team, five sets game, since 1999
   19 (Bulgaria–Croatia, 3–2 [24–26, 23–25, 25–12, 25–20, 15–10],
      6 September 2007)

Smallest difference in points, winning team, three sets game, until 1997
   6 (GDR–Netherlands, 3–0 [16–14, 17–15, 16–14], 5 September 1958)
   6 (Yugoslavia–Bulgaria, 3–0 [16–14, 16–14, 17–15], 25 October 1975)
   6 (France–Czechoslovakia, 3–0 [17–16, 15–13, 15–12], 7 September 1991)

Smallest difference in points, winning team, three sets game, since 1999
   6 (France–Netherlands, 3–0 [26–24, 27–25, 30–28], 7 September 1999)

Smallest difference in points, winning team, four sets game, until 1997
   –7 (Poland against Italy, 3–1 [15–13, 16–14, 2–15, 16–14], 18 September 1983)

Smallest difference in points, winning team, four sets game, since 1999
   –1 (Poland against France, 3–1 [29–27, 25–21, 16–25, 26–24], 13 September 2009)

Smallest difference in points, winning team, five sets game, until 1997
   –15 (Italy against Netherlands, 3–2 [2–15, 17–15, 3–15, 15–11, 15–11],
      7 September 1958)

Smallest difference in points, winning team, five sets game, since 1999
   –7 (Italy against Russia, 3–2 [25–22, 14–25, 15–25, 25–19, 15–10], 11 September 2005)

Most points, winning team, three sets game, until 1997
   51 (Bulgaria–GDR, 3–0 [21–19, 15–11, 15–8], 29 September 1977)

Most points, winning team, three sets game, since 1999
   84 (Italy–Poland, 3–0 [25–21, 34–32, 25–21], 10 September 2001)

Most points, winning team, four sets game, until 1997
   67 (Romania–Finland, 3–1 [22–24, 15–12, 15–10, 15–1], 25 September 1971)

Most points, winning team, four sets game, since 1999
   116 (Belgium–France, 3–1 [31–29, 34–36, 25–20, 26–24], 11 September 2011)

Most points, winning team, five sets game, until 1997
   77 (Czechoslovakia–Netherlands, 3–2 [15–8, 15–8, 17–19, 15–17, 15–8],
      18 September 1983)

Most points, winning team, five sets game, since 1999
   132 (Italy–France, 3–2 [25–18, 40–42, 25–18, 27–29, 15–9], 14 September 2003)

Fewest points, winning team, four sets game, until 1997
   46 (Turkey–Finland, 3–1 [15–11, 1–15, 15–13, 15–6], 6 September 1958)

Fewest points, winning team, four sets game, since 1999
   91 (France–Netherlands, 3–1 [25–17, 25–22, 16–25, 25–20], 3 September 2005)
   91 (Spain–Slovenia, 3–1 [16–25, 25–20, 25–21, 25–18], 6 September 2007)

Fewest points, winning team, five sets game, until 1997
  52 (Italy–Netherlands, 3–2 [2–15, 17–15, 3–15, 15–11, 15–11],
    7 September 1958)

Fewest points, winning team, five sets game, since 1999
  94 (Italy–Russia, 3–2 [25–22, 14–25, 15–25, 25–19, 15–10], 11 September 2005)

Most points, losing team, three sets game, until 1997
  43 (Netherlands–GDR, 0–3 [14–16, 15–17, 14–16], 5 September 1958)
  43 (Bulgaria–Yugoslavia, 0–3 [14–16, 14–16, 15–17], 25 October 1975)

Most points, losing team, three sets game, since 1999
  77 (Netherlands–France, 0–3 [24–26, 25–27, 28–30], 7 September 1999)

Most points, losing team, four sets game, until 1997
  61 (Turkey–Italy, 1–3 [17–15, 18–20, 14–16, 12–15], 30 October 1963)
  61 (France–Czechoslovakia, 1–3 [14–16, 16–18, 17–15, 14–16], 4 October 1985)

Most points, losing team, four sets game, since 1999
  109 (France–Belgium, 1–3 [29–31, 36–34, 20–25, 24–26], 11 September 2011)

Most points, losing team, five sets game, until 1997
  74 (Bulgaria–Hungary, 2–3 [15–8, 15–10, 15–17, 14–16, 15–17],
    15 October 1950)

Most points, losing team, five sets game, since 1999
  118 (France–Spain, 2–3 [30–28, 25–16, 23–25, 31–33, 9–15], 4 September 2005)
  118 (France–Serbia, 2–3 [23–25, 25–22, 23–25, 35–33, 12–15],
    11 September 2007)

Fewest points, losing team, four sets game, until 1997
  24 (Finland–Poland, 1–3 [15–12, 2–15, 1–15, 6–15], 30 August 1958)

Fewest points, losing team, four sets game, since 1999
  69 (Slovenia–Czech Republic, 1–3 [15–25, 25–21, 17–25, 12–25],
    8 September 2001)
  69 (Bulgaria–Russia, 1–3 [13–25, 13–25, 25–20, 18–25], 8 September 2001)

Fewest points, losing team, five sets game, until 1997
  43 (Bulgaria–USSR, 2–3 [15–6, 4–15, 15–4, 2–15, 7–15], 28 October 1963)
  43 (Yugoslavia–USSR, 2–3 [15–13, 15–7, 0–15, 5–15, 8–15], 24 October 1975)

Fewest points, losing team, five sets game, since 1999
  89 (Slovakia–Poland, 2–3 [25–21, 15–25, 10–25, 25–14, 14–16],
    9 September 2009)

Most points, both teams, three sets game, until 1997
  92 (GDR–Netherlands, 3–0 [16–14, 17–15, 16–14], 5 September 1958)
  92 (Yugoslavia–Bulgaria, 3–0 [16–14, 16–14, 17–15], 25 October 1975)

Most points, both teams, three sets game, since 1999
   160 (France–Netherlands, 3–0 [26–24, 27–25, 30–28], 7 September 1999)

Most points, both teams, four sets game, until 1997
   127 (Italy–Turkey, 3–1 [15–17, 20–18, 16–14, 15–12], 30 October 1963)

Most points, both teams, four sets game, since 1999
   225 (Belgium–France, 3–1 [31–29, 34–36, 25–20, 26–24], 11 September 2011)

Most points, both teams, five sets game, until 1997
   145 (Czechoslovakia–Bulgaria, 3–2 [16–14, 12–15, 11–15, 18–16, 15–13],
      27 September 1977)

Most points, both teams, five sets game, since 1999
   248 (Italy–France, 3–2 [25–18, 40–42, 25–18, 27–29, 15–9], 14 September 2003)

Highest average, difference between points scored and allowed per game,
      one edition, team, until 1997
   30.6 (Czechoslovakia, 1948)

Highest average, difference between points allowed and scored per game,
      one edition, team, until 1997
   29.3 (Denmark, 1958)

Highest average, difference between points scored and allowed per game,
      one edition, team, since 1999
   19.1 (Italy, 2003)

Highest average, difference between points allowed and scored per game,
      one edition, team, since 1999
   20.4 (Slovenia, 2001)

Most wins, one edition, team
   10 (Czechoslovakia, 1958)
   10 (USSR, 1967)

Most losses, one edition, team
   10 (Denmark, 1963)

WOMEN'S EUROPEAN CHAMPIONSHIPS

Most consecutive games won, all editions
   49 (USSR, 22 June 1955–6 October 1979)

Most consecutive games won by 3–0 result, all editions
   18 (USSR, 11 September 1949–19 June 1955)

Most consecutive games lost, all editions
   25 (Belgium, 6 November 1967–22 September 2007)

Most consecutive games lost by 0–3 result, all editions
9 (Belgium, 12 October 1979–20 September 2007)

Most editions by player
9 (Elena Chebukina-Ovchinnikova, USSR/Russia/Croatia, 1983–1997, 2001)

Most medals by a player, all editions
8 (Elena Chebukina-Ovchinnikova, USSR/Russia/Croatia, 4 gold and 4 silver, 1983–1997)

Most medals by a head coach, all editions
9 (Nikolay Karpol, USSR/Russia, 7 gold, 1 silver, and 1 bronze, 1979–1981, 1989–2001)

Most gold medals by a player, all editions
5 (Elena Batukhtina-Tyurina, USSR/Russia, 1989–1993, 1997, 2001)
5 (Natalya Morozova, USSR/Russia, 1991–1993, 1997–2001)

Most gold medals by a head coach, all editions
7 (Nikolay Karpol, USSR/Russia, 1979, 1989–1993, 1997–2001)

Most points in a one set, one team, until 1997, without tie–break
20 (USSR against GDR, third set, 3 October 1987)

Fewest points in a one set, one team, until 1997
0 (57 times)

Most points in a one set, one team, since 1999 (rally point system)
34 (Netherlands against Poland, third set, 20 September 2003)

Fewest points in a one set, one team, since 1999 (rally point system)
7 (Israel against Poland, second set, 24 September 2011)

Most points in a tie-break (since 1989), one team
22 (Czechoslovakia against Ukraine, 1 October 1993)
22 (Poland against Russia, 24 September 2005)

Fewest points in a tie-break (since 1989), one team
5 (Yugoslavia against Poland, 28 September 1991)
5 (Netherlands against Poland, 20 September 2003)
5 (Belgium against Serbia, 23 September 2007)

Largest difference in points, winning team, three sets game, until 1997
44 (USSR–Hungary, 3–0 [15–0, 15–1, 15–0], 18 September 1949)
44 (GDR–Austria, 3–0 [15–1, 15–0, 15–0], 24 October 1963)
44 (Netherlands–Austria, 3–0 [15–1, 15–0, 15–0], 26 October 1963)

Largest difference in points, winning team, three sets game, since 1999
36 (Russia–Germany, 3–0 [25–14, 25–9, 25–16], 24 September 1999)

Largest difference in points, winning team, four sets game, until 1997
34 (Bulgaria–GDR, 3–1 [15–3, 15–0, 11–15, 15–4], 26 September 1981)

Largest difference in points, winning team, four sets game, since 1999
  28 (Germany–Belarus, 3–1 [25–10, 25–18, 25–27, 25–17], 22 September 2007)
  28 (Italy–Germany, 3–1 [25–10, 22–25, 25–12, 25–22], 3 October 2009)

Largest difference in points, winning team, five sets game, until 1997
  27 (FRG–France, 3–2 [10–15, 15–3, 14–16, 15–8, 15–0], 23 September 1971)

Largest difference in points, winning team, five sets game, since 1999
  28 (Romania–Slovakia, 3–2 [25–14, 25–10, 22–25, 28–30, 15–8],
    22 September 2003)

Smallest difference in points, winning team, three sets game, until 1997
  6 (Czechoslovakia–Poland, 3–0 [15–13, 16–14, 15–13], 15 September 1949)
  6 (Netherlands–Czechoslovakia, 3–0 [17–15, 17–15, 15–13], 28 September 1991)
  6 (Italy–Latvia, 3–0 [16–14, 15–13, 16–14], 29 September 1993)

Smallest difference in points, winning team, three sets game, since 1999
  6 (Croatia–Poland, 3–0 [26–24, 26–24, 25–23], 21 September 1999)

Smallest difference in points, winning team, four sets game, until 1997
  –1 (USSR–GDR, 3–1 [8–15, 16–14, 15–13, 15–13], 10 September 1989)

Smallest difference in points, winning team, four sets game, since 1999
  1 (Turkey–Croatia, 3–1 [18–25, 25–22, 25–23, 25–22], 24 September 2005)

Smallest difference in points, winning team, five sets game, until 1997
  –10 (Belarus–Bulgaria, 3–2 [15–13, 3–15, 15–13, 9–15, 15–11],
    29 September 1997)

Smallest difference in points, winning team, five sets game, since 1999
  –6 (Slovakia–Czech Republic, 3–2 [25–21, 17–25, 19–25, 25–23, 15–13],
    25 September 2009)

Most points, winning team, three sets game, until 1997
  51 (GDR–Hungary, 3–0 [18–16, 15–6, 18–16], 1 October 1977)

Most points, winning team, three sets game, since 1999
  82 (Germany–Turkey, 3–0 [25–21, 25–21, 32–30], 25 September 2007)

Most points, winning team, four sets game, until 1997
  62 (Romania–Netherlands, 3–1 [15–17, 16–14, 15–7, 16–14],
    19 September 1983)
  62 (Ukraine–Italy, 3–1 [15–17, 15–8, 15–6, 17–15], 2 October 1993)

Most points, winning team, four sets game, since 1999
  105 (Belgium–Bulgaria, 3–1 [25–16, 25–19, 30–32, 25–22], 27 September 2007)

Most points, winning team, five sets game, until 1997
  76 (Romania–Yugoslavia, 3–2 [15–17, 15–8, 15–1, 16–18, 15–9],
    25 September 1977)

Most points, winning team, five sets game, since 1999
   120 (Poland–Netherlands, 3–2 [25–22, 25–19, 32–34, 23–25, 15–5],
     20 September 2003)

Most points, losing team, three sets game, until 1997
   43 (Czechoslovakia–Netherlands, 0–3 [15–17, 15–17, 13–15],
     28 September 1991)

Most points, losing team, three sets game, since 1999
   72 (Turkey–Germany, 0–3 [21–25, 21–25, 30–32], 25 September 2007)

Most points, losing team, four sets game, until 1997
   55 (GDR–USSR, 1–3 [15–8, 14–16, 13–15, 13–15], 10 September 1989)

Most points, losing team, four sets game, since 1999
   98 (Poland–Netherlands, 1–3 [27–29, 25–22, 23–25, 23–25], 24 September 1999)

Most points, losing team, five sets game, until 1997
   70 (Hungary–Italy, 2–3 [15–6, 12–15, 15–13, 14–16, 14–16], 29 September 1985)
   70 (FRG–Romania, 2–3 [13–15, 15–8, 13–15, 15–13, 14–16], 6 September 1989)
   70 (France–Poland, 2–3 [12–15, 15–12, 15–17, 15–7, 13–15], 10 September 1989)

Most points, losing team, five sets game, since 1999
   119 (Russia–Poland, 2–3 [24–26, 22–25, 28–26, 25–20, 20–22],
     24 September 2005)

Fewest points, winning team, four sets game, until 1997
   48 (France–FRG, 3–1 [15–4, 15–9, 3–15, 15–6], 8 September 1958)
   48 (Sweden–Austria, 3–1 [3–15, 15–8, 15–7, 15–9], 1 October 1971)
   48 (FRG–Poland, 3–1 [15–9, 15–9, 3–15, 15–9], 1 October 1985)
   48 (Czechoslovakia–Germany, 3–1 [15–11, 3–15, 15–10, 15–3],
     29 September 1991)
   48 (Russia–Poland, 3–1 [15–6, 15–13, 3–15, 15–7], 2 October 1997)

Fewest points, winning team, four sets game, since 1999
   87 (Netherlands–Turkey, 3–1 [25–18, 12–25, 25–21, 25–20], 25 September 2005)

Fewest points, winning team, five sets game, until 1997
   56 (Switzerland–Belgium, 3–2 [15–8, 6–15, 5–15, 15–6, 15–7],
     6 November 1967)
   56 (USSR–Hungary, 3–2 [8–15, 3–15, 15–13, 15–8, 15–6], 24 September 1983)

Fewest points, winning team, five sets game, since 1999
   99 (Germany–Turkey, 3–2 [25–16, 25–16, 22–25, 12–25, 15–10],
     25 September 2003)

Fewest points, losing team, four sets game, until 1997
   22 (GDR–Bulgaria, 1–3 [3–15, 0–15, 15–11, 4–15], 26 September 1981)

Fewest points, losing team, four sets game, since 1999
   69 (Germany–Italy, 1–3 [10–25, 25–22, 12–25, 22–25], 3 October 2009)

Fewest points, losing team, five sets game, until 1997
42 (France–FRG, 2–3 [15–10, 3–15, 16–14, 8–15, 0–15], 23 September 1971)

Fewest points, losing team, five sets game, since 1999
86 (Serbia–Germany, 2–3 [9–25, 25–23, 27–25, 17–25, 8–15], 30 September 2009)

Most points, both teams, three sets game, until 1997
92 (Netherlands–Czechoslovakia, 3–0 [17–15, 17–15, 15–13], 28 September 1991)

Most points, both teams, three sets game, since 1999
154 (Germany–Turkey, 3–0 [25–21, 25–21, 32–30], 25 September 2007)

Most points, both teams, four sets game, until 1997
114 (Romania–Netherlands, 3–1 [15–17, 16–14, 15–7, 16–14],
    19 September 1983)

Most points, both teams, four sets game, since 1999
199 (Netherlands–Poland, 3–1 [29–27, 22–25, 25–23, 25–23],
    24 September 1999)
199 (Netherlands–Turkey, 3–1 [25–22, 28–30, 25–21, 25–23],
    18 September 2005)

Most points, both teams, five sets game, until 1997
139 (Czechoslovakia–Ukraine, 3–2 [14–16, 15–5, 15–11, 6–15, 22–20],
    1 October 1993)

Most points, both teams, five sets game, since 1999
238 (Poland–Russia, 3–2 [26–24, 25–22, 26–28, 20–25, 22–20],
    24 September 2005)

Highest average, difference between points scored and allowed per game,
    one edition, team, until 1997
33.4 (USSR, 1951)

Highest average, difference between points allowed and scored per game,
    one edition, team, until 1997
35.3 (Netherlands, 1949)

Highest average, difference between points scored and allowed per game,
    one edition, team, since 1999
22.4 (Russia, 1999)

Highest average, difference between points allowed and scored per game,
    one edition, team, since 1999
27.0 (Israel, 2011)

Most wins, one edition, team
9 (USSR, 1958)

Most losses, one edition, team
8 (Sweden, 1967)

Bibliography

BOOKS

Almanacco Illustrato del Volley. Modena, Italy: Panini, various years (1986–1990).
Edelman, Aleksandr, et al, *Voleybol. Spravochnik*, Moscow: Fizkultura i sport, 1983.
Mecner, Krzysztof, *Historia Siatkówki. Mistrzostwa Europy*, Katowice, Poland: PTP, 2005.
Sarić, Novica, *Volleyball. European Championships 1948–2005*, Belgrade, Serbia: Volleyball Federation of Serbia, 2006.
Sviridov, Viktor, et al. *Voleybol. Entsiklopediya*, Tomsk, Russia: Kompaniya "Janson," 2001.

WEBSITE

The official website of the Confédération Européenne de Volleyball: http://www.cev.lu.

NEWSPAPERS

Československý Sport (Czechoslovakia)
Corriere dello Sport, La Gazzetta dello Sport (Italy)
Deutsches Sportecho (GDR)
L'Equipe (France)
Naroden Sport (Bulgaria)
Népsport (Hungary)
Przegląd Sportowy, Sport, Tempo (Poland)
Sovetskiy Sport, Sport-Ekspress (USSR/Russia)
Sportske novosti (Yugoslavia)

About the Author

Tomasz Małolepszy, mathematician, sport historian, and statistician, was born in Sulęcin, Poland, and educated as a mathematician at the University of Zielona Góra, Poland, where he is currently working as an academic teacher with a Ph.D degree on the Faculty of Mathematics, Computer Science, and Econometrics. A longtime sports fan, especially of basketball, he is the author of a basketball book (published in Polish) about the history of the men's European Championships in basketball, *Historia Koszykówki: Mistrzostwa Europy od Szwajcarii 1935 r. do Polski 2009 r.*, and is working on a similar book about the history of the women's European Championships in basketball. He has been a member of the Association for Professional Basketball Research since 2002. He is married to his wife, Paulina, and has one daughter, Karolinka.